The Silver Skeleton

Michael Preston

Published in 2017 by FeedARead.com Publishing

First Edition

A CIP catalogue record for this title is available from the British
Library.

ISBN: 978-1-78697-941-4

Follow Michael Preston on Twitter @PRMikePreston

For Jen

Chapter One

'Careful mate or you'll hurt yourself.'

The bus driver's concerned warning, delivered in a distinctive Eastern European accent, was met with a dismissive wave after Stephen Taylor leaped through the open doors onto the pavement. A sprightly late forty-something, body toned, hair nearly trimmed and his colourful attire as flawless as it was fashionable, he assertively held out the same hand to order the National Express West Midlands bus to remain stopped at the curb side. The bus motionless, he waved an appreciative farewell and jogged across the main road to the central reservation of the dual carriageway.

Piotr Lato smiled, a little jealous at the carefree behaviour of the passenger making his way towards a tree-lined dirt path and a patch of wasteland that served as a shortcut to a housing estate on the other side of the main road. Piotr watched as the man disappeared into the darkness beyond a line of mature oak trees and bushes that bordered the wasteland.

Piotr continued to smile as his focus returned to his final shift on the last number ninety-two bus service of a humid Friday evening that had edged almost unnoticed past midnight into the early hours of Saturday. Three more stops and he would be off the clock. He reached out to press the red button that closed the concertina doors at the front of his bus. Just as the doors responded, three passengers came rumbling down the stairs from the top deck and raced to get off.

'Hold on a minute Polak!' cried one of the agitated teenagers, who had almost missed their stop. Piotr was startled into opening the doors again with a jolt. The noisy trio jumped off the bus, waved two finger salutes and shouted racial slurs in his direction, banging on the front windscreen with their fists as they crossed the road. One even spat on the glass. The repulsed driver closed the doors again and shook his head in dismay. He usually tried to ignore what he had come to expect as predictable insults sporadically directed at people from his part of the former Eastern Bloc. As he prepared to pull away and continue along his route, he noticed an elderly man of West Indian origin sat on the bench seat near the front of the bus. He was smartly dressed and wore a brown trilby hat, which he tipped as he nodded to Piotr.

5

'It was the same in my day, my friend,' he said with a wry smile.

Piotr shrugged his shoulders in dismay, his cheerful demeanour no longer evident. As he checked the large side view mirror for approaching traffic before pulling out, he saw the three objectionable youths making more rude gestures that suggested Piotr would be spending his evening alone aroused by some form of pornographic material, rather than eating the traditional rosól soup his wife Luba welcomed him home with at the end of most late shifts. Once a short line of cars had passed, he pulled out and watched as the youths took off, running across the central reservation towards the cut through.

- - - - - - - - - -

Stephen Taylor paused, bringing his carefree prance along a leaf-littered path to a sudden halt. He was surprised by the silence and darkness shrouding the area of wasteland that connected the main road with the suburban Birmingham housing estate where he lived. Considering the number of nearby streetlights and the glow from the bordering houses, he had expected to find the popular cut through he had not graced in perhaps thirty years easier to navigate. The gloominess and eerie hush amid the arching trees and thick bushes was almost menacing. The foliage had grown significantly since his youthful escapades in these woods back in the seventies and eighties and the leaves were starting to turn and shed as autumn gradually overpowered the lasting grip of summer that seemed determined to hold on into September.

He barely recognised the path he had once ridden frequently on a Chopper bike astride its distinctive elongated L-shaped black leather seat while gripping high and wide handlebars. Owning the pedal version of a Harley Davidson had made him the envy of all his junior school friends back then. Hanging branches and overgrown nettles now obscured secret alcoves he imagined must have survived from his teenage years, even if time and the elements had partly eroded their structure. By digging into mounds of earth around the trees and bushes and weaving together fern leaves to provide cover, he and childhood friends John Garland, Mike Sullivan and Andy Morris used to conceal their whereabouts and become camouflaged within these hideouts, even from somebody wandering along the path that ran only a few yards away. Making a bivouac, where they would occasionally camp

6

out all night some summers, having snuck out of their homes, was one of the few skills any of them had taken away from the teachings of the Cub Scouts. During his time wearing a green jumper adorned with sewn on patches, a neckerchief and a woggle, he had been a proud Sixer, his uniform always dutifully pressed and brushed.

The gang's hiding places began as an innocent means of eluding capture during games of hide-n-seek, then became an occasionally essential refuge during teenage years of minor rebellion and experimentation. Once hidden from view beneath the thick green ferns, they could chug down cheap bottles of Davenports Continental Lager stolen from the storeroom of a local football team's clubhouse and compete to see who could produce the longest sentence while simultaneously burping from the inevitable effects of the gassy beer. They would share drags on Players No. 6 cigarettes sold discreetly as singles to skint school kids by a newsagent nearby and see who could blow the most clearly defined smoke rings. They would occasionally switch to the Consulate brand of menthol cigarettes in a vain attempt to disguise the odour of smoke on their breath from suspecting parents. It was within those secret dens that as an adolescent, Stephen had once dared to arrange a clandestine meeting with another boy similarly short of the consensual age.

Stephen stood uneasily for a moment and felt his stomach turn as he struggled to repress flashbacks from the last time he had trodden this path, which seemed to be leaping from his subconscious. It was not a pleasant recollection; one he had purposely blanked from his memory. Despite living for more than forty years in his neatly manicured semi-detached childhood home in the adjoining Stonor Croft, which he could now just about make out beyond a line of trees, he had not set foot here since one fateful night in the mid-eighties. The exuberance of his carefree dance across the dual carriageway and the mixed emotions of his youthful pursuits within the alcoves of the wasteland had now eroded and he wondered what on earth had possessed him to venture into the darkness of a place that used to haunt his dreams almost nightly. He always traced the pavement back in the direction the bus had come, crossed the main road at the traffic lights and walked the longer route to Stonor Croft; without fail, but not tonight, for some unexplainable reason.

There was a rustling in the bushes that unnerved him, or perhaps it was his imagination, which had by now kicked into overdrive. He wanted to race along the pathway to reach the glow of the safety of the housing estate, but something in the thick bramble caught his eye. Having spent a few minutes in the relative darkness, his vision had adjusted to the dimly lit passageway and he was able to focus on the object. But what was it?

Stephen inhaled sharply and froze with a disbelieving drop of his jaw. A chill ran down his spine as he came within touching distance of the mystery item. It was an old metal chair, likely rusted from decades of exposure to the elements, lying dented and damaged, almost obscured from view beneath the foliage. 'It can't be,' he thought. 'It simply can't be.'

Without warning, he recoiled, gagged, retched and vomited uncontrollably. An evening's worth of fine fresh seafood and several Moscow Mules, his favoured combination of vodka, lime juice and ginger beer, pebble-dashed the pathway.

Spooked by his discovery and eager to escape the suddenly menacing environment and reach the safety of home, Stephen turned and walked along the path and soon quickened his pace. There was no logic to his anxiousness, he thought to himself as he wiped away some tangy remnants from the edges of his mouth. The sight of an old metal chair had awoken a troubling memory, but a short jog away beckoned a welcoming cup of tea and a warm soft bed promising an untroubled slumber deep into Saturday morning. This was the penultimate weekend of his summer holidays before returning to teach a fresh term when he would be introduced as the new deputy head of a local secondary school in addition to his position as head of the English department.

Stephen had barely broken into a longer and more determined stride when he saw the silhouette of two figures blocking the path ahead. Stood side by side, their arms crossed, they appeared intent on halting his progress.

'What, what do you want?' he stammered, his voice trembling and distressed. He genuinely feared the shadows that stood before him. He could feel his heart racing; he sensed his cheeks flush a deep red and felt sweat beads form and multiply on his brow. There was no reply. They just stood there. What did they want? He could hear the deep trunk of an aged imposing oak tree creak as it wavered slightly in the wind, which hissed through its leaves.

'What, what do you want?' he stuttered again.

Then came a voice from behind that made Stephen jump out of his skin. In a moment of shock and pure fear, he instinctively spun on his heels to face an equally terrifying silhouette, which blocked the path back towards the main road.

'You fucking queer,' said the figure menacingly. It sounded like the voice of a young man. It wasn't the deeper tone of the typical forty-something reformed football hooligan who occasionally baited Stephen when he strolled through town to catch a bus or train back home. 'You're a fucking disgrace.'

'Do I know you?' asked Stephen, tense and in fear for his well-being? 'Did I teach you? Were you one of my students?'

The figure lunged towards him, cursing and muttering words that Stephen failed to decipher as he turned instinctively, disregarding the fact that two more apparent assailants blocked his path in the other direction. Before he could break stride, he was punched in the face, with such force that he reeled backwards and fell at the feet of the person who had spoken to him. He grasped at the grass and dirt as he landed, desperate to get back to his feet to flee the assault. His cheek burned and his left eye stung. He staggered to an upright position, dizzy and disorientated by the punch. Next came a blow to the back of the head and then another, this time to his stomach and he doubled over, crashing painfully against a tree that provided unintended but welcome support. His attackers were spitting at him, hurling homophobic insults and kicking and punching him at will. Desperate to escape, he ran blindly between two overgrown bushes that lined the path as a hand grasped at his jacket. He managed to fend it off, break free and burst into a near sprint, but within only a few steps, his right foot became tangled up in the old metal chair he had seen from the path and he sprawled, crashing towards the ground. Stephen reached out with both hands to break his fall, but his reflexes were too slow. His flailing head hit a large rock with a sickening dull thud. Spared further pain and panic, he blacked out, instantly knocked unconscious by the impact.

'Where is he?'

'Where the fuck did he go?'

'Don't let him get away.'

The three assailants were stumbling around in the darkness, each panting heavily and shouting at the other in agitated voices, their adrenaline pumping as they hunted their prey. One thumbed furiously at the metal spark wheel of a cheap disposable plastic cigarette lighter until it caught at the fourth or fifth attempt and the butane liquid hissed and produced a small flame that illuminated the area immediately around them.

The first attacker, whose initial punch had floored Stephen, felt a texture beneath his feet that was inconsistent with the dirt, rocks and bramble. It was the material of a fashionable jacket and beside it laid a lifeless body.

'Jesus, I think he's dead,' cried the teenager as his accomplice held the lighter flame over the motionless figure. He examined the felled body unceremoniously with a callous poke of his foot.

'Fucking hell, I think we've killed him. Let's get out of here before someone sees us.'

Chapter Two

Summer 1986

'You fucking wanker!'

Matt Douglass barely had time to spin around to see who had cursed him in the darkness when a vicious blow to the back of his head sent pain searing through his entire body. The world around him froze briefly, as though he were suspended in time. He felt himself drop to his knees in a pathetic lifeless motion. Exposed in the pose of a condemned man awaiting execution, he squinted to focus on his surroundings and wondered what had hit him with such force. It wasn't a fist or a small blunt instrument, but something more substantial. As he knelt, dazed and vulnerable, Matt felt second blow with the same degree of frenzied force, this time to his shoulders, which sent his helpless carcass crashing in what felt like slow motion, face-first to the ground.

As he turned his head to one side, tasting a mixture of damp grass and dirt with his desperate gasping breath, his eyes focused for a moment on a heavy metal-framed folded chair that crumpled to the ground with a crash, almost as violently as he had. It reminded him of the humorous props he saw wrestlers use back when he would sit on the sofa watching Saturday afternoon sport and horse racing on television in the living room, despite his mother urging him to play outside in the healthy fresh air with the other kids. Disorientated and confused, he remembered an old bout between Giant Haystacks and his favourite wrestler Big Daddy and...

His hazy happy boyhood memory lasted only a few seconds as first the left side of his torso and then his left leg and then his right leg all seared with pain from short sharp blows that pounded him relentlessly. There was no defending himself from the barrage of kicks that rapidly assaulted multiple parts of his body. His ribs screamed out in agony as blows rained down. His chest felt as though it was caving in as it was stamped upon. Desperately, he tried to muster enough strength to respond to his self-preservation instincts and crawl away from the onslaught, but he was powerless. There were three or maybe four of them, frenzied in their attack.

He coughed violently and tasted a bitter spattering of blood. Still the blows came. They were relentless and delivered now with a force even more furious than before. He began to panic. Fighting against a searing pain he had never endured before, he tried frantically to avoid the battering. He curled into the foetal position and covered his head with his arms. He was certain he was going to die and pleaded with his senses to black out from the pain that tore through him. He squirmed helplessly in the dirt of the shortcut through the woods he had taken towards home. Who was doing this to him, and why? He moaned in absolute agony as a kick to his side connected viciously and his bladder released the remnants of several pints of beer he had consumed earlier that night.

Drenched in blood, the stench of urine and aroma of regurgitated Red Stripe, he felt the brutal blows slow and eventually cease. There were just a few straggling kicks to his body, which had become accustomed and almost numb to the pain. Then they stopped.

Through his nose that felt as though it had been split open and spread across his cheeks, the night's cold air stung his senses and he could smell the grass still damp from the day's rain, mixed with the scent of exhaust fumes from the nearby main road. Matt was helpless as he attempted to lift his heavy crumpled frame. The muffled voices of rage he had heard now sounded distressed. He began choking as a string of sharp, deep and painful coughs expelled warm trails of blood, and equally desperate intakes of breath clamoured for air. Matt's heart was racing. His beaten body was shaking uncontrollably. The damp air didn't seem to be filling his lungs. He couldn't breathe. His chest was burning, his ribs felt like they were knives stabbing into the core of his body.

Matt lay still for a moment and his glazed vision cleared slightly. With more effort than he believed he could muster, he raised his head up slowly from the ground, petrified that he would be subjected to another kicking. Despite his ears ringing and his hearing dull from the assault, he could make out the muffled sound of an occasional vehicle from the main road just beyond a line of nearby trees, but no voices. Had they gone? Had he been left to die?

He needed to get to his feet or at least crawl to the road for help. It was no mean feat, raising a 16-stone mass that had been brutally and remorselessly punished, but his powerful arms, which were toned and shaped by countless hours spent pumping free weights at the new gym at the Fox Hollies Leisure Centre, enabled him to move. Matt's thick fingers clawed at the dirt, his fists dug into the soft ground, his elbows began to straighten and his usually solid muscles trembled as what felt like the last possible burst of energy he could muster heaved his body upwards.

'Fucking hell, he's moving!' said a concerned voice in front of him.

For a moment, dazed and certain he was about to pass out from the pain, Matt felt relieved that a concerned Good Samaritan must have found him. Now caked with his own blood, his squinting eyes could make out a pair of black leather ankle boots, just like the ones he wore, with a zip and a silver-buckled strap on the side. There was a second person there too and perhaps a third. Matt could also see scuffed boots with a line of fur where the leather had been turned down at the top. He was sure he recognized them. As Matt tried to peer up, to see who was standing there, both moved aside hurriedly in response to another muffled voice tinged with anger. Where were they going? Why weren't they helping him? For a split-second Matt saw the buckled black boot, blurred by its rapid movement towards his face. He instinctively closed his eyes, shut tight as the most incredible and unbearable pain he had ever experienced ripped ruthlessly through his nose, jaw, eye sockets, cheeks and skull and tore down this throat into every inch of his being. The gripping pain burned down his spine as Matt's head snapped back sickeningly. There was a loud crack.

Matt Douglass was dead.

Chapter Three

'Sully, stop running! Stop bloody running!'

John Garland eventually caught up with Mike Sullivan and breathless, yanked him by the collar of his denim jacket abruptly into a bus shelter, where the pair collapsed, leaning against the structure's graffiti-covered reinforced glass windows. Both bent over with their hands on their knees, gasping for breath and coughing.

'Why on earth did you run?' asked John between bursts of exhaling nicotine perfumed breath, perplexed that his friend had sprinted along the main Stratford Road in a moment of panic. 'We can't be seen running away from…' John struggled to find words to describe the gruesome scene they had hurriedly abandoned on a dirt path several hundred yards away. 'There's people on their way home. They could identify us.'

John ushered Mike, more commonly known as Sully since they had first met thirteen years earlier at infant school, unceremoniously from the relative safe haven of the bus shelter, quickly across the pavement to a gap in an eroded old church wall. The pair slumped down on a patch of grass, sitting with their backs against the cold grey stone, while facing several uneven rows of unkempt ancient gravestones. Equally breathless and concerned, Andy Morris, who had been trailing some distance behind, had seen his friends duck for cover and also scrambled onto the damp sod of the graveyard and lay prostrate beside them.

'Why the bloody hell did you run?' demanded Andy between bursts of breath.

John was poised to escalate the inquisition when Sully, his elbows rested on his knees and face buried in his hands, looked up and hissed in a loud whisper 'because we just killed Matt Douglass. We fucking killed him! And where's Stephen?'

The three stared at each other for a moment, catching their breath and examining their surroundings, which were suitably hidden from the main road and would shelter them from any passer-by. Andy glanced at his silver-metallic wristwatch and pressed a button on its left side to illuminate the digital screen. Blue LED figures glowed to display *1:22AM*. Two hours had passed since the local pubs had started to turf out their patrons and the last bus of the evening had long since departed, so foot traffic nearby would be at a minimum. There might be people staggering home while digesting a curry, chips, or the delights of the nearby Kentucky Fried Chicken takeaway in various states if inebriation, perhaps unlikely to concern themselves with the sight of three young lads who also appeared to be making their way home.

A car cruised past slowly and stopped within sight of the entrance to the cemetery, causing the three nervous teenagers to freeze in fear of being detected. There were cheerful voices, some lewd banter and a car door slammed shut before footsteps came in their direction. Nobody dared move. The footsteps stopped. The three glanced at each other, their frowns deeply concerned. At first there was no sound, but then came a barely audible trickle of liquid that grew more forceful and was accompanied by a loud sigh of relief from the person who was standing barely six feet from them. Sully's frown broke into a wide smile and he had to clamp his hand hard across his mouth to suppress the fit of giggles he was desperate to release, almost as urgently as the man had apparently needed to relieve his bladder. John held out an alarmed hand to motion Sully to remain silent. There followed the sound of a zipper closing, another relieved sigh and a sharp fart, followed by erratic footsteps that dimmed into the distance.

'Good job he didn't see if he could piss over the wall,' laughed Sully, his jovial disposition in stark contrast to that of a few minutes earlier.

John was less buoyant. 'Do you think anyone saw us running up here?' he asked in a deadpan tone. Both friends replied with decisive shakes of the head. His tongue was pressed firmly into his right cheek and he drummed four fingers together rapidly; familiar traits he exhibited when stressed. He collected his breath and thoughts and leaned forward with an air of authority.

'We didn't kill him.'

'What!' cried Sully in disbelieving response, which was met by an instant and frantic chorus of desperate and prolonged hushing sounds as John and Andy both motioned with agitated hands for him to be quiet. John imagined the man who had stopped to piss against the stone wall turning back in their direction out of intrigue if he had heard the raised voice.

'What?' demanded Sully again in a quieter but equally perplexed tone. 'We kicked the shit out of him and that loud cracking sound as his head snapped back. I can't even bear to think about it.'

Sully's voice tailed off as he cupped his hands to cover his nose and mouth as he gulped for air and sounded as though he were hyper ventilating.

'I know we gave him a kicking, but I don't think we killed him,' resumed John. The other two exhibited a strain of disbelief that crumpled their faces.

'Right now, that bastard is squirming in the dirt, crawling home and suffering from a beating we all know he deserved. What he did to make us do that...'

John stopped mid-sentence, rage etched across his face and he punched the grey stone barrier beside him with the side of his fist. Nobody spoke. Andy reached for his inside pocket to retrieve a packet of Players No. 6 cigarettes but was stopped immediately as Sully administered a sharp whack to his chest with the back of his hand and shook his head. He indicated that the light from the burning ash could betray their hiding place. Still nobody spoke.

After a pause of a few minutes, in a hushed and calmed voice, John explained his logic.

'It takes a lot more than what we just did to kill someone. Broken bones, bruises, serious injuries, yeah, sure, but not dead. Either he'll get home, or someone will find him when they're out walking their dog in the morning and he'll recover. His ugly face will be a fucking mess, but he'll recover.'

Sceptical at such a theory, Sully wanted to interrupt, but John held an assertive index finger up in front of him and continued to whisper.

'Stephen ran when you ran, but in the opposite direction because he lives the other side of the cut through. So, he must be home by now.'

John had seen the fourth member of their group race away when Sully turned tail and fled and he and Andy followed. Stephen Taylor, who completed the quartet of childhood friends, was a neighbour of the victim they had just brutally beaten.

'We don't have to worry about Stephen. Right now, we need to get home and make believe we were back a while ago because we can't be tied to this.'

Andy was rocking back and forth, shaking his head, muttering almost incoherently such was the pace of his chatter.

'I've never so much as punched someone. I've never started a fight. At school, I always stood at the back when we fought with other schools, we all did, and now this. We're not football hooligans or striking miners. We're not violent. How the fuck did this happen?'

John paused to allow Andy to vent, but still the vision of Matt Douglass lying lifeless in the dirt was embedded at the forefront of everyone's mind as John continued to outline a hastily composed plan.

'Look Andy, we all have to get home quickly and calmly and wait to see what happens. He won't be able to identify us because when I hit him with the chair he was still walking away from us. He never saw it coming. He was covering his face while we were kicking him and then he was disorientated, at, well, at the end.'

John's voice held little conviction to support his theory that Matt Douglass might still be alive. The hesitation in his low whisper betrayed the concern he really held that murder and not just a vicious assault was their true guilt. Sully and Andy nodded, but were visibly unconvinced.

The three lived in the same direction from the churchyard and on nights when they drank at local pubs, or caught buses returning from town, would wander or stagger along in unison. Now they hatched a plot to follow separate routes home. Andy was visibly upset and agitated and was the most eager to reach his safe haven, so it was quickly decided he would take the shortest route home. Sully would follow the main road, but since his was the course most likely to bring him into contact with other Friday night stragglers and passing traffic, he agreed not to run as he had done earlier. A late-night jogger in boots and denims might arouse suspicion. John volunteered to track the back streets, making for the longest journey home of the three. He could navigate the shortcuts and hidden alleyways with his eyes closed if necessary. Those trails were burned in his memory from the days when he and Stephen would ride their Chopper and Grifter bikes around Hall Green and neighbouring Shirley every single day of the summer holidays. Such carefree times now seemed a world away.

Just before the trio vacated the safe shelter of the stone wall, Sully suggested they each establish an alibi. John agreed, wishing with a tinge of jealousy that he'd had the foresight to include that aspect in his plan. A friendly rivalry had long existed between the two and these would register as valuable bonus points for Sully if they ever totted up a score. Andy faced the biggest challenge of sneaking quietly into his house unheard because his dad was a notoriously light sleeper, but he planned to immediately lie down on the sofa in the living room with the television switched on and the sound turned down, giving the impression he had fallen asleep while watching a late-night film.

'Make sure you know what was on the telly about an hour ago,' warned John. 'Check the Radio Times to see what was on. And take your boots off. We can't traipse mud from the...' John paused. He was about to say crime scene, but it sounded so clinical and, he had to admit, criminal. 'Just be smart. You never do your own washing, so don't put your clothes in the machine to get any mud and blood off or it will look suspicious. Do it when nobody's home.'

John faced no such challenges. His parents were away enjoying their annual two-week summer holiday in Southbourne, a seaside town traditionally popular with residents of the Midlands, just a few miles along the south coast from Bournemouth. Chris and Marie Garland had reluctantly allowed their son to remain home alone for the first time, accepting that family holidays were now most likely a relic of the past, especially since John was poised to fly the nest to take up a place at university in London the following month. The eighteen-year-old had eagerly accepted the coveted set of keys to the Garland home and was entrusted with its safety. There were lovingly prepared frozen meals diligently labelled by his mother that almost overflowed from the chest freezer in the garage and written instructions not to so much as open the drinks cabinet let alone consume its contents. A laundry list of dos and mainly don'ts underlined concerns over excessive hot water usage, locking the front door, not hosting parties and strict visitation rights of friends. 'So long as you don't burn the house down or kill anyone,' his dad had joked as he waved a cautious farewell from the open window of the family's luggage laden Ford Mondeo.

John put his hand on his friend's shoulder. 'I know you ran because you were shitting yourself Sully, and so was I, but we need to be smart about this. Nobody saw us, or we're pretty sure they didn't. We got away with racing up the Stratford Road at one in the morning and now we have to get home without incriminating ourselves. Andy...'

'I know,' said Andy, somewhat agitated. 'Be smart and check the Radio Times.'

19

Chapter Four

Five Weeks earlier

'Mom, do we have to?'

While Craig Jones was helping the woman he hoped might one day become his mother-in-law find every last speck of dust to brush diligently from his pristine uniform, Siobhan Murphy was less enthusiastic about the grooming task at hand.

'Can't we stop doing this every year? Please? Mom, it's embarrassing.'

'Nonsense,' retorted Marion Murphy. 'This is a tradition. We've been doing it for, what, twelve years now?'

'Thirteen, Mrs Murphy,' Craig corrected her. 'Since Siobhan was five years old.'

Siobhan rolled her eyes and cursed the day she herself had inadvertently initiated this tradition of the dreaded now annual photograph as a little girl celebrating completing her first year at Peterbrook Infant School. Back then, thirteen years ago as Craig so dutifully noted, she had impulsively posed for the camera, stood with both hands on her hips, her head tilted precociously to one side with her wavy dark brown hair falling gently on her shoulders. She was stood beside Craig Jones, who her friends readily admitted was the best-looking boy in middle infants, a year older than her. Now, aged eighteen, she felt far less enamoured by the boy formerly of form 2C, who delighted in encouraging her mother in staging the painful annual photo re-enactment.

'You looked a proper little miss back then,' said Siobhan's dad Frank, deliberately antagonising the situation as he recalled the initial picture he had taken and those that had been recreated every single July since, despite Siobhan's protestations.

The willing annual participant in front of the camera was of course Craig, Siobhan's long time on and occasionally off boyfriend, who had stood rigorously to attention by her side that fateful last day of school in 1973. Back then in the early seventies he had been as smartly dressed as any six-year-old, in a navy-blue jumper adorned with a green badge that said 'Tidy', which had been awarded for

21

picking up litter from the playground during lunchtimes. A blue and white striped kipper tie offset his stiff white shirt, while his grey shorts, embarrassingly tight by modern standards, exposed pasty legs pinked by that year's early summer sun and knees scraped by endless games of football played with a worn tennis ball in the school quad. The discolouring old original photo of the pair still held pride of place on the Murphy home mantelpiece.

As the years went by and the taking of the photo became a staple of their growing up together, Siobhan initially hammed up her pose for the camera, exaggerating her 'I'm a little teapot' stance, but since reaching her teens, had become a reluctant participant in the end of the school year ritual that she had come to loathe. Two years ago, her mother had created a mortally embarrassing Murphy family Christmas ornament adorned with the photo that hung from the plastic tree in the living room and was shown to every festive visitor, even to random carol singers on one occasion. Another time Siobhan's cousins all received the awful pose in a stand-up frame as a gift, and, well, there were just too many painful instances to recall.

'Oh my, where have the years gone?' wondered Marion Murphy, as she did every year, her soft Irish brogue still as clear as it had been the day she arrived in England from Enniscorthy, some twenty years earlier. She was a slim, attractive woman of average height, Siobhan her only child in stark contrast to a family tradition of procreating in large numbers. Despite being contently settled in Birmingham, she missed her home desperately and had been counting down the days until the Murphy family planned to visit her siblings in Ireland in five weeks' time, at the end of August.

Now aged eighteen, Siobhan was the spitting image of her mother at the age at which she had emigrated. She had inherited Marion's striking porcelain features and an infectious smile that could betray as much mischief as happiness. Her stubborn streak came courtesy of Frank. Encouraged by his father to abandon his native Dublin and accept an offer of work and temporary accommodation from a relative in the Birmingham suburbs, Frank Murphy had set sail for the promise of new adventures in a relatively foreign land in the mid-sixties. Within a year of finding steady employment and less excitement than he had anticipated, Frank had 'bedded and wedded' as he liked to boast, much to his wife's chagrin, Marion McConnell, herself only a matter of months removed from County Wexford. Siobhan was welcomed into the world in the waking hours of a freezing cold February morning in 1968, six months after a band of gold had been slipped onto Marion's finger at a sparsely attended service at the Birmingham registry office on Broad Street. Eighteen years later, Marion was eager to marry off her own daughter to the ideal son-in-law, Craig Jones. She basked in the family tradition of recreating the photograph of her tempestuous daughter and the literal boy next door who had been a welcome and likeable presence in their lives throughout the years.

'And this year we have police constable Jones in our photo,' observed Marion. 'I wonder one day if we'll be taking photographs of you two walking down the…'

'Stop Mom, just stop!' complained an irate Siobhan. At the suggestion of wedded bliss eagerly promoted by her mother, she angrily brought both hands down hard on her hips and turned her head to the side, glaring at the perpetrator. Her father Frank was barely able to hold back a snigger as he quickly captured the moment, depressing the shutter button on the same Canon AE1 35mm camera he had used for every portrait since 1973. Siobhan snapped her head back towards him in response to the flash that lit up the living room. She glared. She quickly warmed and smiled back at her Dad as she realised her frustrated posturing mirrored the annually captured moment. Unintentionally, but as if to complete the pose, Craig had stood stiffly to attention in his smart new police uniform, startled by her irritation.

'Oh, I'm sure that's perfect,' said Siobhan, now enthusiastic at the prospect of a humorous version of the dreaded annual photo. 'I think we're finished Mom.'

Marion disagreed and would be content only once she was certain her husband had snapped the textbook pose to add a collection that uniquely documented the young couple throughout their years together, maturing at Peterbrook infant and junior schools and continuing when both attended different secondary schools. Reluctantly and under protest, Siobhan recreated her hands-on-hips stance and tossed back her head. She felt Craig's arm extend around her waist and let out a defeated sigh.

Flash! The tiresome deed was done.

'Wait!' said Marion as Siobhan walked towards the door to go upstairs and change into less formal attire. 'We have something for you both. For you, our darling daughter, to say well done for what are sure to be grand A Level results, and to Craig to celebrate recently completing your police training. You look so smart in your uniform and I'm sure one day you'll become the Chief Constable!'

Siobhan's A level results were due to be announced shortly and everyone was confident she would achieve the grades necessary to accept a conditional offer to read biology at Liverpool University, starting in the autumn. Siobhan felt almost as relieved as she was excited at the prospect of heading to Merseyside. She loved her parents unconditionally and imagined the relationship between the three of them was healthier and happier than that of most teenagers and their mother and father, but she needed to move away from home and forge an independent life of her own. Frank was supportive and had secretly encouraged Siobhan to apply to a university beyond the convenient distance of a short car ride, Liverpool being some 100 miles to the northwest. When Siobhan explained to her less-enthusiastic mother that she was leaving home at the same age as both her parents had vacated Ireland, Marion reminded her that she had also settled down and married at a similar time and of course Craig's name would be slipped deliberately and approvingly into the conversation. What use might she have for a university degree anyway? Girls her age… and at that point, Siobhan would tune out the conversation, eager to avoid further conflict.

Marion fumbled in her handbag and just as her husband started reaching over to assist, she produced a plain white envelope and handed it to Siobhan.

'They're something we think you want,' added Marion excitedly.

Siobhan was not sure why, but she felt a twinge of anxiousness as she opened the unsealed envelope and peered inside. She looked at Craig, his deep blue uniform an awkward fit, but a proud one. All Craig had ever wanted to do, at least since the dream of becoming a professional footballer had faded, as it did for most boys at some point in their early teens, was become a policeman. Now, he could combine both loves anyway, also turning out for West Midlands Police FC in the local Midland Combination league. Rather than run out at Anfield or Villa Park, he would play matches at the oddly named Tally Ho Sports Ground against such obscure local clubs as Highgate United, Boldmere St. Michaels and Northfield Town. Her mother used to say he was a born policeman, whatever that meant. Since completing mandatory time at the Ryton Police Training Centre in nearby Coventry, Craig had been dispatched onto the streets of the West

Midlands and was even riding as a passenger in panda cars as Siobhan insisted on calling them, pacing the beat as a real policeman.

Much as she despised posing for the summer snapshot and was frustrated by Craig's ridiculously willing participation, Siobhan loved him. She had since they first met when she was five years old and he six, even if their friendship had got off to a rocky start.

Overwhelmed at such a young age by the apparent vastness of the Peterbrook School playground and the swarm of noisy pupils buzzing around playing leapfrog and hopscotch, she and an equally shy friend managed to avoid joining the general population at morning break and lunchtime. For three weeks, they sat together, detached from the rest of school society, sat leaning against a small concrete wall below a classroom windowsill reading books, while hidden among the rose bushes. Their idyllic arrangement lasted until a sunny lunchtime, when her friend was absent, struck down by the chicken pox. Mr Lewis, a maths teacher with a booming Welsh accent, who was already established as their least favourite educator, ushered a solo Siobhan into the abyss. Once out in the open playground, her head spinning, she thought skipping might help decrease the feeling of agoraphobia, so she pranced her way from the main school building towards the far fence, but just as her fears began to subside, a tennis ball struck her leg and bounced away from a nearby pile of blue jumpers that had been set down on the ground.

'You stupid idiot!' bellowed an angry voice. It was Craig Jones, the tall handsome boy she had seen leading the chorus to the football song *Blue is the Colour* that all the boys in school had adopted and sang regularly at break time while they kicked a small ball around and scuffed their once shiny shoes. 'That would have been a goal. It would have been my hat trick.'

Siobhan had no idea what a hat trick was, but she was terrified of the angry boy from the year above, turned back towards the school in tears and tore across the playground, bouncing off a startled Mr Lewis as she raced to reach the safe confines of the brick building. After Siobhan was comforted by the headmaster's secretary in her office, Craig was summoned to apologise and threatened with the slipper, corporal punishment's softer version of the dreaded cane, if he ever upset another pupil over such a trivial matter again. Siobhan reluctantly accepted his sorry plea and an embarrassed red-faced handshake, but vowed never to so much as look at, let alone speak to, horrid Craig Jones.

Three weeks later, the Joneses moved into number 25 Salford Lane, next door to the Murphy family.

Siobhan defiantly kept up her unfriendly façade during the cold winter, but thawed along with the spring temperatures of 1973 and by the end of the school year, willingly posed for that first fateful end of term photo with her now best friend. In later years in junior school, he was the first boy she kissed, allowing herself to deliberately be caught by her equally determined pursuer in a game known as *kiss chase*. She could no longer remember the rules of the game, which had probably since been banned in the name of political correctness, other than it presented eager boys and girls with an opportunity to make their affections known in a playful and less embarrassing manner than despatching a friend to deliver the line 'my mate fancies you.' Senior school presented a parting of the ways of sorts, albeit only a few miles apart within the same catchment area, to a one of the new Secondary Modern establishments in Craig's case and a traditional Grammar School education for Siobhan. Craig remained loyal, making it known that he had a girlfriend who lived next door, but Siobhan was a pretty girl who regularly attracted the attention of admirers throughout her time from first form to upper sixth. Would be suitors were plentiful when hanging around aimlessly and harmlessly on the wooden bench outside Jack's Fish & Chips Shop, where all the local kids sought to be seen, to being walked home from the Baptist Church Friday night disco and eventually accepting offers of a date at Solihull Cinema to see films like *Top Gun* or *Back to the Future*. Craig remained among those whose affections Siobhan accepted and by the time Craig committed to A Level studies, the teenagers were simply considered boyfriend and girlfriend by all who knew them. Now, despite a pending geographical parting, as far as Craig was concerned life would always be this way: him and her. She might be bound for Liverpool to continue her studies, but each could visit the other and as the old saying promised, absence would make the heart grow fonder. Besides, Craig was now P.C. Jones, career copper, whose goal was to become a detective and join the prestigious, or in some eyes, the infamous West Midlands Serious Crime Squad.

For Siobhan, the break from their daily dating was long overdue. The three words that had loomed large in the early days, which he had uttered before she, had merely become a prerequisite before returning home from an evening spent together. Often, he would whisper it gently in her ear after sex before fumbling for a cigarette. She expressed her love with irregularity, but Craig either failed to notice or was unconcerned. She admitted to herself that she loved him, but their relationship had slipped into a pattern more of convenience and familiarity than passion and excitement. Neither had been tempted by an opportunity to seek a different partner and they felt safe with each other. The spark might have dulled, but there seemed no reason to part ways or consider an alternative.

'Well?' asked Marion in anticipation. 'Are you going to open it or not?'

Siobhan was stunned for a moment, and pleasantly so as she peered inside the envelope. Her face broke into a smile that her parents felt they saw too rarely during her adolescent and late teen years as she transitioned through all the emotion and angst that seemed to dramatize her life on a daily basis.

'How did you get these?' asked Siobhan, astounded, but delighted by the gift. 'This gig has been sold out for weeks. I know people who would die to have these tickets!'

She handed two rectangular pieces of paper, each perforated a quarter of the way down one side, to Craig, who appeared less surprised and excited. Printed on both sections of the lightly shaded blue paper was bold black lettering, which read:

The Odeon, Birmingham
Friday 29th August
At 7.30 p.m.
Phil McIntyre presents
THE SMITHS
Plus support
£6-50
(£4-50 UB40 Card Holders)
Front Stalls
B32
Conditions of sale printed overleaf

'I bloody love you Mom! These are fantastic. Thank you. Thank you. Thank you. You too Dad.'

They were going to see The Smiths, the band their friends either loved or loathed, whose singer Morrissey was either a charismatic genius or a suicidal pessimist, who waved bunches of flowers around on stage and wailed hit songs like *This Charming Man* and *Heaven Knows I'm Miserable Now*. Like Siobhan, The Smiths were fervent vegetarians, illustrated by the name of their album *Meat Is Murder*. She had cried when she first heard the title track and when the twelve-inch vinyl frequently spun on her antiquated Dansette record player at 33rpm, she would sing along solemnly to the lines condemning the consumption of flesh as an unpunished form of murder.

The Smiths. She was going to see The Smiths! Siobhan already planned to burst into the nearest Woolworths store on Shirley high street the following day and eagerly buy a copy of the band's new single *Panic*, which was due to be released. What a perfect start to the week, she thought to herself.

'You can thank Craig for getting the tickets,' explained Marion, breaking her delighted daughter's celebration.

Siobhan was puzzled. Recently Craig had grudgingly admitted he admired the style of Johnny Marr, the band's innovative guitarist and chief songwriter, but his music tastes were of a much heavier variety. Judas Priest, Black Sabbath, Led Zeppelin, Queen and local bands Quartz, Magnum and the Mean Street Dealers usually spun on Craig's turntable and blasted out from his speakers.

Delighted that her ideal future son in law was the catalyst for such celebration from her daughter, Marion Murphy encouraged Craig to explain how he had managed to secure the in-demand tickets to see The Smiths.

'Some lads who were in the lower sixth when I was finishing my A levels, well I've seen them in the Bull's Head a few times recently, so we've sort of become mates. They'll all be at my friend Stephen's house when we go around there tomorrow, so you'll meet them then.'

Craig had a knack of spinning the shortest and simplest of yarns into long convoluted tales and much to Siobhan's delight, her mother was making a clockwise circular motion with her index finger to encourage him to hurry along to the point he was trying to make.

'Well anyway, a few weeks ago, your mom and dad asked what you might like for a present and later that night I was in the pub and Stephen said he was going into town to queue up to buy Smiths tickets, which were on sale the next day, so I, asked him if, you know...'

Siobhan did not need to hear any more. Lovely, lovely Craig, who for all his frustrating yet forgivable faults was always thinking of her. She walked towards him, put her finger on his lips, thrust both arms around his neck and kissed him, more passionately than either Frank or Marion Murphy felt comfortable witnessing. She released an awkwardly self-conscious Craig from her grasp and brushed down his blue uniform where she had ruffled his smart jacket and straightened his tie. She looked at him admiringly. As her parents also embraced, albeit less fervently and smiled proudly at the young couple, Siobhan rose up on her tiptoes and softly whispered in Craig's ear, causing him to blush awkwardly.

'You deserve a reward P.C. Jones. Do you have any handcuffs to go with this uniform?'

Chapter Five

'You're finally going to get your hands on a pair of tits, Stephen.'

Two startled customers and a red-faced shop assistant cringed as John Garland shouted to his friend across a sparsely furnished ladies clothes store that was in its final week of an 'everything must go' sale. Since the store was closing and relocating to new premises, even fixtures and fittings were either being sold off or given away along with the final few heavily marked down items that hung, unwanted it seemed, on two rusty metal bargain rails.

Grinning mischievously, John dumped the top half of a mannequin that had no arms and was bald in the absence of a feminine wig into the outstretched arms of Stephen Taylor. Two protruding features provided a natural means by which to carry the lifelike torso and Stephen's hands cupped around them as he steadied his load. John lifted up the lower half of the stiff body and placed the open legs around the back of his neck, holding onto the ankles to balance his cargo.

'Thank you very much,' John cried out. Bemused onlookers were joined by a second shop assistant, who shook her head as she emerged from the store room. 'I suppose boys will be boys,' she muttered as the bell that signalled the opening of the shop door pinged and the two eighteen-year-olds sauntered towards the Robin Hood traffic island, where five major roads intersected, intent on brightening the day of passing motorists. The morning rush hour and congestion of housewives returning from delivering infant offspring to the school gates had subsided and some of the few drivers now traversing the relatively unobstructed local roads honked their horns or called out from open windows as they passed the odd sight.

'She's not my type,' chuckled Stephen as he led the way towards his house, hands clamped onto fibreglass mammaries and a blank painted-on expression staring back at him.

By the time they reached number five Stonor Croft some fifteen minutes later, their friends Andy Morris and Mike Sullivan had arrived in Sully's car and were perched on the red terracotta front doorstep. They sat smoking the last of their Players No. 6 cigarettes, the empty packet crumpled and tossed into a nearby plant pot, littering an otherwise pristine front garden. Both stood up slowly, bemused looks on their faces. Sully wolf-whistled, while Andy echoed John's earlier observation.

'That's a first for you isn't it Stevie?' he laughed.

'What are you going to do with, um, 'her'?' inquired Sully, inspecting the fibreglass skin-toned curves as John assembled the two pieces, joining top and bottom halves by inserting a sturdy metal rod that poked up from the waist into the upper torso. He stood back and admired his naked new friend.

'Not what you think! But if Stephen's mom has some old clothes we can borrow, we can have a laugh with this.'

Mary Taylor, who had raised her only son as a single mother since he was three years old, was away on holiday in North Wales. Her former husband, a travelling salesman who embraced all the stereotypical temptations associated with his profession, had left home with his samples briefcase one Tuesday morning in 1971 never to return. He was the father Stephen never knew and the spouse Mrs Taylor only ever heard from once again, in a letter several weeks later that confirmed but failed to truly explain his soon to be permanent absence. The taboo of an abandoned young mother and infant son fuelled the gossip tanks of the curtain-twitching neighbours of the middle-class suburb for many months.

Now Mrs Taylor had entrusted the home she had fought hard to retain and maintain over the years, while barely making ends meet, to her usually sensible son Stephen. Some of the pranks he and his friends had pulled during the short time she had been on holiday at her sister's cottage near Llandudno ranged from harmless to downright dangerous and would not have met with her approval. The Saturday morning taxi, which had taken her to the dingy National Express bus station in Digbeth to begin a fortnight of relaxation, had barely turned the corner out of Stonor Croft when the high jinks began. That lunchtime, Stephen and John had decided to remove the entire contents of the living room and reassemble them in the back garden to create an outdoor lounge as a unique setting for a party they had planned for that evening. The three-piece suite, sideboard, television, magazine rack, family portraits, drinks cabinet (which was locked and the key safely stored in Mrs Taylor's purse), ornate lamp and a well-worn antique footstool had all passed through the French windows and were rearranged on the browned grass outside. Even an old painting of a horse and cart passing through a ford, its frame a heavy bronze ornate design, was hung from a nail protruding from a large oak tree in the garden. Only an antiquated three bar electric fire remained in place beneath the Art Deco mantle, which was a permanent fixture. The wall-to-wall carpet also escaped relocation.

The outdoor party hosted that Saturday night had welcomed numerous invited guests only, though Matt Douglass, the obnoxious next door neighbour and former school classmate of Stephen's, had gate-crashed briefly before he headed off to work as a nightclub bouncer at The Dome, a popular late night haunt in Birmingham city centre.

'There's no birds here,' he had observed bluntly, mocking the party hosts and running a dismissive rule over the female revellers who did not measure up to his apparent expectation. Having grunted a string of obscenities aimed at nobody in particular, he left by climbing over a manicured hedge, taking with him two cans of Tennant's Super lager, which were already in short supply. Nobody dared challenge the Neanderthal as he ambled towards the Stratford Road to catch the number ninety-two bus into town.

'Now you're a proper copper, can't you nick him for robbing those cans and do us all a favour?' John Garland had asked Craig Jones, a friend of Stephen's he had met for the first time a few weeks earlier in a local pub. Over a beer and a smoke, the pair had discussed the upcoming life changes both faced as they bode farewell to the relative innocence of youth and swapped schooldays for the realities of the adult world. John had booked a one-way coach ticket to journey to London for his fresher year at university and sparse digs on the Isle of Dogs, while Craig had recently completed his training towards becoming a fully-fledged member of the West Midlands Police force and had already taken his first steps out on the beat. Just as had been the case had when they supped pints in the Bull's Head a few weeks earlier, John was struggling to warm to Craig, with whom he felt he had little in common. Their music tastes differed and political views clashed and while John favoured the unpredictable though often unfulfilling escapades associated with being a single male looking to catch a girl's eye, Craig was settled contentedly in a relationship. He occasionally referenced how he planned to marry his girlfriend once she had completed her upcoming course at university.

'Yeah, maybe I could arrest him,' Craig had confirmed, unconvincingly. 'But I'm off duty, aren't I? He's right though, about there not being much talent here tonight. I'll bring my girlfriend

Siobhan to the next party with some of her friends so we can show him we're not a bunch of queers.'

John winced at Craig's choice of phrase and small-minded attitude and soon wandered away to seek further alcoholic refreshment and alternative company.

- - - - - - - - - -

Now standing beside an expressionless mannequin that Stephen had dressed in an eclectic assortment of garments and a woollen hat, all found in a bag that was bound for the local Oxfam store, the four friends surveyed the dummy.

'What next?' asked Sully.

John had been rummaging around in the old garden shed that had seldom been used since Mr Taylor had gone AWOL in 1971. From beneath a pile of dusty old blankets, he produced a length of frayed rope that he proceeded to contort into a noose-like knot, which he held up in front of Sully, Andy and Stephen.

'Well I know Stephen's been a bit depressed lately, but his mum won't be happy if she comes back next week and finds him hanging.' Sully looked deadpan at Stephen, who did not appear to be amused by the comment.

'No, this is for her,' said John, motioning to the mannequin. The three confused friends followed as John, carrying the rope, led them down an alleyway between the houses on Stonor Croft, towards a row of garages and a patch of wasteland that bordered an area of trees and bushes, which served as a shortcut to the main Stratford Road. Sully carried their catatonic female friend, dressed in all her hand-me-down glory, as the group of friends sauntered across the nearby open area of grass, laughing and making immature jokes about the potential of the mannequin for the loneliest among them. They disappeared within the bushes that lined the dirt path that led to the main road.

Once there was a sufficient break in the traffic and no sign of approaching vehicles, John dashed from the cover of the line of trees beside the main road and hastily attempted to lasso the short end of the noose over a short piece of metal that protruded from a lamppost. At the third attempt, the loop caught and he could dart back into the foliage before a car passed by, its occupants failing to notice the inconspicuous hanging noose, or the hidden youths. When a lull in activity on the road presented an opportunity, all four mischievously scrambled out into the open with the mannequin and quickly hoisted it up and slipped its head through the noose, which pulled tight when the dummy was lowered. Maggie, as they had christened her in dubious honour of the nation's leader, hung swaying slightly in the breeze. For a moment, all four friends stood oblivious to the previously paramount concern of being caught by a passing motorist or pedestrian. They grinned and clapped in brief celebration before quickly hiding again, each behind a tree trunk that ensured a clear view of Maggie and the road beside. Now they just had to wait.

Within a matter of seconds, there was a screech of tyres as a car came to an abrupt halt on the opposite side of the dual carriageway beside a bus stop. The driver initially stared open-mouthed, clearly in shock at the sight of a person hanging from a lamppost, presumably dead. His passenger, similarly stunned at first, was now laughing and patting his acquaintance on the back to reassure him that they had not happened upon a gruesome suicide, but merely a convincing prank. The driver did not seem amused.

John, Stephen, Sully and Andy were either doubled up with laughter, or pounding fists against the tree trunks in hysterics at the success of their practical joke. More cars passed and while some slowed and then sped off, the drivers either chuckling or shaking their heads in dismay, others tooted their horn and waved at the four friends who by now had grown bold enough to stray from the cover of the trees. As Sully and Andy bowed and accepted the applause of three girls whose shrills amplified from a battered old blue Mini, John tapped Stephen rapidly on the shoulder as he spied a pedestrian in the distance who was heading towards them, walking a boisterous boxer dog on a taut lead.

'Quick,' urged John to the others as he motioned towards the approaching figure. They ducked into the natural camouflage and waited. As he came within sight of Maggie, who was now swinging in the wind, the man slowed and edged cautiously towards the lamppost. The lean muscular dog was eagerly pulling on its lead and growled and barked at the hanging body. The man's face was steeped in terror but he was unable to stem a perverse urge to close in on the apparent suicide, a cigarette hanging precariously from between his lips. Once he had edged to within just a few yards of the dangling mannequin, he peered over his metal-rimmed glasses, his tense shoulders slumped back, and he let out an audibly relieved sigh and a guttural cough as he threw the cigarette butt to the kerb. His dog continued to bark incessantly as the man could hear laughter from within the line of trees.

'You sick bastards,' he yelled in the direction of the unknown pranksters. 'I'm calling the police when I get home. Come on Blaze, let's go.'

Unconcerned by the threat of their unwilling victim, the amused quartet of friends continued to milk the spoils of their prank for the best part of another half an hour.

- - - - - - - - - -

'We should go back now,' suggested Sully after more drivers and pedestrians had been duly duped. The gag was losing its appeal.

'It's lunchtime and I'm starving. We can heat up some of those frozen meals John brought over from his parents' freezer.'

Before they could lift Maggie from the noose and retreat to Stonor Croft, Andy caught sight of blue flashing lights in the distance. A shiny white Mk2 Ford Granada, with a distinctive luminous green stripe down each side, was speeding towards them along the opposite side of the dual carriageway. All four hid instinctively as the police car raced past them and began to slow as it neared a gap in the central reservation that enabled U-turns about a quarter of a mile further down the road.

'Quick!' yelled John. 'Get Maggie and then leg it before the coppers catch us.'

Stephen wanted no part of the action and turned and ran towards home, tearing through the bushes lining the dirt path, with Sully in quick pursuit. Andy and John knew they had enough time between the police car squealing as it braked to U-turn and double back along the Stratford Road towards them, to retrieve the mannequin and make their own retreat.

The noose instantly broke free from the lamppost as Andy clambered up the frame, the soles of his black monkey boots gripping the metal, and pulled frantically at the rope. The pair disappeared behind the line of trees and stumbled along the cut through bordered by bushes and bramble. As they reached the open area of wasteland beyond the foliage, John felt the dummy fall to the ground and he lost his grip as Andy jogged past him.

'Fuck this for a game of soldiers! Leave her here and let's get back to the house.'

John wasn't throwing in the towel so easily. Quickly, he grasped the lifeless body by its ankles and while running backwards, dragged it unceremoniously across the open patch of parched grass. He reached a crumbling concrete strip that ran beside a row of garages and paused for breath for a moment. He heard the screech of tyres as the police car came to an abrupt halt at the scene of the debatable crime and a dog barked beyond a fence bordering a nearby garden. John pulled a now grass-stained cream-coloured worn jumper that had ridden up over Maggie's head while being dragged, back down to cover her nakedness and two lifeless eyes stared hauntingly back at him.

His friend Sully's beaten old orange Morris Marina was parked beside the garages. Knowing the rusted locks were faulty and rarely functioned, he hastily tried the boot and the metal creaked as it opened to reveal a completely empty storage space. John dumped the mannequin into the open boot and slammed the lid closed. Hearing voices approaching from the cover of the trees, he turned and raced down the alleyway between the houses on Stonor Croft, heading for the sanctuary of number five.

Stephen, Sully and Andy were cowering but sniggering as they hid in the upstairs spare back bedroom, each daring the other to peer out of a window that overlooked the garages and wasteland and risk exposing their identity to the policemen, whose agitated muffled tones they could hear. John joined them, crawling along the floor to remain incognito, breathless and laughing as he struggled to speak.

'You bastards! Why on earth did you run?'

John rolled onto his back, catching his breath as he stared at the ceiling and listened to the chatter outside that mixed with crackling voices broadcast loudly on a police radio.

'Don't worry, by the way,' he whispered. 'Maggie's safe.'

- - - - - - - - - -

Shortly after any hint of probing voices had faded from outside the rear of the anonymous Taylor residence in Stonor Croft, four sheepish teenagers ventured into the back garden and peered over the wood-panelled fence. The boot of Mike Sullivan's Morris Marina was still closed and there was no sign of irate policemen, items of second hand clothing or mannequin body parts.

The hoax suicide had generated enough excitement and humour to furnish countless tall tales to tell down the pub in the coming weeks, but Stephen in particular was nervous that the group's antics would upset neighbours and land him in trouble. He suspected the chain-smoking old man with the snarling boxer dog who lived a few doors down had made good on his threat to dial up the local constabulary. Despite the protests of his three friends, he began returning the living room furniture that had been resident in the garden since the weekend's party to its rightful place. As the four struggled under the weight of the sideboard Stephen inquired after their missing mannequin.

'Where's Maggie, John? You told us she's safe, but what did you mean?'

John laughed as the bulky sideboard was eased back onto a darker patch of living room carpet that had not been exposed to the many years of sunlight that had slightly faded the majority of the red shag pile.

'Well, you bastards didn't care enough to save her from being caught by the fuzz, so I'm not telling you. Don't worry, you'll see her again.'

The final item moved inside was the ornate wooden drinks cabinet and Stephen struggled to resist the pleas of his friends to jimmy open the lock since their once plentiful supply of cheap beer that had stocked the fridge had been consumed at their party the previous weekend.

The friends were heading into town later that evening to see a gig at Peacocks, a venue in Birmingham, fashionable with fans of what had become dubbed the indie music scene. The Burning, a local group growing in popularity and attracting interest from major record companies, were playing that night and all four lads were eager to see them live.

Stephen grabbed hold of Andy's arm and glanced at his silver-metallic digital wristwatch.

'Hey, John, are you still going to Woolies to buy the new Smiths single? I told that lad Craig from the pub that we'd have it this afternoon and he said him and his bird might come round for a listen.'

Panic, the latest seven-inch vinyl release by the Manchester group, whose popularity now ranked higher than U2, The Alarm and Echo and the Bunnymen among the four friends, was poised to hit the shelves at Woolworths on the bustling Shirley high street that afternoon. John was eager to add the single to an impressive record collection he had started when only nine years old during the post-punk boom of the late seventies. He then planned to rush urgently back to Stephen's house to share that special moment when the stylus of a record player crackles into the groove of revolving black vinyl to magically reveal the notes and tones of a previously unheard and much anticipated tune for the first time. All four had borrowed, begged and in some cases stolen to afford tickets to see The Smiths live at The Odeon in town in a month's time. The release of a new record only served to heighten their excitement. The gig promised to be the highlight of their last perfect carefree summer together.

John fumbled in his pocket and waved his wallet in the air. Five minutes later, he wandered through the wasteland cut through to the main road, smirking as he passed the lamppost where they had hung Maggie, and walked towards Woolworths on Shirley high street.

Chapter Six

'Are you expecting rain?'

John Garland perched on a green plastic seat inside a muggy bus shelter as the afternoon's sun streamed erratically through three graffiti-covered reinforced glass windows. He thumbed nervously at a plastic Woolworths shopping bag as he wished he had conjured up a more impressive ice-breaking line aimed towards the beautiful girl who sat on the opposite end of the bench. A large umbrella rested beside her. She too held a Woolworths bag, which dangled casually from her finger as she swayed lightly from side to side. She appeared to be humming and mildly singing to herself.

John had almost breezed past the bus stop, having planned to walk the short mile or so from Shirley high street back to his friend Stephen Taylor's house where his arrival, or rather that of the new seven-inch single release by The Smiths, was eagerly anticipated by his waiting friends. A glance inside the vandalised bus shelter had stopped John in his tracks. Sitting alone, staring disinterested at the bustling Stratford Road, was a girl of about his age who looked at John, smiled warmly then returned her gaze to the blur of traffic that sped by. John was stunned by her beauty. He checked the ridged plastic seat for chewing gum, the scourge of many a bus traveller, and sat pensively, staring at the most striking girl he had ever seen.

When she turned again and saw John's expression that seemed to be awaiting a reply, that melting smile amplified and curling her shoulder-length auburn hair behind her right ear with her fingers, she removed a small white earpiece attached to a thin wire that led to a whirring Sony Walkman tape cassette player. She spoke, slightly embarrassed.

'I'm sorry, did you say something? I couldn't hear you.'

Her voice was as soft and seductive to John as her effortless beauty. Now she was going to think him an idiot for his lame comment, unless he could think of a better line, despite his mind being a blur. He couldn't. His delivery of what he had originally considered a witty observation was unimpressive

'Rain. Are you, um, expecting rain?'

The girl shifted on her seat and looked thoroughly confused until John pointed to the umbrella and motioned to the shards of sunlight that pierced through the spray-painted shelter. The beautiful girl again broke into that melting smile.

'Oh, no. It's for my Dad. I just collected it from Woolies for him. It's for when he plays golf.'

John frowned and the girl responded with a confused look of her own, especially when John provided his observation of the umbrella.

'That won't be any use for golf. The balls are small, the holes are a long way away and he won't be able to hit anything with that.'

John shifted cautiously along the bench so that he now sat beside the girl, breathing in her white musk perfume. He picked up the umbrella, inspecting the brown hard plastic handle at one end and the metal point at the other. The girl laughed as he continued his appraisal.

'You see, golf clubs have a metal piece at the end, angled to a certain degree. Seven irons, sand wedges, woods. They're all designed to hit the ball, but this thin point here, well, this just isn't going to work.'

He handed the umbrella back to her, shaking his head dismissively with a mocking smile.

Now laughing and rolling her eyes at John's absurd observation, the girl stood up and chinked a few coins in her hand, nodding towards the road where a double-decker bus approached. She didn't speak, but smiled warmly again at John, who was delighted that his obscure humour had served as a conversation starter after all.

As he heard the umbrella tip tap along the aisle and saw the girl choose a seat near the back of the bus, John fumbled in his pocket for money having not originally planned to pay for public transport on his way back to Stephen's house. He produced barely enough coppers for the driver to press a button on his console that dispatched the change loudly to an unseen destination somewhere within his cab and produce a blue and grey ticket from a machine mounted higher up to the right. John grabbed the thin strip of paper, which he stuffed into his pocket and noticed the girl was now glancing up from inspecting the contents of her Woolworths bag and was smiling at him.

He sat sideways on the passenger-worn double seat in front of her, stretched his arm confidently across the length of the backrest between them and leaned his back against the window. He motioned as if to request her approval for his seating choice and she nodded and spoke, having placed both her Walkman and earphones into her bag. There was an undertone of caution in her voice.

'I'm only going a few stops, as far as Robin Hood Island.'

John smiled, unconcerned that her journey and their time together would last four or five stops at the most and perhaps barely as many minutes.

'Me too, that's where I'm getting off, just outside the Kentucky.'

John protested as the girl questioned the coincidence. He imagined that corny one-liners and excuses to abandon a bus ride conveniently at the same stop as her must have been commonplace. She must surely have a built in repellent reflex, he thought.

'No, really, I'm visiting a friend's house near there so we can listen to this.'

John fumbled for the plastic bag placed beside him on the seat and pulled out the latest addition to his record collection. A black and white photo of an actor from the sixties, whom John did not know was Richard Bradford, a star of the screen from a time before he was born, peered up at the girl from the cover and at big sky blue lettering that simply read 'SMITHS.' The girl laughed, not mockingly, but in a moment of pleasant surprise at John having produced *Panic*, the band's new single, released earlier that day.

'Mine's bigger than yours!'

She opened her similar white Woolworths bag and proudly showed off the larger 12-inch version of the same single with a satisfied smile.

'They told me they'd just sold out. The person at Woolies before me had bought the last…'

John's voice trailed off as the identity of the customer, who had denied him a copy of the vinyl containing an extra track on the B-side, became clear. They both laughed and she reached to press the red button that rang a bell in the driver's cab to request a stop. The bus slowed and came to a halt and John followed the girl down the aisle, her hair flicking as she snapped her head to the side to confirm John was behind her.

She was perfect. She liked The Smiths, she was dressed in a fashionable white jacket with the sleeves rolled up over a loose black t-shirt, fitted Lee denim jeans and soft brown leather ankle boots. She looked over her shoulder again, this time with an enticing smile before they both stepped onto the pavement and she thanked the driver as the concertina doors closed. The bus pulled away in a stale trail of diesel fumes.

'So, which way are you going really?'

She was testing John, to determine if the point at which he had followed her off the bus was genuinely his intended destination. John stretched out his hand and coaxed the girl towards him. She responded, amused by his confidence and they walked hand in hand away from Robin Hood Island, John leading the way, uncertain as to whether she was humouring him or also planned to head in that direction.

They talked of a shared love of The Smiths and other bands and of tiresome A Level studies that both were delighted to have recently completed. Neither was concerned over their likely exam results, both confident they had achieved grades sufficient to confirm the university placements of their choice. He introduced himself fully as John Garland, but she playfully refused to tell him even her first name despite pleas and protests.

John was determined not to let go of the gorgeous girl's hand and she made no effort to lessen her grip, enjoying the flirtation. The tightness in his gut that had punched him the moment he spied her sitting in the bus shelter was still raging. Usually calm and indifferent when out on a date, John had never truly experienced this sickening yet addictive feeling. His emotions were in turmoil. He was truly captivated by the mystery girl walking beside him.

As they waited to cross a side road, John stared at her beauty as she searched in her pocket for a scrap of paper that confirmed the street number of the house where she was heading. She was perfect, he thought. Her skin was like porcelain, not tanned or blemished by the summer sun, so smooth he wanted to touch her cheek. She had mysterious deep brown eyes, a slightly elongated but cute nose and soft high cheekbones; a look he imagined would have endeared her to popular society back in the 1920s. Who is this girl, he wondered to himself?

Her smile lit up as she caught him staring. Embarrassed, John searched for a witty comment, but instead his heart sank as she loosened her grip and let his hand slip away.

'I have to go down this road here.'

Coincidentally, John was heading the same way, but fearing this might be the moment she would vanish from his life after an all too brief encounter, he asked for her phone number, optimistic after the playful and natural connection he felt on the bus and during their short walk together.

'No! Fucking hell, no!'

John was taken aback and rocked on his heels at the ferocity of her reply. He had asked for her phone number, not a shag. Before he could respond, the girl clamped both hands on the side of her head, massaging her temples as she squinted her eyes closed and shook her head.

'No, no, it's not that. I left the umbrella on the fucking bus!'

Her eyes were now wide open, her hands still clasped to her cheeks as she stared at the floor in disbelief.

'My dad waited weeks for that thing to come in and he'll be so pissed off with me for losing it.'

John looked at her blankly, a smirk gradually emerging on his face. She tried but failed not to laugh.

'Stop it. It's not funny. I can't believe I lost the umbrella. It's all your fault!'

John held his arms out to the side, his palms facing skyward as he gestured that he was innocent and bemused by her accusation. She walked briskly along Stonor Croft, the quiet road they had just reached, and again scanned the piece of paper, double-checking the number against those mounted on the sides of the white pebble-dashed houses. She looked over her shoulder at John, shooting him the same mischievous and enticing look as she had on the bus and laughed loudly, her smile stoking that crippling fire burning in John's stomach.

John smiled back, but then his belly ached and his heart sank again as he saw her standing outside a house he recognised.

'Hold on. Are you Siobhan?'

She turned abruptly at the end of a short lightly-gravelled path that led to a dutifully scrubbed terracotta step and a house clearly identified as number five Stonor Croft by a large wooden number painted red that was affixed the wall. Her eyes narrowed and she stared at John bemused.

'Oh Jesus, you're going to marry Craig the copper!'

Siobhan laughed mockingly. She responded with a short cluster of exasperated questions.

'What? Who told you that? Did Craig, because it's news to me if he did. Did he really tell you that? When? Is this where you're going too? To Stephen's house?'

John trudged slowly along the path as Siobhan pressed the white plastic doorbell that produced a loud shrill and brought Stephen Taylor to the front door. He looked confused to see an unknown female standing beside his friend John, both carrying matching white Woolworths carrier bags.

'Hello, I'm Siobhan, Craig's wife. Mrs Jones if you like. Pleased to meet you.'

Siobhan waltzed past Stephen, following the loud sound of music emanating from the back room and opened the door to a welcoming smile and the outstretched arms of Craig Jones.

Thoroughly bemused, Stephen stared at John, who still stood on the step outside, brushing his feet on the stiff wire mat before entering the house. He laughed and patted Stephen on the shoulder as he entered.

'Don't even ask mate. She's gorgeous, but I think she might also be a little crazy.'

Sat awkwardly at a small wooden table in a darkened corner of Peacocks Bar, Craig Jones was noticeably aggrieved. His entire frame appeared to tense as he craned his neck towards the stage where a local post-punk group, The Burning, were pounding their way through a unique new wave version of the Motown classic *Band of Gold*. The multitude of colourful flashing lights flickering around the venue made it impossible to determine which of the merging silhouettes among the swirling crowd were John Garland and Siobhan Murphy. His girlfriend and the boy she had returned with from Woolworths had gradually found their way to near the front of the packed dance floor to seek a prime view of the band, followed by Andy Morris and Mike Sullivan, who had both since returned to the table in the corner for liquid refreshment. Craig deliberated over which of the collection of tall glasses of lager was his before making his selection and downing the best part of half a pint.

'It's sweatier than a rugby player's jockstrap up there,' gasped Andy, who used the sleeve of his cotton shirt to mop perspiration from his brow. 'The band are bloody great though aren't they? That guitarist's Mohican is just tremendous. Never seen anything quite like it.'

Andy failed to stir any such enthusiasm from Craig, who thought he caught a glimpse of Siobhan until he realised she was actually a he, with similar long brown hair. Stephen Taylor returned from the toilet still cursing a large and visible damp patch that embarrassingly highlighted the crotch of his jeans where his friend John had accidentally knocked an entire pint into his lap earlier in the evening. The hand dryer in the men's room had barely breathed enough hot air to even partially dry his sodden jeans despite three attempts.

Craig was now standing beside the table, arching his neck like a giraffe as The Burning launched into a cover of *King Rocker* by Generation X and the Peacocks hordes let out an appreciative cheer in response to the crowd-pleaser. This evening, his girlfriend seemed to prefer the company of John, from their shared delight at the dulcet tones of the new Smiths single, to critiquing Stephen's record collection together in his living room, while managing to belittle some of Craig's differing musical preferences. Squeezing the six of them into Sully's rusty old Morris Marina for the drive into town had necessitated four passengers cramming onto the back seat together. Siobhan had somehow become positioned on John's lap, her legs stretched out across Craig and Andy. Perhaps Craig was unduly concerned and the combination of a frustrating day out on the police beat and having paid two quid to watch a local band he thought unimpressive was just gnawing at his paranoia. His foul mood was also fuelled by the laugh everyone else had enjoyed at his expense when they left Stephen's house earlier that evening.

Having been subjected to the song *Panic* multiple times, while draining the last of several bottles of lager that had briefly replenished Stephen's fridge, Craig had mentioned how earlier that day he and a police colleague had responded to a complaint call in the Stonor Croft area while out on patrol. His anecdote seemed to perk the interest of John, Andy, Sully and Stephen who listened intently, proving to be an unexpectedly captive audience. Craig told of how a relatively routine Monday to begin his third week accompanying a veteran constable patrolling the suburbs in a smart and shiny police car had sprung into life when they responded to a call. The pair had just wrapped up dealing with a minor a shoplifting offence at a supermarket in Shirley by issuing a caution when an alert came through on the radio that a concerned pensioner had observed three or four youths hanging a woman by her neck from a lamp post. Craig's colleague tore down the Stratford Road at such a rate of knots that Craig was certain he was about to deposit the lunch he had consumed a short time earlier all over the dashboard, but at the same time thrived on the rush of adrenaline he felt as they swerved between traffic, their blue lights blazing and siren screaming. Craig had been thrilled at the prospect of being the first responder to an attempted murder case.

He was exhilarated as the police car screeched to a halt beside a cut through that led to the rear of the houses on Stonor Croft and he leaped out in pursuit of the fleeing criminals. He became less enamoured with the apparently false lead when there was no sign of either a noosed woman, or a band of youthful killers. The experienced nose of P.C. Edmonds, Craig's fellow bobby, smelled a rat and although there appeared to be marks in the grass betraying a dragged body, he was unconvinced. A clearer explanation of the crime committed was provided by the elderly neighbour, who, between barks and yelps from his agitated dog, explained it was a showroom dummy that had been hanging from a lamppost and that some young hooligans were responsible for the prank.

Listening to Craig recall his brush with master criminals, John had been curious about the outcome of the wild goose chase. After the group walked through the alleyway beside Stephen's house towards the old orange Marina that would transport them to Peacocks, they watched an animated Craig point out some of the suspected hiding places he and P.C. Edmonds had searched while seeking the perpetrators. John had decided to press for more information.

'So, did Starsky and Hutch catch the mannequin murderer, or should Stephen sleep with a cricket bat beneath his pillow tonight?'

Craig had showed his displeasure for John's mockery with an irritated two-finger salute that he made sure everyone noticed. As John stepped away from the back of the car, he flipped the boot open and Craig let out a shriek that echoed between the rows of garages close by.

'Fucking hell, I thought…'

Craig soon composed himself and was now peering into the boot, no longer shaken, but surveying what turned out to be a lifeless mannequin dressed poorly in women's clothes, which were dusty and dirty from clearly having been dragged along the nearby path.

'Aargh, ooohh!' mocked Sully, adopting a startled expression and animated pose that might have been borrowed from a low budget horror film as he mimicked Craig's reaction. To make matters worse, Siobhan had been testing the working of a small instamatic camera and captured Craig's panicked expression for posterity. He was not amused.

'You bastards! Me and P.C. Edmonds spent a good fucking hour responding to that call, not to mention all the paperwork we had to submit back at the station. And all along it was you immature tossers playing a prank. I should nick you all, right here.'

- - - - - - - - - -

With the house lights now up to illuminate two roadies, as they dragged away amplifiers, speaker cabinets and various components of a drum kit after The Burning's gig, Peacocks was exposed as being a dark, dank, beer-soaked and cigarette-stained hovel from wall to clammy wall. It was essentially a disused function room at the rear of the long-established New Imperial Hotel that provided local bands with a stage for their burgeoning talents. The doors of Peacocks led onto Needless Alley, a narrow thoroughfare between the shops of New Street and the grounds of Birmingham Cathedral, known affectionately as Pigeon Park, since it was home to a thriving population of the city's feathered friends. John and Stephen had joined a group engaged in conversation with the singer and guitarist from The Burning, who were triumphantly sipping beer from tall green cans of Tennant's lager provided as part of their backstage rider. Siobhan was candidly shooting photographs of the scene, capturing John's image more deliberately than those of the band.

As Sully herded his friends towards the exit to return to his car, Craig was examining the bar's notice board and frowned at the names of some of the groups booked to play at Peacocks in the coming weeks. 'The Reformation Club featuring Prehistoric Pets, Partners in Crime, Fetch Eddie and Major Hero,' he read aloud from a Letraset poster. 'They all sound a bit weird to me. How did you find this place anyway? I mean that hotel next door has a very dodgy reputation. My Sarge tells me that every now and then there's a call at the station to come and sort out a disturbance and it's usually a bit strange what's going on there.'

Craig felt a sharp pinch of his bum, which startled him and made him jump in shock. Expecting to see Siobhan's playful smile, he was instead greeted by a muscular man, all of six feet tall, who minced, as his colleagues at the station would say, in the direction of the exit. The man, dressed in a tight white string vest and even closer-fitting black leather trousers, beckoned to him with an authoritative index finger.

'If you lot have homes to go to, make your way outside please. Or we do have rooms available at the hotel next door if you have something else in mind.'

Craig felt particularly uneasy when the man winked at him. He joined Sully in encouraging the others to exit.

- - - - - - - - - -

Once outside, the midnight air felt cooler than the humidity of Peacocks and John tugged the cuffs of the denim jacket he had worn faithfully since unearthing it at the Birmingham Rag Market in March down over his wrists and folded his arms tightly in front of him, letting out a slight shiver. He noticed Siobhan also pull her jacket closer to beat off the mild chill and shook his head as Craig ignored her, rambling on about the nature of his hastened departure from Peacocks as the group ambled up the alleyway. John gazed at Siobhan, who smiled back just as she had multiple times that afternoon, only now her signals had evolved considerably. During one of the songs, when they stood close to the front of the crowd watching The Burning, she had unexpectedly taken his hand. He had known her only a matter of hours, but the romantic glances, the passionate discussions of shared musical interests while in Stephen's living room, sitting on his lap in the car, taking his photo, holding his hand; surely, they were signs, weren't they?

They skirted the edge of Pigeon Park, heading for a weathered plot of abandoned land that doubled conveniently as a night time car park. John waved his TSB bank card aloft and proclaimed theatrically that he would be drawing the princely sum of ten pounds from the cashpoint located at the corner of Temple Row and Cherry Street. Earlier that evening, Siobhan had lamented her need for money to replace the umbrella she had unintentionally discarded on the bus. Producing a similar blue and white card from her purse, she followed John. The others continued and gradually wandered out of sight, passing the back of Rackhams department store, where a couple embraced in the shadows and another appeared to be talking full advantage of a nearby shop doorway darkened by the lack of illumination from streetlights in disrepair.

Her transaction complete, Siobhan nestled her bank card beside two crisp ten pound notes in her small red purse and she turned to thank John for his gallantry after he had offered to stand guard over her and repel any danger that might emerge from the empty streets. His was a humorous chivalry, but the city had indeed suffered a spate of muggings of bank customers withdrawing late night cash in secluded locations.

John peered beyond Siobhan's shoulder to confirm the others were no longer within eyesight and almost lunging forward, forcibly kissed her, nearly knocking Siobhan backwards and down the bank steps. His arm steadied her as it arched around her waist, while he brushed her hair away from her face that at first had contorted with shock at his kiss, but was now relaxed and soft as she responded. Siobhan returned his impulsive gesture with equal passion and John felt her tense body ease as she wrapped both arms around his neck and pulled him closer. They kissed again and then paused briefly, each breathing heavily and paralysed it seemed by the spontaneous moment. They stood, foreheads and noses touching gently as they kissed lightly, almost guiltily, but relieved and overwhelmed at their embrace.

Sully's sudden cry from a distance shook them and they became individuals again, standing alert, side-by-side, concerned that they had been so locked in passion that the others had tracked back and discovered their clandestine embrace. Relieved that the call to catch up had come from a few hundred feet away, John reached for Siobhan's hand, but she pushed him away, hurried down the steps and urged him to follow.

'No. We can't. Not now.'

What did she mean? Can't explore the undeniable connection John knew they had unearthed and surely had to pursue? Or was her concern only for this specific moment, with their friends and most pointedly her boyfriend in such close proximity? Perhaps her hesitation was of a broader nature, suggesting she would remain the girlfriend of Craig the copper for the foreseeable future and was reluctant to sever their dreary and monotonous relationship.

John stood confused, his shoulders slumped, frustrated that the most meaningful and gut-wrenching instant of passion since he had first locked lips with a girl, had him in turmoil. Kissing Siobhan Murphy, who was unquestionably the most beautiful girl he had ever met, should have left him elated, eager to loudly proclaim his love from the steps of the TSB bank to trigger the flock of sleeping pigeons into flight. Instead this indescribably euphoric emotion was sobered by a presumably equally conflicted Siobhan hurrying along to catch up with the others, and of course, her long-established boyfriend, Craig.

By the time he had meandered the same dim route, John spied his friends, who had wisely chosen to cross Corporation Street, rather than dice with the unpredictability of one of the city's many pedestrian subways that lurked below. He focused on Craig's shielding arm draped loosely across Siobhan's stiff shoulders as they walked together awkwardly. John slouched along at the rear of the group.

Once at the makeshift car park, a defensive Craig shepherded Siobhan into the front passenger seat of Sully's car and squeezed uncomfortably and awkwardly in beside her, assuring the others that this painful travelling arrangement was preferable to the previous distribution of bodies on the inbound journey. Craig boasted that if intercepted between the city centre and the suburbs by an unimpressed police patrol, he could flash his warrant card at an intervening fellow officer and deflect any threat of prosecution.

Sully laughed at the ridiculous sight of Craig contorted between his girlfriend and the door, which he locked from the inside to ensure they did not unintentionally alight a member of the party on the way home. Then he navigated between Siobhan's curves and the dashboard to reach the car's cassette player and rewind a tape of The Smiths, a band it turned out all six of them were going to see live at the Birmingham Odeon just a few weeks later. He fought the gear stick into first and drove cautiously out of the pot-holed car parking space, heading towards Digbeth and the Stratford Road.

'I wish one of you buggers would learn to drive so that I could have a drink once in a while.'

John protested Sully's complaint with a reminder that he too had the ability to engage a motor vehicle, but admittedly lacked the legal certification to do so, having failed his driving test a few weeks earlier.

The spooling tape made a familiar clicking sound once rewound and clunked as it slipped into auto-play mode. After a brief silent pause and the hiss of a recording untreated by Dolby, the unmistakable haunting riff of *How Soon Is Now* pierced the speakers. All sat in appreciative silence at the guitar genius of Johnny Marr, though John's mind was consumed by his undeniable moment of passion with Siobhan beside the TSB hole in the wall.

What had she meant by *not now*?

'How Soon Is Now?' asked the song. How soon indeed, John thought while appropriating the lyrics to align with his own current state of mind. How could he create an opportunity for them be alone together, even briefly, so he could tell her how he felt and discover if she was equally as besotted? He threw back his head against the rear of the back seat, closed his eyes and exhaled a deep frustrated sigh. Stephen was already sleeping to his left, while to his right Andy was nodding, eyes closed and tapping his fingers, transfixed by the hypnotic beat of the song blaring from the tape deck.

So, whose fingers could John feel tracing his knee, as if spelling out letters? John sat upright, bemused and saw Siobhan's hand reaching back between the front seats of the car, unbeknown to Craig, who was struggling to focus his blurred and somewhat drunken vision on the street lights as they passed by rapidly. Siobhan's finger seemed to trace either a letter L or a number seven on John's knee, unseen by the other passengers. She caught his confused expression in the rear-view mirror. John silently mouthed 'seven?' and she nodded in confirmation. Siobhan turned to gaze nonchalantly out of the windscreen and listen to Craig's tipsy mutterings, while with her finger, she traced the shape of a number four and then another four on John's knee. Suddenly he realised they were the first three digits of her phone number, which she was secretly sharing with John. He let out a relieved laugh that briefly disturbed Andy from his musical trance, to which he quickly returned as Siobhan revealed four further figures.

John had it! He had Siobhan's phone number.

As Morrissey sang, John understood that Siobhan had literally meant that right now, tonight, they had to temper their romantic instincts, but that the following day, he could call the beautiful girl with the porcelain skin and the melting smile to steal her away from Craig Jones. How soon is now? Tomorrow would dawn soon enough and John would make his move. He reclined against the seat back again, this time content with the night's outcome, repeating the seven figures to himself, to burn them indelibly into his memory.

Chapter Eight

Five weeks later

'No Siobhan, you can't! You just can't!'

Marion Murphy was perplexed. She angrily threw a damp tea towel, its crumpled print depicting the Ring of Kerry and other favoured Irish tourist spots, faded from several years of use, onto an unfashionable Formica kitchen counter. The towel hit a dried juice glass, which skidded towards the edge of the counter, but stopped short of falling to the floor below.

'I bloody well can, Mom, and I have. It's my life, you know!'

Siobhan Murphy wanted to pick up the glass and smash it against the beige tiled wall, imagining a million pieces shattering across the kitchen to amplify her frustration and satisfy her anger. She hated these heated rows with her mother, particularly when the catalyst was her relationship with Craig Jones. She walked calmly from the kitchen to the lounge, resisting the temptation to slam the doors to either room, and slumped onto a large soft brown sofa that wrapped itself around her as she landed. Her mother was not finished and trailed behind her.

'How can you, Siobhan? Poor Craig. He's always been such a sweetheart and now you're dumping him for some lad you've just met? What about that concert you're supposed to be going to tonight?'

Siobhan banged the back of her head several times against the spongy sofa, while staring blankly at the ceiling. She let out a guttural sigh that was loud enough to illustrate her displeasure. Calmly, as she made eye contact with her mother, who stood over her demanding an answer, Siobhan confessed.

'Actually Mom, I haven't just broken up with Craig. It happened a few weeks ago, but I didn't tell you because I knew how you'd react. I've seen John, who, yes, is my new boyfriend, almost every night since then and every weekend. You just assumed it was Craig I was seeing, but it wasn't, okay?'

Marion attempted to interject to voice her objection, but Siobhan's vitriol was gathering pace.

'You honestly assume that because you think Craig is wonderful, I'm just going to stay in a relationship regardless of my feelings. Well I'm not, Mom. Yes, Craig is a lovely person and I upset him when I broke up with him, but I've met someone else. It's as simple as that. Can't you just let me do what I want to do? What difference does it make who I'm going out with?'

Agitated and angry, rather than unleash an opinion of Marion's smothering parenting she might regret once their spat calmed, Siobhan rose from the sofa and edged past her mother as she stood in the doorway. She stomped up the stairs; some creaking louder than others as her feet pounded the worn maroon carpet.

'I'm going to the Smiths gig tonight with John, okay? Craig told me he's sold his ticket to someone. I hope that's okay with you Mom. Oh, and I'm surprised Dad didn't tell you about this because I told him a couple of weeks ago.'

The bedroom door proved too tempting a target. Slammed shut, it bounced back open a few inches before Siobhan closed herself in the bedroom loudly and purposefully with her foot, causing family portraits, including one of Siobhan and her former love posing for their annual end of term photograph, to shake slightly on the landing wall.

Disappointed but not defeated, Marion returned to the kitchen to extinguish the gas flame burning beneath a tarnished stainless steel kettle that had been whistling throughout the tail end of the argument. She took a West Midlands Police Force mug Craig had given her husband as a present the previous Christmas, which already contained a splash of milk and a PG Tips tea bag, and poured in boiling water. Drumming her fingers on the kitchen counter as she waited for the leaves to steep, she smiled to herself. The following morning, she, her husband Frank and Siobhan would jump into the family's already luggage laden Hillman Avenger estate car to embark on a four-and-a-half-hour crack of dawn drive to Pembroke in Wales, regardless of how tired Siobhan might complain she was after the effects of attending the Smiths gig. There they would catch a sea ferry to Rosslare and eventually arrive at her family home in Ireland. The main purpose of the excursion, other than to enjoy a boozy ten-day reunion with her sisters, many cousins and old friends in Enniscorthy, was to enjoy a final family summer holiday on the emerald isle before Siobhan left to take up her place at Liverpool University.

Marion contentedly stirred two heaped teaspoons of white sugar into her brew and took a sweet sip of tea as she hatched a plot to revive the relationship between Siobhan and Craig. By the time she had scored points almost equal to those totalled by the bright contestants on Channel 4's *Countdown* quiz show, which she watched routinely at this time every afternoon, Marion was convinced she could talk some sense into that daughter of hers. She would wear her down during the long and arduous journey to Ireland. Marion drank her tea and switched off the television, smiling at the prospect of P.C. Jones being reunited with his destiny and the Murphy family.

Matt Douglass planned only a brief pause to bid his mother goodbye, between pounding down the stairs at number three Stonor Croft and slamming the frosted glass front door shut behind him as he raced away to catch a bus into town. An inconveniently timed phone call from a local police constable had already caused him to be running late by a few minutes.

'Alright, you old bag, I'm off. I'll see you next weekend, or maybe the weekend after.'

Rosemary Douglass shifted in her comfy armchair, calling after her son, puzzled by his rapid farewell.

A stark mop of spiky blonde hair poked around the living room door.

'I thought you weren't leaving until tomorrow morning, Matthew. Are you off now instead?'

Matt entered the room, which apart from a recently rented colour television might have been time-warped from the 1950s, its decor bland and unfashionable. Agitated at having been slowed by his mother's inquiry and her short-term memory issues, he cleared a spot on which to perch among a mass of knitting and sewing patterns that covered a fraying old sofa. He cursed the sharp poke of a stray knitting needle that protruded from an eclectic pile of balls of wool and tossed the offending long metal pin onto a low wooden coffee table, where it bounced and rolled before coming to rest against another supply of yarn. He reached over to the Baird television set, the theme tune from the popular soap *Coronation Street* blaring out loudly enough for Rosemary to hear comfortably and for Mrs Taylor next door to routinely bang on the wall to register her complaint. Matt turned the volume all the way down.

'I know you're deaf Mom, but I did tell you what I'm doing. I'm going to see a band called The Smiths tonight at the Odeon in town then I'll have a few beers with some mates and come home. I've packed my suitcase. It's in the car, which is in the garage, so I can get up early tomorrow and drive to London. I should be back next weekend, or the one after, unless I find a job and then, who knows. I won't wake you, Mom, but I'll give you a ring from The Smoke.'

Rosemary appeared to be processing the information Matt had already shared the previous day as she motioned to the television, requesting her son restore the volume since there was movement inside the Rovers Return and the show she never missed had started.

'Okay, love, just be careful. Here, I thought you couldn't get a ticket to that concert.'

Matt rolled his eyes, again frustrated and a little concerned at his ageing mother's apparent inability to retain simple information. His father had died from a heart attack only four years after the unexpected delight of welcoming a child into the world despite the odds being stacked against parenthood with both in their forties. Now retired, having worked as a secretary for countless years at a small insurance company, Rosemary survived on her pension and the amount her son was willing to contribute, depending on the fluctuation of his erratic monthly income. Matt seemed to spend as much money as he earned as a nightclub bouncer on alcohol and Saturday afternoons spent in the smoky atmosphere of the bookies by Robin Hood Island. The unexplained work he did for a businessman with a shady reputation furnished a lifestyle of which Rosemary disapproved, but rarely confronted. Matt regularly crashed through the front door drunk and staggered noisily up the stairs to bed in the early hours and slept off his hangover deep into the afternoon, sometimes woken only because of the raised volume of the television and game show contestants selecting another vowel or consonant. Rosemary could gauge when Matt's work was scarce, or when the drinking bouts intensified, by how often five-pound notes disappeared from the purse she left nightly on the sideboard in her living room.

'I told you yesterday, Mom, I got a ticket from a copper, of all people. I was filling in a form at the police station after finishing my community service and he was pinning an advert to a notice board trying to sell one. I bought it from him right there and then.'

Rosemary nodded and pretended that she remembered.

'So, do you think you'll be late tonight?'

Matt laughed, irritated. She used to complain when he was younger that anything she said went in one ear and out the other. Now the shoe seemed to be fitted snugly on the other foot. He turned the volume on the television back to beyond a reasonable level and mockingly yelled his reply as he exited the room.

'I don't know, Mom. What difference does it make? Bye Mom!'

'No. No. No. Hold on fellas. No chips on the bus. You know the rules.'

Winston Roberts kept hold of the handle that cranked the concertina doors at the front of his double-decker bus, leaving them open as two teenagers climbed aboard, their fare in one hand, white crumpled paper packages in the other.

'Oh, come on Winston, you know us. We won't make a mess. We don't want to wait twenty minutes for another bus.'

Stephen Taylor's impassioned plea drew a reluctant smile from the bus driver who recognised the pair as two of the more polite youngsters who had hopped on and off his platform since they were in short trousers, rarely giving him cause for concern. He tipped his brown trilby hat, which contravened regulation attire, but afforded him some form of individuality.

'Okay then, but no mess and no leaving your rubbish upstairs, or I won't let you two back on if you catch my bus when it's time to come home.'

John Garland gave a thumbs up sign, his mouth crammed too full of deep-fried wedges of potato to speak in appreciation. Their fare deposited in the automated slot and tickets dispensed, they clambered noisily up the metallic steps to the top deck, choosing to sit all the way at the back. Sprawled across a long blue-coloured bench seat capable of hosting five passengers, John and Stephen delved into their large bags of salt and vinegar-soaked chips that had been freshly fried at Jack's Fish & Chips Shop.

By the time the bus had navigated half a dozen more stops, they were deep in discussion about John's favourite subject, Siobhan Murphy.

Five weeks had passed since with great urgency, John had scrawled seven large digits that comprised Siobhan's phone number across his bedroom mirror with a blue felt tip pen that had not seen the light of day outside an old plastic pencil case since his final hours at senior school. He had sat contented on his bed, reading out loud the ten-inch high numbers that were already imprinted in his memory. His parents were less impressed at the sight of the vandalised furniture, the marking indelibly etched there for posterity. Since then, John and Siobhan had become inseparable. Their relationship had been consummated more rapidly than either had expected, in large part because John and Siobhan had regularly snuck into an office building in the city centre where he, Sully, Stephen and Andy all held down part time jobs at evenings and on occasional weekends. Each was furnished with a key to the premises and John took full advantage of his access and a soft sprawling sofa in an upstairs room on a regular after-hours basis.

Siobhan had won the approval of Mr and Mrs Garland and more importantly the acceptance of the close-knit circle of friends, none of whom particularly objected to a fifth wheel spinning yarns with them during regular Friday and Saturday ventures to the Bull's Head pub. The occasional accompaniment of Siobhan's friends added a welcome female element to the social circle and helped fuel the romantic pursuits of Sully and Andy in particular. There barely seemed to be a day or evening when John and Siobhan were not together, either enjoying a live gig at Peacocks, seeking seclusion in the darkened office, drinking in the pub, pooling together for a bag of chips to scoff on the bench outside Jack's, or on one special occasion splashing out on a slap-up meal at the posh Italian restaurant opposite the Bull's Head. Craig Jones no longer frequented their local pub, preferring the company of fellow police officers at the Tally Ho Social Club following a Saturday afternoon kicking lumps out of opponents on the football pitch. Rumour had it that Craig was also dating someone, but neither John nor Siobhan showed any intrigue, so encompassing was the passion and excitement of their relationship.

John screwed his empty chip paper together tightly, letting out a loud burp that morphed into a muffled mix of a cough and laughter as a couple sat all the way at the front of the upper deck turned and shot a disapproving look in his direction. He spied a long thin window cracked open enough to provide an unintended release for his unwanted litter, but Stephen grabbed at the wrapper, placing it beside his on the bench seat.

'Don't you dare, or Winston will kill us.'

60

John gazed out of the bus window and observed the buzz of activity below on the hectic pavements of Sparkhill. The ageing Birmingham suburb lined with endless rows of old Victorian terraced houses had become home to the city's burgeoning Indian, Pakistani and Bangladeshi population in recent years. Once it had housed mainly Irish and then West Indian migrants from an influx of workers granted citizenship in exchange for swelling a work force decimated by the loss of life in the Second World War. As the lure of immigration had shifted to Asia, popular Indian restaurants and takeaways had sprung up like a rash beside specialist stores selling silk and other materials essential to Asian costume, and a seemingly endless chain of grocers, Halal meat suppliers and spice emporiums. John was fascinated by the diversity of the culture he felt enriched the city he called home. He rejected the counter opinion that a once respectable neighbourhood had fallen into disrepair, arguing that the ethnic minorities had simply transferred their way of life to a new and surely daunting habitat, thousands of miles from familiarity. After all, British enclaves were sprouting up across Spain where expats dined on steak and chips with HP Sauce and boozed their way noisily through pints of lager and bitter rather than sample paella and sangria in a mirrored wave of migration. What was the difference, he wondered?

John's deliberation was broken by an ambiguous question posed by Stephen, who sat nervously fumbling the two spent chip papers as he awaited a reply. Stephen had to repeat the question following an awkward silence.

'How long have you known?'

John's unconvincing response betrayed his feeble attempt to deflect the question.

'Known, what? What do you mean?'

Stephen smiled, shaking his head and stared blankly at the pair's chip papers as he rolled them into one ball. He elected not to speak, but instead waited for John to stammer on.

'I mean there was that time last summer when Sully set you up with that blonde girl from Swanshurst School. What was her name? I can't remember. Anyway, her sister said you hadn't so much as tried to kiss her. You never really showed much interest in girls, did you?'

Stephen was perversely enjoying watching John drown in a torrent of meaningless memories as he avoided confronting the obvious fact that he had been aware of his old friend's sexuality for quite some time. Their clique often made what they considered humorous remarks regarding his ongoing lack of female companionship, or the perceived preservation of his virginity. None of them had ever felt comfortable enough to simply address the somewhat taboo topic that was now unexpectedly out in the open.

John stopped babbling and sat back on the seat, staring up at a bus ceiling he noticed was stained by countless nicotine fumed journeys, searching for a more appropriate response. The words that followed were more thoughtfully chosen.

'You remember a couple of weeks ago, we were in the Bull, the night Andy had finally replaced his old monkey boots with a pair of leather boots with the fur-lined top? Well, actually, it was Siobhan who convinced us, when you were at the bar, getting a round in.'

Stephen shifted in his seat, remembering the evening indeed, while intrigued by the revelation that the probing of Siobhan had instigated the debate.

'Me, her and Andy had walked to the pub from mine and on the way there, she asked if you'd ever admitted, well, you know. Andy told her it was all just an act and that you were shy and had always been a little, what's the word? Effeminate.'

Stephen laughed and nodded, enthralled by the tale of how his homosexuality had been summarily recognised, dismissed and, he hoped, accepted by his closest friends. He encouraged John to continue with the story.

'Siobhan was dying to tell us something in the Bull. When you went off to the bog, she tried, but someone came over and talked to us. I can't remember who it was. Anyway, you came back and she couldn't finish what she was saying. Then when you were at the bar, she pointed out the love bites on the back of your neck as proof of, well, you know.'

Stephen did know. He blushed as he covered his face with both hands, chuckling as he rocked back and forth before clapping mockingly, though not intending to belittle his friend.

'So, you wankers have been around me for probably, I don't know, thirteen years, so most of our lives, basically, and you weren't really sure. Yet in five minutes, Siobhan has sussed it all out and convinced you. I knew I liked that girl!'

John laughed too; one of relief that the elephant in the room was finally charging down the top deck of the number ninety-two bus, blowing its trumpet at full blast.

'So, what do you think?' asked Stephen, his question again vague enough to intrigue John. After a pause for reflection, John squinted both eyes and scratched his chin as he pondered.

'Well, I'm pretty sure I'm not your type.'

Stephen lunged playfully towards John, wrapping his arm around his neck, while grabbing his crotch with the other hand, wrestling as they used to many years earlier as children.

'Come here you sexy bastard and I'll show you how much you're not my type.'

As John and Stephen laughed and grappled on the back seat, they failed to notice that their bus had stopped to collect passengers stranded briefly by the side of the busy Stratford Road, who had abandoned a forlorn bus that had broken down earlier. A puzzled driver and engineer stood examining an unresponsive engine that had puffed a cloud of thick black smoke from beneath a large metal panel at the rear of the vehicle. Among those transferring from one bus to the other was Matt Douglass, Stephen's obnoxious next-door neighbour, who now pounded his way between the rows of top deck seats, heading in their direction.

'Look at you pair of fucking queers. I always knew you were. I thought you were shagging that tart, the one who used to go out with that copper. I'll take her off your hands if you like, show her a good time.'

Matt grabbed his crotch with his right hand that bore a crudely applied green tattoo on each finger, spelling out the upside-down letters L O V E, while making a forward jerking motion with his hips as he smirked and snarled at John and Stephen, goading them to react. Stephen cowered, cautious to remain in the middle of the seat should he need to fight his way along the aisle to reach the stairs and bolt to safety.

Single parenthood forced unexpectedly upon both their mothers through death and divorce in the early seventies, Matt and Stephen had been innocently thrust together as five-year-old next-door neighbours considered ideal playmates, given their matching ages and similarly fatherless predicaments. The anticipated friendship never blossomed and Stephen would beg not to be left alone in Matt's company, fearing another in a long episode of physical torment as he was bullied and teased mercilessly by the wrestling-obsessed buddy from hell. Only years later, when Mary Taylor's presence was requested by the junior school nurse to explain a rash of bruises that set off an alarm warning of suspected child abuse, did Stephen hysterically blurt out a stream of painful misdemeanours of which Matt had been guilty during their play dates. Perhaps this explained the bed-wetting and the acute anxiety exhibited when the kid next door came calling. Rosemary Douglass dismissed the accusations as nonsense. Matt might have been a burly child with a tendency to play a little rough, but he was just another mischievous and harmless little boy as far as she was concerned.

John had witnessed Matt's random intimidation of Stephen throughout years spent at secondary school, sometimes stepping in as arbitrator, occasionally to his own cost. He had often thought the world would be a better place without the hulking bully who by the age of eighteen had now worked 16-stone of mass and muscle onto his frame that stood beyond six feet tall. The low roof of the bus caused him to stoop menacingly over them. John was powerless to intervene or object to the insult Matt had uttered about Siobhan, but regardless, clenched one fist, hidden from view by the seat in front of him, unafraid though reluctant to enjoy the advantage of the first punch and engage in a physical fight if necessary.

Matt leaned forward and reached inside Stephen's jacket pocket as he sat rigid with fear, unable to object to the removal of his half-full packet of cigarettes. Matt tucked one behind his own ear and placed another between his lips, lighting it before tossing the packet into Stephen's lap. He blew smoke into Stephen's face then raised his eyebrows as he glanced at John.

'Nice boots, mate,' he said butting the toe of his own black leather boot against John's identical choice of buckled footwear. John nodded, unsure as to whether he should break eye contact to avoid the risk that Matt would accuse him of trying to stare him down. Matt blew Stephen a mocking kiss and turned away to focus his attentions on harassing a couple of teenage girls who had also transferred from the stricken bus, which now disappeared from sight out of the rear window.

'Not your type either I suppose?' whispered John, hoping to lighten the mood.

Stephen laughed, though more out of relief than in humorous response. He shook his head and tucked his lightened cigarette packet back within his jacket pocket.

The bus soon reached New Street, the city's main thoroughfare where all passengers would alight. John and Stephen planned to meet

Andy, Sully and Siobhan, who were travelling into town together, outside the Birmingham Odeon, the city's traditional meeting point for friends, lovers and nervous couples beginning a first date, which was also the venue for the night's highly anticipated gig. An hour or so later, The Smiths would come on stage and Stephen could again banish traumatic memories of Matt Douglass, while the wistful tunes of Morrissey and Marr filled the concert hall and make this a night to remember for far more pleasurable reasons.

John looked Stephen up and down as he leaned against a wall beside the entrance to the Odeon, while waiting for their friends to arrive. Stephen coaxed the flame of a flickering match towards the tip of a cigarette pursed between his lips that he shielded with a cupped hand. He pulled in a sharp breath of smoke as it caught light, speaking after he inhaled.

'What?'

John shrugged, almost apologetically.

'Look, Stephen, you're my best mate and no matter what other people think about you being gay, as far as I'm concerned, what difference does it make?'

Chapter Nine

The sinister tones of Prokofiev's *Dance of the Knights* swirled menacingly around the murky Birmingham Odeon, the music's intimidating onslaught of horns, brass and strings marching like a battalion across a sea of heads crammed like sardines between the front rows of theatre seats and the precipice of a stage shrouded by shadows. An aggressive, almost violent energy emanated from the cavernous concentration of bodies that swayed as one dark mass.

Siobhan Murphy's heart raced and she gripped the sweaty palm of John Garland tightly as the brooding classical music swept her deeper into the chasm of bodies. In the darkness, she spied a silhouette slip behind the drum kit risen at the back of the stage. Another ghosted over to her left, a bass guitar slung casually just above his hips, and then to the right she caught sight of the distinctive outline of a Gibson guitar, a bobbed haircut and a baggy suit. She felt her barely audible gasp wrenched from her lungs by the collective cries of appreciation that rose up noisily from the restless crowd. The Smiths were poised and ready on stage. The strings and horns that pierced the chilling atmosphere peaked at a high-pitched crescendo and there he was, lit up like a god, looking down upon his devotion of disciples.

'Hello!'

The mob erupted, cheering in unison in reply to his rally cry. Tom-tom drums pounded and the thrashing of a cutting guitar sparked a horde of leaping, air-punching bodies into life. Lights of all colours flashed and pierced the theatre manically as Morrissey balanced and swayed on his standing leg, kicking the other repeatedly towards his hypnotised audience. In one hand, he cracked the lead of his microphone like a whip and in the other trailed a placard he waved defiantly above his head as the night's opening song stormed into its chorus. *The Queen Is Dead* proclaimed the undisputed king Morrissey with his treasonous wooden banner.

The force of the crowd lifted Siobhan at will from her feet and dragged her, with John clinging on desperately in tow, among likeminded fans bobbing and dancing and singing along to the rebellious lyrics. She was breathless, but exhilarated, captivated by the music and the lure of the mass of bodies that churned before the stage.

There was a brief lull between songs as a sea of clapping raised hands voiced unanimous appreciation of the opening number. Then an unfamiliar drumbeat teased a fervent audience curious to guess the identity of the night's second song. Suddenly a bright shrilling guitar riff exposed the disguised intro as *Panic*, the new single that had been spinning on Siobhan's Dansette record player on a daily basis for the past few weeks. A huge roar greeted Morrissey as he emphasised the mention of the proud audience's home city of Birmingham in his opening verse. As a mass chorus echoed that society should '*Hang the DJ*', Morrissey spun a noose demandingly above his head and spurred the brutal mood of a crowd now swelled beyond comfort by the arrival of alcohol-fuelled latecomers descending from the Odeon bar.

The pace and relentlessness of the collective energy of band and audience continued for three further songs, eventually slowing to the gentle sway of *There Is A Light That Never Goes Out*, which provided a welcome respite from the boisterousness. Its lyric of tragic devotion brought Siobhan and John together in an appreciative embrace, both oblivious at being uncomfortably sweaty from the exertion of the gig's opening bombardment. John stood behind Siobhan and held her tightly, almost protectively, as they rocked gently as one to the slower tune, both singing along wholeheartedly.

When The Smiths launched into *The Boy With The Thorn In His Side*, with the audience also in full voice, John felt a frantic tapping on his shoulder and turned to see an overjoyed Andy and Sully singing along excitedly to the cheerful tune. Andy was attempting to yell something in John's ear with limited audible success over the noise of the band. 'This is fucking mad! Down the front... hope they play...' Then, as the song *What She Said* revived the fevered madness, he pointed to the unmistakable figure of Matt Douglass, gyrating violently among the masses.

'Look at that fucking idiot!'

The neighbourhood bully's imposing frame, shirtless and muscular, towered over those around him as he waved his white t-shirt manically above his head. Sweat sprayed from his spiky blonde-mopped mane as he head-banged ferociously to the music.

The Smiths appeared to be thoughtfully pacing their dedicated audience, alternating slow and sombre numbers with up-tempo tunes that demanded drawing on another reserve of energy from the pit of fans crushing and crashing in waves against the stage. Eager to force their way through to as prime a vantage point as possible, Andy and

Sully merged into the silhouette of bodies that swirled before John, Siobhan and Stephen. They were instantly swallowed up by the crowd, leaving their friends on the edge of the cauldron, leaning against a strained row of archaic theatre seats that bordered on buckling under the tension.

The unmistakable haunting guitar introduction to *How Soon Is Now* provoked a near hysterical roar of approval from the audience. As they swayed in unison, Siobhan began to trace a number seven and then two fours on John's leg. They both laughed as John held Siobhan tighter and more passionately than he thought he ever had before. He was never letting go of her. This was their song, the melody that had brought them together. It was their secret romantic trigger that would always provoke a loving smile of affection wherever they might be when hearing its driving beat and hypnotising sound. They were so in love and immersed in each other. Siobhan had never been happier. Neither had John.

'Thank you, goodnight,' waved Morrissey as the band's epic anthem crawled to a close.

Siobhan turned to face John and they locked in a gentle loving kiss as the crowd bayed for more from The Smiths. John curled sweaty strands of Siobhan's hair behind her ear, gently caressing her damp porcelain cheek as he breathed in her beauty. She turned her head slightly to acknowledge his touch and gently bit at his finger. They stared into each other's eyes, oblivious to the crowd's impatience for encores, which would soon be satisfied. John didn't need to repeat the three words they had whispered lovingly throughout the past few passionate weeks together. He could see the love in Siobhan's eyes and she in his.

'Look, look, look!'

Stephen broke their trance unceremoniously as he pointed excitedly in the direction of the stage. The rhythmic scratching of Johnny Marr's guitar had signalled the return of The Smiths and the introduction to the classic *Still Ill* and much to their delight, the appearance on stage of Sully. He had clambered up from the mass rank of fans and now hugged a bemused Morrissey and raised his arms in triumph before diving headfirst into the swelling mass of bodies below. John was beyond jealous.

Siobhan urged John to rush forward and become swept up by the whirlwind between them and the stage. Desperate to emulate Sully, he hesitated and then before she could protest, grabbed Siobhan by the hand and dragged her along with him, into the storm. The jangling tempo of *Still Ill* whipped the Smiths faithful into a frenzy that took control of all who dared to enter the fray.

Siobhan's feet no longer touched the beer-sodden floor. As The Smiths blasted into a finale rendition of *Bigmouth Strikes Again*, she had leaped as high as she could manage in an attempt to catch a better view of the band. The uncompromising surge of bodies had clamped themselves around her, trapping her, suspended and powerless to control her own movement. Her legs simply dangled. Her left arm was stretched almost to the point of pulling clear of its socket as she fought to hold onto John's hand. He too had become a slave to the undertow of the crowd and the tide was twisting him towards the opposite side of the stage. Unable to resist the pull, John could no longer turn his head to see Siobhan and he felt her fingers slip slowly from his grasp as the power of the mob overwhelmed him.

John Garland would never hold Siobhan Murphy's hand again.

Chapter Ten

'Where are they? I'm bloody freezing.'

John Garland was fast losing patience with the absent Siobhan and Stephen as the sweat-soaked paisley shirt that had steamed in the pressure cooker atmosphere of the Birmingham Odeon now clung to him uncomfortably, chilled by the cool end of summer air outside. His friend Sully also folded his arms tightly across his body, alternating rubbing his biceps frantically with blowing into cupped hands to generate warmth.

John had succeeded in emulating Sully by clawing his way onto the stage just as The Smiths powered through the final bars of their farewell number. He had hugged Morrissey, who cowered slightly and smiled awkwardly at the latest in a couple of dozen stage invaders to profess love for their idol. Unlike Sully, who had face-planted back into the mass crowd, John made a beeline for guitarist Johnny Marr, but was intercepted by a frustrated and overworked member of the venue's security staff, who hauled him abruptly to the side of the stage and locked him in a vacant spare room off an anonymous corridor. There, he was ordered to remain, along with three similarly triumphant Smiths fans, with the threat of a visit from the authorities and, they imagined, the punishment of a public order caution. That would be a small price to pay for having embraced the iconic singer of his favourite band and made definite eye contact with Johnny Marr. Instead, approximately twenty minutes later, John and fellow felons were released without ceremony from the makeshift cell, into a dank alleyway at the rear of the building. Triumphant in his quest to maul the beloved Morrissey, John set about gradually navigating his way around to the Odeon entrance via a twisting service road. A shorter and more convenient route was blocked by security guards preparing to usher the exiting Smiths onto a waiting coach.

An equally buoyant Sully and Andy hugged their victorious friend as he arrived at their prearranged post-gig meeting point. A competitive conversation lauding the band and the atmosphere, and of course the successful scaling of the Odeon stage summit, rang out as they waited for Stephen and Siobhan to appear from among the final stragglers meandering from the foyer out onto New Street. They never emerged.

A burly security guard, dressed head to toe in black, wearing an intimidating frown, began to bolt shut the top and bottom of each of a row of glass doors, all patrons having vacated the premises.

'Hey mate, I don't think everyone's come out yet.'

The bouncer shrugged nonchalantly and continued about his business. John's impatience, fuelled by the discomfort caused by his cold sodden shirt spilled over.

'Are you deaf? Don't just ignore me. My girlfriend and best mate haven't come out yet.'

The security guard stiffened, pushed out his chest and raised one menacing eyebrow, questioning the wisdom of John speaking to him in such a manner. He patiently bolted closed the last of four doors, shutting himself inside the Odeon and with an authoritative index finger, beckoned John to come closer. 'Maybe she's run off with your best mate then,' came his reply, muffled by the glass barrier between them. He slowly turned his back and walked away. Andy pulled John back before he could aim a kick at the closed door.

'They're probably just at the bus stop waiting for us. You were backstage a long time after the gig, you know. Let's walk to Bull Street. I'm sure they'll be there.'

Andy was right. Both he and Sully had remained pinned near the front of the stage after the gig and had spent several minutes pleading unsuccessfully with one of the road crew to furnish them each with one of Mike Joyce's spare drum sticks as a memento of the occasion. Siobhan and Stephen would surely have exited first, from the rear of the crowd swell, long before they, and were likely waiting for them, equally as impatiently, at the bus stop a few streets away.

'Hold on a minute, let's wait.'

Andy hoped they could duck the bare-chested Matt Douglass who was striding along New Street in their direction, grasping a sodden white t-shirt in his hand. He pounded over, baiting them into confrontation.

'So, what are you queers hanging around for? Have you got your autograph books? Isn't it past your bedtime?'

Shaking loose the white sleeveless garment that smelled as rank as it was damp, Matt slipped it over his head and shuddered in response to its cold touch. He surveyed the three friends, counting them off slowly and loudly.

'One. Two. Three. You're missing the queer and the slag.'

The shrill of a loud car horn stole everyone's attention and Matt waved in recognition of the driver and passenger of a sleek black Saab Turbo saloon car.

'My ride to The Garryowen,' he sneered, referencing an after-hours drinking club renowned for its volatile atmosphere. Before approaching the car, Matt slid the middle finger of his right hand beneath his nose in a slow slashing motion, breathing in deeply as if sampling an exclusive cigar.

'Ah, fishy fingers! I've had my share of that tonight, lads. Now for a few pints and maybe a few punches to finish things off nicely. Goodbye, ladies.'

'Come on, I can't hold the bus up any longer. You're either getting on or you're not.'

Winston Roberts waited a moment longer and then closed the doors of the last number ninety-two bus of the evening. He departed from the city centre stop located on Bull Street, bound for Hall Green. Mike Sullivan and Andy Morris each slotted correct change into the ticket machine and slowly climbed the stairs to seek two open seats on a packed and raucous top deck buzzing with Friday night revellers. They watched through graffiti-blurred windows as John Garland scuffed the soles of his boots against the pavement, his head drooped, as he shuffled, alone, in the direction of a wooden bench outside the Oasis indoor market stall entrance.

Neither Stephen Taylor nor Siobhan Murphy had been waiting for them at the bus stop. John was at a loss. He was convinced that Siobhan would not have simply returned home without him and consequently suspected something untoward had taken place. But where was she and where was Stephen? John took comfort in knowing that Stephen would have remained with Siobhan in the event of there being a problem, but still, their absence made no sense. He had called the Queen Elizabeth Hospital and confirmed Siobhan had not been admitted to the emergency room and had even visited nearby Steelhouse Lane Police Station to make inquiries, but without result.

John had convinced Andy and Sully to take the final regular bus of the evening to Jack's Fish & Chips Shop, where they often congregated following gigs at the Odeon or Peacocks. He would follow forty-five minutes or so later, on the first after-hours night bus, having scoured some of the main streets that dissected the city centre. He would either meet them at the chippy, or alight at the stop closest to the wasteland cut through leading to Stephen's house. Concerned and pessimistic, John spent half-an-hour wandering along Corporation Street and New Street and traced a familiar route along Needless Alley past Peacocks, the TSB Bank and the back of Rackhams department store. He roamed along Colmore Row to the night bus stop having failed to locate either Siobhan or Stephen. There, he boarded the double-decker, sitting alone and despondent.

Having spied no sign of life outside a shuttered Jack's, John was relieved to discover Stephen stood casually beside Sully and Andy at the second designated meeting point as he frantically leaped from the bus platform to the pavement.

'What the hell's going on Stephen?'

John immediately saw concern etched across the faces of his friends.

'And where's Siobhan?'

Stephen moved towards John and attempted to put his arm around John's shoulders, but was rebuffed by an immediate swat of the hand. Stephen held both hands up defensively, indicating he had done no wrong. He spoke slowly, almost reluctantly.

'She's ok, John. She's at home. But something happened. And it's not good.'

John glanced at Sully, who was staring at the floor. He scanned Andy's face as the equally hesitant friend bit his lower lip and was not forthcoming with any information.

'Will someone tell me what the fucking hell is going on? What's happened? What happened to Siobhan?'

Stephen massaged the temples on either side of his head while squinting and nodding affirmatively. He paused for breath; his eyes staring at John as he searched for the right words to best devastate his best friend. He coughed lightly; almost emitting a laugh, frustrated that the phrasing he sought eluded him.

'Fuck, Stephen! Spit it out! What. Happened. To. Siobhan. Tonight. Just go through it, step by step! Tell me everything that happened.'

John's was yelling as much out of frustration as anger as he shook his friend by the shoulders, causing Stephen to recoil and slump against a tall old oak tree that towered over the main road.

'Okay, okay. This isn't easy, you know.'

Stephen clasped his hands together, as if praying for divine inspiration and as Sully and Andy pensively surveyed John for what they knew would be an explosive reaction, Stephen inhaled a deep breath of courage. His narrative was as clinical in its delivery as it was heart-breaking for John to digest.

'When you were separated by the crowd, Siobhan was swept over to the opposite side. I moved back a few rows, quite a few rows actually, and stood by some empty seats. The three of you had fought your way up to near the front.'

John was immediately agitated. He inhaled and exhaled a loud deep calming breath, impatiently wishing that Stephen would simply cut through all the background and get to the point. He covered his face with both hands, gripping his forehead almost forcefully with his fingers, his eyes shut tight, anticipating bad news.

'I lost sight of Siobhan, but then she came rushing past me before the last song had finished. She was really upset, crying hysterically. I thought you two had a fight or something. I ran up the aisle after her and she raced out one of the emergency exits and she just ran. I went after her, shouting, but she wouldn't stop. She ran all the way to New Street Station.'

Stephen paused and nervously made eye contact with John, whose face was expressionless. His eyes seemed black in anticipation of rage and two clench fists now hung loosely by his side, his fingernails digging into his skin, his knuckles whitening. Stephen glanced briefly at Sully and Andy before returning his focus to the concrete of the pavement, his head hung as he resumed.

'She got into a black cab and I managed to get in with her. She was distraught and I just comforted her. Then she told me what had happened. So that you know, she went straight home. I paid for the taxi and I suppose she's off to Ireland in the morning with her parents, as planned.'

John was pacing the pavement, psyching himself up to absorb the bad news. He wanted to scream at the top of his lungs for Stephen to spit out the devastating news that seems to be lodged in his throat.

'John, this isn't easy to tell you and I'm sorry. Someone was behind Siobhan in that crowd. She was being crushed, her arms trapped by her side. She felt a hand touching her from behind. She screamed but nobody heard because of the music and the crowd singing. She just couldn't get free. He, well, Matt Douglass, you know. She was wearing a short skirt, and his fingers…'

John was numb. The fury he felt would tear from his core in furious response churned like lava poised to erupt, but immediately he was overwhelmed by pure sadness. His girl had been abused, assaulted. He had to see her, to make everything right. His pained expression sought comfort, one by one, from each of his three friends. They stared back helplessly.

Before John could insist they walk the couple of miles to Siobhan's house for him to comfort her, a raucous laugh, an exchange of colourful banter and a slammed car door broke his focus from across the deserted main road.

'Fishy fingers! That bastard. I'm going to fucking kill him.'

As the same sleek Saab Turbo that had collected Matt Douglass from outside the Odeon went tyre spinning off into the summer night, John strode purposely across the dual carriageway, oblivious to an approaching car forced to slow to allow him to pass. He quickened his pace as he crossed the grassy central reservation, Sully trailing him by a few yards, while Stephen and Andy followed not far behind. Matt Douglass slipped silently beyond the first line of trees bordering the cut through to Stonor Croft, oblivious to the following pack.

'That bastard was right behind Siobhan as I let her hand slip.'

John was enraged, snarling as he half turned to spur his friends on in pursuit. He beckoned to them with an authoritative subtle wave of his hand, as if leading troops forward, into a doomed battle. He paused until all four reached the edge of the tree line. John's eyes were narrowed with a stare of intense hatred. He breathed rapidly through gritted teeth and shot each of his friends a volatile glance before racing blindly into the darkness that shrouded the dirt pathway.

Stephen followed first, initially in a mild panic at the terrifying prospect of confronting Matt Douglass, but soon a surge of adrenaline and the perverse urge to reap revenge on the lifelong bully wrested control of his actions. As he stumbled along the path, he spied John ahead, raising a large object that looked like a metal-framed chair that must have been dumped on the wasteland. John cried out as he swung it purposely, crashing the improvised weapon violently against the back of Matt's head, felling him instantly to his knees.

'You fucking wanker!'

Chapter Eleven

'Come on Ellie, they're just having a couple of beers. She'll be eighteen in a week's time.'

There was clear exasperation in John Garland's voice, just as there always seemed to be when he spoke to his wife.

'It's not as if they're getting pissed in the pub, which they do most Friday nights if you hadn't noticed, and…'

'Okay, okay,' snapped an antagonised Ellie Garland in response as she thumped both fists against the soapstone surface of her kitchen countertop. 'Okay so it isn't a big deal. They can do whatever the hell they want.'

John didn't bite. He stretched the inside of his right check with his tongue, drummed his fingers and turned away, not wishing to show his displeasure, though his body language betrayed his mood. The arguments between the two had become commonplace, not only on a daily basis, but now at an hourly rate if the couple had the misfortune to be in the same vicinity. He massaged the temple on the right side of his head with his thumb and ran his fingers across his brow in a deliberate and frustrated motion. They hadn't always fought like this, but it was increasingly difficult to remember the last time they had even been civil to each other, let alone communicated in a manner befitting a married couple. He stared blankly at the kitchen floor, noticing how frayed and tatty the light brown linoleum surface had become where it bordered the skirting board, which was overdue a new coat of white emulsion. He let out a sigh and frowned as he wondered how much longer either of them could cope with such constant agitation in their lives.

'Dad, Dad, we found this photo. It's hilarious!'

Vicky Garland was giddy with a shriek of laughter that broke the tension as she burst into the kitchen. She waved a dog-eared photo in the air, smiling gleefully at her discovery that had been gathering dust in the attic, where she and a friend had been searching for a retro eighties video game console her father had assured her was packed somewhere among a mound of old boxes. She had heard her parents arguing, but during the months, or perhaps it was years that they had fought, she had grown immune to the conflict. Occasionally at night she would pull her bed covers up over her head to blank out the commotion, or since she had been given what she assured her dad were the latest and hippest line in noise-cancelling headphones the previous Christmas, would clamp those cans over hear ears to maximum effect. Vicky would drown out domestic worries with the music of Kasabian or the Arctic Monkeys, rather than listen to her parents fight.

'Sophia found it!' she exclaimed. 'It says 'Peacocks 1986' on the back, so I worked out it must be from when you were about my age.'

Sophia, Vicky's best friend since longer than anyone could remember, had followed Vicky into the kitchen and took a sip from her bottle of Leffe Blonde Belgian beer that John had allowed the two girls to consume, much to the annoyance of his wife.

'You look cute in the photo, Mr Garland,' said Sophia with a smile that was as innocent as it could be interpreted as flirtatious, as she took the photo from John's hand.

'Oh please,' muttered Ellie Garland in a mocking tone, loud enough for all to hear as she left the kitchen, pouring her second, or perhaps it was her third glass of red wine of the evening, unconcerned that a few errant drops spilled onto the worn linoleum. She had become used to the attention of other women that her husband seemed to effortlessly attract, which was one of the many sources of tension in their marriage. 'He's old enough to be your father,' she called out dismissively.

Sophia cringed slightly but pretended not to hear Ellie's comment as she inquired further about the photograph that provoked such curiosity. The picture had been taken at Peacocks, a live music venue in Birmingham city centre popular with local bands, sandwiched between Mr Bill's Bier Keller and a specialist classical music record store on Needless Alley. John smiled when he saw his highlighted hair and a denim jacket that he had worn almost religiously that year. He remembered his friend Sully had bought an identical jacket, much to John's displeasure. He recalled immediately whom he was with when that photo was taken and the band they had gone to see at Peacocks.

'The Burning,' he said, as both Vicky and Sophia looked quizzically at the photo and then at him. 'Me and my friends had gone to see a band called The Burning at Peacocks. The place was packed and they were incredible. I remember sitting at a table before the gig and I was waving my hands around as I talked, like I always do, and I knocked a full pint of lager over my friend Stephen who was sitting across from me. It landed in his lap, completely soaked him, and of course when he stood up it looked like he'd wet himself!'

The girls laughed. Vicky enjoyed listening to her dad's anecdotes, which were plentiful and often inappropriate. Her mom would routinely discourage John from sharing tales of his teenage misdemeanours, concerned that their daughter might emulate the unseemly actions of a misspent youth. 'She's too sensible to do the things I did,' John would claim dismissively as he recalled such juvenile antics as a stealing hubcaps from vehicles on car showroom forecourts, or the time he and his friends hung a mannequin by its neck from a lamppost, causing passing traffic to screech to a halt in fear that a woman had committed suicide beside a busy main road.

Sophia studied the photo closely. She looked first at the fresh-faced eighteen-year-old with a suspect haircut that might have been fashionable at the time, but was truly awful by today's standards, and then compared the matured, greying features of her friend's dad as he sat on a stool at the kitchen counter. She listened as John indulged in the memory of his youth and bemoaned that there had been some talented local bands in Birmingham at the time, but that the London-based record company executives were reluctant to venture north of the Watford Gap in search of such talent.

'Who took the photo?' inquired Sophia, who was more interested in its origins and the possibility of an intriguing back-story than the musical attributes of England's second city.

'A friend of mine,' replied John, not wishing to delve into his past beyond recalling a tall tale or two to amuse his captive audience. 'I remember she took some great photos of the band that night. The guitarist had a wild Mohican and it was so hot in there, you could see sweat steaming off the audience.'

'She? Was she your girlfriend?' Sophia persisted; intrigued by the idea that John had a romantic past from a time before he met Mrs Garland.

'Okay girls, you need to start planning for next weekend's birthday party or it will never happen,' said John, cutting short the line of inquiry. 'You can keep the photo to give your friends a laugh but don't you dare scan it and put it on Snapface, or whatever it's called.'

Vicky snatched the photo from Sophia's hand, more in a playful motion than to underline the irritation she felt at her friend's ambiguous flirting with her dad. She too studied it closely and noticed how happy he appeared in the photo. There was a warm glow to his eyes and his mouth turned up at the edges in a subtle smile. She rarely saw him looking so content at home these days. She wondered what the relationship might have been between John and the mysterious female friend armed with a camera. While Sophia asked John another question about the eighties and the fashions of the day, Vicky felt a tinge of sadness as she imagined how her dad must surely miss those happier times and his old friends, given his current dissatisfaction at home.

'What happened to them?' asked Vicky, interrupting the kitchen conversation.

'The Burning?' said John. 'They recorded a single I think, then split up like all bands do.'

'No, silly,' Vicky laughed. 'What happened to your friends? Was it Steve, who you poured beer all over? And the girl who took the photo.'

John paused for a moment, uncomfortable with the question. 'I don't know,' he replied dismissively, hoping to disguise his true emotions. 'I moved down here to London to go to Uni and never really went back to Birmingham. I hear from Stephen every now and then, but not often.'

Vicky started to press for a better explanation when John's phone pinged, signalling that he had received a text. 'Ok, I need to reply this,' he said. 'It's work.'

'On a Friday night?' complained his daughter.

John gave Vicky a warm hug and squeezed her as tightly as he always did. She knew that although her mom and dad's deteriorating relationship was a strain on both of them, his love for her was unconditional. John rapped the top of Vicky's bottle with two fingers and winked to remind her not to waste the beer he had permitted her to drink. He left the kitchen, peering first towards the lounge to confirm his wife was still occupied by a glass of wine and the television, as he anticipated she would be. He slipped quietly into the room at the rear of the house that was designated his home office and closed the door behind him with a barely audible click before discreetly replying to the text on his smart phone, a mischievous smile emerging as he tapped at the screen.

Chapter Twelve

Her husband's knuckles already whitening from gripping the arms of his chair at the headlines on the BBC lunchtime news, Siobhan Jones wondered if there was any hope of a passive resolution by the time the newscaster delved into the nitty gritty of the topics of the day. She questioned why Craig was so intent on watching a programme that filled him with such frustration. His bitter views on immigration and his apparent sympathy for some of the more extreme right wing political parties always seemed to be at odds with the daily bulletin. When she considered the other shows he watched, she observed a similar outcome. *Match of the Day* provoked complaints of 'we were better than these millionaire wankers when I played in the old Midland Combination.' All those stupid reality shows that she refused to even entertain dredged up abusive remarks better left festering in the depths of the interview room at Steelhouse Lane police station. When American cop dramas such as *Law & Order* or *Criminal Minds* hit the airwaves, she knew better than to sit around in the living room to listen to the onslaught of an irate Detective Inspector Craig Jones and instead retired to the spare room to play meaningless social media games on the computer. Siobhan rarely kept her opinions to herself either, but they usually contradicted those of her husband, as the oh so helpful marriage councillor had so expertly observed on the couple's first and only session a few years earlier.

The home phone that perched on a shelf in the hallway rang out three sharp tones, which were seldom heard these days since each member of the Jones household relied on their own personal mobile phone for communication. The couple's teenage daughter Aimee lifted the receiver a moment before her agitated father had chance to shout a warning from the living room.

'Don't answer! It'll just be a bloody sales call.'

- - - - - - - - - -

There was a trace of concern in Aimee's voice as she entered the back room where her parents both gazed blankly at the television.

'Mom, there's someone from Solihull Hospital on the phone. They're calling to see if you know a Stephen Taylor?'

Craig shot his wife a puzzled stare as she brushed past him with a concerned look on her face while hurrying towards the hallway. He and Stephen Taylor had become acquaintances, but little more than that, in the mid-eighties, while studying for A Levels. Stephen, along with three childhood friends, had attended the same sixth form as Craig. They were a close-knit group who would sip pints most nights at the nearby Bull's Head pub. While Craig joined them socially on a handful of occasions, he always felt like an outsider, denied acceptance into their clique, and when one of the group briefly stole the affections of Siobhan, their interactions ceased. Craig and Stephen now moved in very different social circles. Both continued to live in the same leafy Birmingham suburb, so it was inevitable they would bump into each other a handful of times each year, perhaps in a local supermarket or their old stomping ground, the Bull's Head. Neither divulged more than minimal and polite information about their lives when they met, turning the conversation instead to music or politics, though their tastes and opinions of both subjects differed greatly. Craig knew that Siobhan, whom he had introduced to Stephen and friends, back then in the eighties, had retained infrequent contact with Stephen through social media and occasionally in person. He was intrigued to know why the hospital was calling his wife regarding their old acquaintance. His detective instincts rather than a concern for Stephen Taylor led him to the hallway.

- - - - - - - - - -

Aimee Jones stood helpless at the foot of the stairs, gazing down anxiously at her mother, Siobhan, who had crumpled to the floor, sobbing uncontrollably, the retro-style telephone receiver dangling from the shelf in the hallway. Tears flooded her face. Craig Jones, having heard his wife cry out in despair, knelt beside her, genuine concern in his voice. He caressed her shoulders tentatively and peered up at his daughter with a quizzical look that searched for an explanation and then turned back to his wife.

'What is it love? What's happened?'

Siobhan was inconsolable. She was sat with her back against the cream painted wall, her knees pulled defensively up beneath her chin. Her hands were clasped together tightly at the back of her neck, her fingers interlocked and her forearms squeezed against either side of her head, her elbows almost touching. She had stopped crying, but was breathing rapidly and gazing at the floor. Her eyes stared through the carpet. Slowly she began to cry again, her breath omitted in short bursts before she let out a vast sigh and moaned 'no, no, no.' Her eyes again welled with tears.

This was typically the cue for Craig to leave the room having usually been the root of Siobhan's despair at the conclusion of their frequent arguments, but he cradled his wife as she rocked forward and nestled the side of her face against him. He felt awkward. Breaking tragic news to the family member of a victim of assault, a fatal accident or very occasionally a murder had never been his forte at work. He would routinely and willingly allow his detective partner to be the catalyst in triggering the sudden emotional response of a family bereavement on such occasions. He held her, but said nothing.

Aimee was upset that her mother was clearly distraught and stood helplessly in the hallway. Craig motioned for her to go and sit in the living room with a reassuring wave that he had the situation under control.

'It's Stephen,' said Siobhan quietly, still staring at the ground. 'That was the hospital. He was attacked last night.' She spoke slowly and in a tone of disbelief, but the emotion overwhelmed her. As she attempted to provide an explanation, tears and weeps of misery engulfed the words that were choked back inside her.

'Stay here and I'll get you a glass of water, or something stronger,' offered Craig, eager to help, but feeling helpless.

'No, no,' Siobhan interrupted. 'I'm fine.'

She sat upright, stretched out her legs and looked up at Craig, who was now standing beside her, and at Aimee, who had half emerged from the doorway to the living room. She drew in a deep breath and slowly exhaled, as she might when being examined at her annual physical. She wiped her reddened eyes with the palms of both hands and sniffed into a white tissue Craig had handed her from a square box that sat on the shelf next to the phone. Its receiver was now sat back in place in the cradle. She waited, again staring blankly at nothing in particular, her face overwhelmed by sadness. She leaned her head back against the wall as if defeated and spoke very deliberately, almost emotionless, to prevent the next inevitable flood of tears that were welling up inside her from bursting free.

'Late last night, he was attacked in some woods near his house. They don't know why, or who.'

Siobhan composed herself further with another deep inhale and exhale. Her captive audience looked on with concern.

'They found him this morning and he's in a coma. He carries this little diary.'

Siobhan's hands were trying but failing to illustrate something amid her state of shock and confusion.

'It has. Hold on. He had my name and number written where it says who to contact in an emergency, so they called me. They're not certain if he's going to...'

Before she could finish the sentence, but having painted a grim enough picture for Craig and Aimee to appreciate, Siobhan stopped talking. She hid her face in her hands and cried again, this time almost silently, as if she was resigned to the fate of her friend. The caller from the hospital had shared additional information, but it seemed immaterial.

Craig stared solemnly at his wife, again feeling powerless to help in any meaningful sense.

'Aimee, go make your mom a cuppa will you love.'

That was usually his duty while his police partner shared devastating news with the bereaved. Strong and not too hot, with two or three sugars, though they never really tasted it anyway.

'I can give the lads at the local nick a call; see what they know.'

The combination of a loud and annoying telephone ring tone and a noisy vibration as his smart phone buzzed across the polished top of a bedside table woke John Garland suddenly from his slumber. He blinked for a few seconds, confused briefly by his whereabouts. A bitter taste coated his tongue and drool seeped from one corner of his mouth. The sun had dipped beneath a picturesque collage of buildings and trees outside, but the diminishing rays of the early Saturday evening still lightly illuminated the bedroom.

'We must have dozed off,' he said, still not quite fully alert. As he reached for his phone, the ringing stopped. He squinted at the screen, which read 'Missed Call. 6.12pm.' They had fallen asleep more soundly than intended for more than two hours, but then their afternoon activity had been somewhat vigorous.

The ringing blared out unexpectedly a second time, almost causing John to drop his phone. The number prefix was 0121, the Birmingham dialling code. Who could be calling him from Birmingham?

'Hello?'

John's tone betrayed an element of trepidation, as he slid from the compact double bed onto his feet, standing, yawning and stretching his shoulders back, making no attempt to hide his nakedness.

'Is that John Garland?' asked the caller, in a mild Birmingham accent.

'Yes, it is. Who is this?'

'It's Craig Jones,' replied the caller to a prolonged silence. 'Hello? John?'

'Yes, I'm here. Sorry. Craig Jones?'

John knew a Craig Jones, or at least he had what seemed like a lifetime earlier when he lived in Birmingham as a teenager, before moving to London to attend university. The pair had not had made contact through so much as a phone call or an email, having fallen out irreconcilably in the eighties. John was shocked to hear his voice.

'Yes. Craig Jones. I know we haven't spoken in, well, a long time, but I have some, um, bad news.'

Intrigued and slightly concerned, John sat on the corner of the bed, gripping the phone between his shoulder and ear as he pulled on a pair of blue boxer shorts and denim jeans that lay abandoned on the carpet. He should have been preparing to return home by now anyway and oversleeping was an inconvenience. Dazed from his unintended afternoon nap and the surprise identity of the caller, he failed to respond, but Craig elaborated as John sat and listened.

'Siobhan wanted to call you, but she's too upset, so I'm making a few calls for her. She got your number from Sully, I think.'

John could not remember the last time he had heard Siobhan's name mentioned, though he thought of her often. His mind wandered for an instant then he listened as her husband explained the reason for his intrusion.

'It's Stephen, Stephen Taylor. I know you two were close once. I'm really sorry, but he's in hospital, in a coma. It happened last night and the boys at the station are investigating, but they don't know much at this point.'

John frowned and put his phone on loudspeaker mode. 'What station, Craig? What do you mean by investigating? The police? What's happened to Stephen?'

John stood shirtless and shocked, his brow taut and his eyes squinting, disbelief etched across his face. Rachel Turner sat upright in bed with a crisp cream-coloured sheet pulled up to her neck to conceal her nudity, and stared back inquiringly to a dismissive shake of the head as John indicated he was listening intently to the caller's every word.

Craig explained that their mutual friend Stephen Taylor appeared to have been attacked late the previous night, or possibly in the early hours of the morning and that an elderly couple out walking their dog had found him lying unconscious. Once the hospital had called Siobhan with the news, Craig had immediately contacted a former colleague now working at Solihull police station to glean more information.

'How bad is he?' John inquired with a blend of anger and distress. 'And why would someone do this to Stephen, of all people?'

Craig's voice wavered and he now spoke in a pessimistic and resigned tone. 'Not good, mate. They seemed surprised at the hospital that he was still alive. He'd been given a real beating. If you can get up here, well, I think you should.'

Neither spoke. The toll was telling on Craig, who was making the last on a long list of morose calls. Plus, he had just reluctantly suggested that the person he had been delighted to see vacate

Birmingham permanently in the eighties should return home to visit. John could not comprehend that his old friend he had known since he was five years old, with whom he seemed to speak less frequently with every passing year, now lay dying in a hospital.

'I can come up tomorrow,' replied John, wiping away a tear he had fought to prevent from spilling from the corner of his eye. Rarely did he make any form of obligation without first consulting his busy business calendar, but in this instance, work commitments felt immaterial. He sniffed and rubbed the end of his nose with his finger. 'Is this your number that came up on the phone, so I can get in touch?'

'It is, but I'll be working tomorrow so…' Craig's voice tailed off and there was hesitancy in his voice as he resumed the conversation. 'Let me text you Siobhan's mobile number. She'll be going to the hospital and meeting with everyone else afterwards. She's there now actually. Your friend Andy's driving up from Wales in the morning and Sully will be around, so they suggested all meeting in the pub at some point on Sunday night.'

John and Craig shared an awkward and muted goodbye. John tossed his smart phone dismissively onto a nearby armchair where a few hours earlier, in a thrill of Saturday afternoon passion, he had eagerly discarded a light blue shirt he was now buttoning and tucking into his jeans.

Rachel Turner had tears streaming down her face. She had overheard enough of the conversation while sitting in bed to decipher the heart-rending news.

'God no! Why Stephen?' she asked of the loveable character she remembered from when she too lived in Birmingham and had moved on the fringes of John's close-knit circle of friends.

John stood helplessly in the middle of the bedroom of his lover's small flat, his shoulders slumped, and stared at the ground shaking his head. 'I have to go up there. I need to go home first and pack a bag, but I can't. I need a drink.'

John deliberated and then spent the next minute texting, interrupted briefly by Craig sharing Siobhan's contact details.

'I just sent Ellie a message,' he explained, wandering into the small kitchen to retrieve what would be the first plundering of his favourite Belgian beer from a fridge populated by brown bottles with golden-foiled tops. 'Told her me and the lads are having a few more in the Bricklayer's Arms. She'll believe that.'

He laughed dryly. There was no joy in his bitter smile, just a multitude of emotions flooding his thoughts. John walked over to Rachel's side of the bed and perched on the edge, draping a consoling and resigned arm around her cold trembling shoulders. Helpless to answer her question, he could not even begin to fathom why someone would wish to hurt their friend.

The couple's depressed embrace was interrupted by a ping from John's phone that signalled the arrival of a text message. John glanced at Rachel and then as they both reached the same spontaneous conclusion, he sprang towards the armchair, eager to discover likely news of their friend from the text. He read the message intently, but soon chuckled, this time allowing himself a respite of light relief. The shake of his head confirmed what Rachel already knew; that he had not received an update from the Midlands.

'It's from Dom. *Crap game, crap team, crap manager. Drew 1-1. I'm sure your shag was more fulfilling. Programme with the doorman. C U Monday.*'

Dominic Hunt, John's old university roommate and now business partner in a range of entrepreneurial ventures, also doubled as a regular Saturday afternoon alibi. For the past few years, he had enabled the long-standing affair between the lovers to remain anonymous. John and Rachel enjoyed a passionate liaison most weekends at a small Bloomsbury flat that, unbeknown to all but his accountant and a handful of trusted allies, John owned and made available to Rachel at a token rent. The quaint, tastefully furnished one-bedroom dwelling overlooked pictorial Tavistock Square, an oasis amid the London hustle. The tranquillity had been shattered a few years earlier when a terrorist bomb tore the roof off a passing double-decker bus and blew out the windows in most buildings, but the serenity soon resumed. The flat was ideally located a short tube ride from the private medical practice where Rachel worked as a secretary and was a convenient distance between John's office off the famous King's Road and his family home in the suburbs.

Every Saturday that featured a home match for Fulham Football Club provided a smokescreen and an opportunity for the covert couple to indulge in their long-time secret affair. Dom referred to the arrangement as 'the genius of deceit.' John and Dom were season ticket holders in the Hammersmith end at Craven Cottage, dating back to the seasons in the nineties when they were still able to stand on the terraces. Back then Fulham had gained promotion to the

Premier League, where they remained until the disastrous reign of two managers, whose tenure John preferred to forget, relegated them to the misnomer that is The Championship, the dreaded second division of English football. Having grown disinterested at the prospect of a Saturday afternoon that ultimately ended in defeat, John regularly handed down his match ticket to an employee or a customer, whereas Dom remained blindly faithful to the Cottagers. As far as John's wife Ellie was concerned, her insufferable husband was thankfully still dragging himself across London to Fulham for all home and even occasional away matches and she had little reason to doubt his alleged whereabouts on Saturday afternoons and the odd Tuesday here and there. To underpin the pretence, Dom would purchase a match day programme as soon as he entered the ground and on his way home afterwards, would dutifully deliver the magazine to Julian, the doorman at Tavistock Court. After a quick thumb through the glossy colour pages before he finished his afternoon shift, Julian would ride the creaky old lift that was original to the refurbished art deco structure up to flat 407 and post the programme through Rachel's letter box. His illicit rendezvous consummated, John could then return home, usually having allowed enough time for a phantom post-match pint and a delay on the Tube to occur, before opening the front door, muttering about the failings of Fulham FC and tossing his printed alibi onto the kitchen table. It was the genius of deceit indeed.

As if on cue, the afternoon's match programme dropped through the letterbox onto the welcome mat and Julian's footsteps faded down the hallway. John retrieved the programme and while a distressed Rachel found comfort in a running hot bath and pouring a glass of wine, he stretched out on the living room sofa, flicking disinterested through the 84 glossy pages. His head was filled with thoughts of his comatose old friend, Stephen.

John paused, picked up his phone and stared at Siobhan's number. He had often wondered what on earth had possessed the beautiful emerald isle girl to marry Craig the copper. He deliberated, his finger hovering over the call option on the screen, took two indecisive swigs of his wheat beer and selected the 'cancel' option on his phone.

'I'll see her this week,' he murmured to himself.

John reclined and slowly sipped his cold beer until the foamy dregs were all that remained. He rearranged the cushions behind his head and closed his eyes, hoping to blank out images of how Stephen

Taylor must now look, on the brink of death, lying in a coma in a sterile and unwelcoming hospital ward, tubes protruding from his beaten body. He forced his mind to recall more pleasant memories of their last period of meaningful time together. It had been during the summer before John had left Birmingham to attend university in London.

A smile eased the stress that had formed across John's face as he remembered an infamous week when Stephen's mother had entrusted her son with the keys to her home while away on her annual summer holidays. The mischievous pair, partnered in crime by their good friends Sully and Andy, had embarked on several dubious pursuits that infuriated the neighbours and almost landed them in trouble. They were four irresponsible eighteen-year-olds, desperately fighting off the unavoidable onset of adulthood and behaviour expected of young men embarking on new journeys in their lives. Siobhan had come along that summer too, the new girl on the scene.

Chapter Fourteen

'You know what mate, drop me over there before the island, just by the chippy.'

John Garland had not said so much as a word to the driver of a taxi ferrying him to Hall Green since slumping into the black leather seat of a shiny new Mercedes black cab at Birmingham International Station. His voice no longer pounded in his head as it had two hours earlier when he rather abruptly informed a chatty woman on the train that due to his severe hangover and less than jovial mood, he would not be exchanging pleasantries all the way from London Euston to the station servicing the National Exhibition Centre and Solihull, or even as far as the first stop. Instead, he placed the lightweight jacket he was carrying unsociably up over his head and hoped he would snore loudly enough to serve as a reminder that he did not wish to be disturbed throughout the journey north. He imagined the woman would consider him a typically unfriendly southerner, who rarely ventured north of the Watford Gap, which he was, but with sociable origins in the Midlands at least.

John met the taxi driver's eyes in the rear-view mirror for the first time since depositing himself in the cab fifteen minutes earlier and they looked as bloodshot as his felt. He fumbled for enough notes in his wallet and declined both the few pounds change and a receipt as he stepped out onto the pavement and shut the heavy black door.

'You know the Bull's Head is further down there, right mate?'

John had walked from the pub of his misspent youth along Highfield Road to soak up several pints with a generous portion of greasy chips and sometimes a saveloy sausage at Jack's Fish & Chips Shop more times than he could even begin to remember. He smiled at the driver's directions, which while well intended, were completely unnecessary.

'Yeah, I'm good thanks. I fancy some chips before I hit the beer.'

John slung the strap supporting an expensive black leather Tumi garment bag over his shoulder and walked towards Jack's which was now called the Highfield Fish Bar. Jack had been a hardworking Greek or Cypriot immigrant; John couldn't remember which. Along with his cheery wife and two young sons, Jack had served fish n chips at all hours to the locals of Hall Green for generations. John liked to think that Jack was now comfortably retired somewhere warm, perhaps on a Greek island, though probably still trying to rid himself of the unmistakable stale smell of fried food that greeted John as he pushed open the shop's heavy glass door.

Cod and chips set him back six pounds twenty, a far cry from the days when a handful of small coins could buy enough chips to fill a teenage craving and Jack would scrape the corners of the fish cabinet to add a sprinkling of loose bits of batter for those kids who asked politely. Salt and vinegar were still applied as liberally as ever. John's eye caught a large vat of pickled eggs sat on the counter top and he winced as he remembered the time his friend Sully had accepted a dare to eat as many of the foul acidic ovals as he could stomach after a bout of drinking. Sully had burst suddenly out of Jack's, projectile vomiting several eggs and just as many pints of beer onto the pavement at the feet of a mix of disgusted onlookers and cheering drunken blokes saluting his bravado. Two hours ago, when boarding the Virgin mainline train, John might have suffered a similar reaction at just the memory of those pickled eggs, but after a solid hour napping beneath his jacket on the journey from London, his hangover had subsided. He was now ravenously hungry and even felt the inkling for a few more pints.

The previous night he had pounded a stream of bottles of Leffe Blonde Belgian beer to the point where Rachel Turner had forced him to phone for a taxi to take him home to his wife and his bed. Unconcerned by whether Ellie Garland suspected he had ventured beyond his alibi of Fulham's Bricklayer's Arms, he had eventually collapsed on the living room sofa, though not before polishing off the remainder of his wife's second bottle of red of the evening. Ellie was unsympathetic the following morning and made no effort whatsoever to temper the noise generated by her cooking a breakfast omelette, which was amplified by John's horrific hangover, until he explained the catalyst for his drinking. Her immediate compassion filled John with guilt, especially when she rushed to iron three clean but creased dress shirts to pack for his impromptu excursion to Birmingham.

John sat on a weathered old bench outside Jack's former chippy and wondered if these were the same wooden slats he had graced some three decades earlier. As he tore at lumps of fish and batter with a small wooden fork and poked thick chips that were almost too hot to eat, he remembered the times spent on that bench. He had kissed two girls there and been chased away once by a pair of rockers who took exception to the line of Two-Tone record label badges he wore down either side of the zip on his fashionable Harrington jacket celebrating bands like The Specials, The Selecter and Madness. He had convinced Siobhan Murphy to dump her boyfriend Craig Jones while they sat on that bench one night on a perfect summer evening. Another time he had fought Craig outside Jack's, long after the closing shutters had been drawn.

John felt happy to be home, if he could still call this home, having not set foot on still familiar streets since he was a teenager. As he screwed up the chip paper, empty apart from the wooden fork, John thought about Stephen Taylor. He too was a fabric of this bench's memory. They had sat there together watching boy racers in finely tuned Mini Coopers approach the adjacent traffic island at speed and on occasion navigate its curve on two wheels, while perversely hoping the posers would lose control and crash into a parked car or perhaps flip onto their roof to provide genuine entertainment. He watched a bus breeze by, remembering how he and Stephen would often share their deepest secrets and fears on the back seat of the top deck over bags of chips bought by pooling the cash they had scraped together by various means.

Disposing of his rubbish in a squat council-supplied bin that was concreted to the pavement, John again banished the picture he had in his head of Stephen connected to tubes and machines that blinked and beeped. His reunion with Sully and Andy and whoever else planned to join them in the pub would likely be emotional enough without him arriving sniffing and teary-eyed. He ambled the five-minute or so walk along Highfield Road to the busy intersection with the main Stratford Road. He passed houses of people he had known at school, remembering the names of some, but searching his memory banks unsuccessfully for others and wondered what might have become of them, not that he honestly cared.

A number ninety-two bus breezed by, exceeding the thirty miles per hour speed limit, and John watched as it sped towards Shirley, the next adjoining suburb. The sporadic traffic ceased, but John did not cross the dual carriageway, the Bull's Head awaiting his arrival on the opposite side. He watched the bus hurtle along the main road, transfixed, paralysed almost, for perhaps a minute or more as it gradually disappeared beyond the horizon. A few stops further on, the bus would pass the leafy cut through where John, along with the friends he was poised to meet and his comrade who lay dying in a coma, had once committed murder. Or at least they believed they had.

The body of Matt Douglass, kicked into submission, brutally beaten and surely killed, had never been discovered. There were no reports the following morning of a dead body discovered by an unsuspecting passer-by and no traces or remnants of a vicious assault. There were no hospital records of anyone being treated for life-threatening injuries. None. Matt Douglass, dead or alive, had simply vanished that night. If he had survived the brutal assault, the hulking bully had failed to return to the streets, buses, pubs, clubs and shady haunts of Birmingham. If anybody anywhere was aware of the location of Matt Douglass, they had kept it a closely guarded secret for a lengthy period that now spanned a generation. Any mild intrigue that lingered regarding his whereabouts had gradually faded. He became an unsolved and eventually a forgotten mystery, but still a potential threat to the liberty of four friends.

Chapter Fifteen

'A pint of UBU please, mate; I've heard good things about that beer.'

These days in pubs, John tended to drink the bottled offerings of local micro-breweries or a smooth glass of Argentinean Malbec if available, even the occasional cider, but chose to mark the return to the scene of his youthful drinking days with a pint of the amber ale a Brummie friend had recently recommended.

John looked around a familiar old pub he barely recognised. Wooden partitions created intimate new alcoves; a false floor elevated shiny-seated areas, and gone was the beer-stained maroon carpet, tacky to the touch and the stale smell of cigarettes, long since banned from such establishments. A new generation of drinkers was thinly scattered throughout a pub struggling to attract clientele on a Sunday evening. There was no sign of either Sully or Andy.

'Haven't seen you in here in a while.'

John ignored the comment at first and then realised it had been directed at him by the barman pouring his tall chilled pint. He looked understandably confused.

'What?'

'Haven't seen you here in quite a while.'

John narrowed his eyes as he studied the perhaps forty-something overweight man in ill-fitting dark grey trousers and a stained black polo shirt worn by every member of the bar staff bearing a brewery's logo on his left man boob. John thought he looked vaguely familiar as the pint glass was placed on a Guinness bar towel and he handed over a ten-pound note.

'I used to wash glasses behind the bar when my old man ran this place in the eighties. Never forget a face, me. I remember you and your mates used to sit over there in the corner. I manage the place myself now.'

He took the money and walked over to the till, returning with change that jangled as he placed it in John's hand. John vaguely recalled a much younger man, perhaps five or six stone lighter whose job was to place pint pots on top of spinning bristle brushes as jets of warm water cleaned the glass. Beer would be poured into them immediately on busy nights when clean glasses were in short supply, warming an already tepid beverage that punters still downed without complaint. He was impressed at the man's memory.

'I think I remember you.'

John wasn't lying out of politeness, but he wasn't certain either.

'I've been away, but I'm back to visit some friends.'

The barman nodded and moved along to serve another customer. John laughed to himself as he realised the reference to his absence had been misinterpreted as being a period of incarceration. Many of the old boozers from the Bull's Head had been away, their absence enforced rather than by choice. He leaned against the bar taking a sip of a pint some several degrees cooler than the last one he had tasted in this particular pub and began texting Rachel Turner, informing her he had successfully reached Birmingham and their old local.

- - - - - - - - - -

'Aye, aye, it's the crafty Cockney!'

Mike Sullivan's gripping hug was as passionate as his smile had been wide when John peered up from his phone and spied his two old friends. Andy Morris moved in next and he and John patted each other on the back enthusiastically in a slightly more relaxed embrace.

The trio sized the other up and down briefly. John tapped Sully affectionately on his pronounced beer belly.

'I know mate; I'm expecting twins! Carling and Guinness, I'm going to call them although the missus thinks they're going to be girls.'

The three of them laughed. Immediately to John it felt as though they had never been apart and in a sombre moment he hid with a smile, he wished that could have been true. They exchanged more playful insults, before Sully ordered two more pints of UBU and they chinked the full glasses together loudly, spilling celebratory drops of beer over the brims.

'To Stephen,' said Sully, instantly sobering the mood. Each took significant gulps, swallowing solemnly.

'Can we not talk about it for a while?'

Andy had arrived a few hours earlier from the Welsh seaside town of Tenby he now called home and while John was finger-deep in cod and chips, he had been enjoying the warm hospitality of the

Sullivan home, which included a lovingly prepared Sunday roast and a waiting welcoming bed for the night in the spare room.

Andy dutifully returned to the suburb, where his now pensioner parents still lived, two or three times every year and at least annually he made a point to sink a few in his former local, though this was the first time that pilgrimage did not include Stephen's presence. On this occasion, Andy had hurriedly cashed in an owed week of holiday time to permit his urgent absence from work.

The others agreed to delay mourning for their absent friend and instead set about catching up on almost thirty years apart, avoiding the reality as best they could that Stephen lay prostrate only a few miles away, knocking at death's door.

Sully had been happily married since as long ago as 1994 to the first girl he fell in love with. She was as doting a wife as he was a devoted husband and life for the couple had sauntered along just as both had envisioned and hoped. Marriage, two kids, and a mortgage they were paying off comfortably since Sully had reinvented himself as a financial adviser after being made redundant from the alternator assembly line at the local Magneti Marelli car factory. It was an anonymous life that John imagined would have bored him to tears, perhaps worse, but Sully was a picture of contentment, a cheerfully chubby chap sharing family photos on his smart phone, pausing to highlight his pretty wife, offspring who had posed reluctantly for the camera, two dogs, a cat and a sensible four door family saloon. He admitted he would soon dip into the savings to buy one of those wonderfully economical Honda Fit cars if his son ever managed to pass his driving test. Twice already, Sully's son had moped into the house still carrying L-plates, confirming the negative outcome his parents had been praying against. Mike junior would inherit the family four-door and all its future maintenance challenges if only he could earn that coveted pass mark.

Sully sensed John was concerned that his former running mate had failed to realise his ambitions, having not lived and breathed the life of a rock star they had both dreamed and talked about as teenagers. By his own admission he was mister ordinary, an anonymous, tax-paying conformist, who was sauntering through life, though wonderfully content with his lot.

'Who's your favourite poet, John?'

The question floored John completely, as he put down his pint and sat back, wondering in which direction this line of questioning would take the conversation.

'I already know your answer, John. You loved W.H. Auden at school. His poems spoke to you. I remember you telling me that. Your favourite was *Epitaph on a Tyrant*. I loved him too. My favourite was *A Permanent Way*. I can't remember all the lines, I mean, blimey, it's been a long time, but he wrote about a train sticking to its rails. It sticks rigidly to those tracks, which are laid out in a permanent direction and, well, the train can't be led astray, no matter what temptations come along, can it? That's me John; the train. I'm following Auden's *Permanent Way*.'

John smiled at the familiar imagery and while he remembered every stanza, such was his love for the poet whose works he had studied dutifully both at school and university, he chose not to recite them. Sully's simple life was no different in ambition or accomplishment than the server behind the bar, the man carrying a tray of drinks and a selection of Walkers crisps to his acquaintances in the corner alcove, or the latest pair of anonymous patrons who had entered through the main door of the Bull's Head. It was the norm.

'I've been travelling that permanent way my entire life, John. You followed what Auden called new-fangled trails, but me, well, I chose this existence, this direction. After what happened back in eighty-six, well, I took a different perspective on things. I stayed here and worked instead of going away to university because that appealed to me. I don't mean to upset anyone, but I'll bet I'm the most content of all of us at this table.'

Andy raised his eyebrows, his bottom lip protruded and he peered towards the ceiling, humming as he nodded slowly in agreement.

'Can't really argue with you on that one mate, can I?'

Back at the time of his late teens, Andy had initially struggled to banish the fear that one day his world would come crashing down if Matt Douglass was indeed discovered as having been murdered and his demise should be attributed to the quartet that had left him for dead. John had moved to London for his studies, Sully increasingly devoted nights previously spent in the pub to his new love, and Stephen rented a bedsit a more convenient distance from the city centre, where he worked and mixed in different social circles. Andy had become withdrawn and sought solitude. His parents owned a shabby old caravan near Tenby on the Welsh coast and at their insistence as that summer drew to a close, he spent a convalescent week gazing at the ocean and breathing in the salty sea air. He drank as heavily as his thin finances would permit to numb the guilt that gnawed at him constantly. Two weeks later there was an urgent rapping at the caravan door and so shocked was Andy at the sight of two policemen that he backed away from them in a panic and tripped over his own feet, falling and crashing to the floor, convinced he was about to be arrested for murder.

'Your mam and dad are worried about you,' the concerned officer informed Andy as he helped haul him back onto his feet. 'They said you haven't called them like you were supposed to. Be a good boy and phone home, will you?'

As requested, that evening Andy rang his parents, who had originally suggested he stay longer than the prescribed week at Kiln Park, where their caravan resided, but had anticipated at least a brief status report on their son's well-being and confirmation that he was to extend his absence. As a last resort, they had contacted the local authorities to investigate. Andy soon returned to Birmingham, but only to pack up as many belongings as he could carry before resuming his isolated existence in the ramshackle seaside structure, which barely survived the wintry winds that howled in off the ocean later that year. A dingy bedsit and later a smarter studio flat in the less touristy neighbouring town of Saundersfoot replaced the soon to be condemned caravan accommodation and Andy hopped from bar work to odd jobs during the first few years he lived in Wales. Ironically the caravan park that was in the process of demolishing his lapsed summer getaway advertised for a fulltime maintenance man and since his friendly face had become well known about town, Andy was hired without much fuss.

'It wasn't easy at first, but all I really needed was enough money for beans on toast, the odd bag of chips, my fags and my beer and I was all set. Then the caravan park job meant I was working outside all summer and I could spread the bigger offseason work, like replacing cookers and fixing broken bunk beds through the quiet half of the year. Before they knew it, I was indispensable. I have been for more than a quarter of a century now!'

Andy put the telling of his relatively Spartan life story on hold as he took a reassuring sip of what remained of his pint.

'I don't spend much, so I save up for the odd holiday here and there and to visit me mam and dad. A mate who owns a local garage found me a cracking old car that runs like clockwork, so that's all I need really.'

John nodded, in quiet admiration. He smiled at the hint of a soft Welsh accent that had overpowered Andy's once dulcet Brummie tones. He reprimanded himself for having judged his two old friends and having measured their achievements against what he considered his own success.

'So, what about you John Garland? What the fuck have you been up to all these years?'

Sully knew of course, or was at least familiar with the basics. John and Stephen had remained in sporadic touch and occasional updates were shared with those who cared when John's name cropped up in conversation, which it seemed to with less frequently as time passed.

'Well, I'm a successful businessman running my own very profitable company, with a comfortable lifestyle in the suburbs, a wife, a grown-up son, a charming teenage daughter and, you know; things are great.'

Sully leaned forward, his belly causing the table to tilt slightly and all three instinctively reached to steady their glasses. He stretched out his arm and ran his finger over John's light blue shirt and nodded approvingly at what appeared to be an expensive garment paired with exclusive designer jeans and smart brown Italian leather shoes.

'These goods don't come cheap mate, that's for sure, so you must be doing alright.'

Sully paused and sat back, silently inviting John to come clean. His friend laughed and shook his head.

'Okay, so I don't have to bullshit you two, do I? Look, work really is great. It's been fairly easy to be honest and my partner Dom has become a really good mate over the years. We've cleaned up in the industry and my expertise and his sales savvy have been the perfect combination. I still love my football and we go to watch Fulham, drink too much, you know, all that good stuff.'

John took another swig of his beer and pursed his lips.

'Ellie and I met through friends, not long after I went down to Uni and she got pregnant. Use a condom and all that bollocks; well I didn't bother of course, did I? We planned to get married, you know, do the right thing, but we didn't have to in the end because it turned out to be a false alarm. We should have called it quits around then, but we didn't and we were on and off and on again for a couple of years. We'd pretty much moved on and were both seeing other people when I bumped into her in a pub the night England beat Cameroon in Italia 90, the World Cup quarter final, while I was out with some mates. One minute I was singing away with the lads and the next, she was on her back thinking of England and that was it. Nine months and a ring on the finger later, along comes John junior. I wanted to call him Gary, after Lineker, but Ellie was having none of it. She said Gary Garland sounded like the souvenir bear they sell at the airport, Gary Gatwick.

'My daughter, Vicky, she's great. She came along by accident seven years later. No football celebration this time, but it might have been after Ellie and I had both been pissed up, singing *Wonderwall* by Oasis in a karaoke bar. She'll be eighteen this week. If there's one good thing that's come out of our marriage, then she's it.'

John rested both elbows on the table and perched his chin on top of two gently clenched fists. He lowered his voice, which carried a more serious tone as he confided in his friends. This outpouring felt like a therapy session. Rarely had he opened up so freely. Sully was shocked that he had managed to squeeze more than a few droplets of information from his inherently impervious friend.

'I never tell anyone about this. There's no need to. Stephen knows about some of it and Dom of course, but that's about it. So, this is between us lads, okay?'

Sully and Andy nodded in unison. Their chairs seemed to have edged even closer to John in anticipation of a confession.

'Me and Ellie row constantly. We fight every day; there's always something that agitates us. I can't remember a time when it wasn't like this. John junior got a scholarship to a college in America and has stayed out there to live. Can't blame him really. So, for all the material things... Look, I was probably never meant to be a loving husband with kids, but that's where I've ended up. Well, at least... you know what I'm trying to say.'

As John sat back in his seat, both Andy and Sully nodded again, neither truly able to relate to such circumstances, but sympathetic nonetheless. John finished off his second pint and circled a finger around the top of his glass, his thoughts elsewhere, prompting Andy to reach for his wallet.

'It's my shout.'

Andy was adamant at first, but relented when John insisted on dipping into his pocket again.

John was ready to resume what felt like some sort of declaration of guilt when he returned clutching three pints that Andy helped him steady onto the table. He waited before asking an unexpected question that intrigued both his friends.

'Do you remember Rachel Turner who used to drink in here sometimes?'

Sully let out a raucous laugh that drew the attention of two couples sat in one of the nearby partitioned alcoves.

'Sorry, I didn't mean to be so loud, but I'm sure we all remember her. How many times did you walk her home? It must have been a dozen, perhaps twenty and although she wasn't a religious girl, she would always kneel in appreciation at the feet of the one she worshiped!'

Sully was pleased with the graphic imagery of his contribution to the conversation, which was more humorous than he typically managed these days. Then he stopped talking and shot a confused glance at both John and Andy.

'But why are you asking about her?'

John gathered his audience closer to avoid broadcasting his admission, but before he could reply, Sully chimed in.

'No! You're not still tapping that are you? You're still walking her home?'

John cringed at Sully's choice of phrase, but was hardly in a position to admonish his friend, considering the personal misdemeanour of which he had been guilty for almost the past five years.

'A few years ago, Rachel moved to London. She'd been through some tough times. There was an abusive ex-boyfriend, a lecherous boss, and her mom had died from cancer not long before. She needed to see a friendly face; someone who could help her out.'

The explanation failed to make sense as far as Sully was concerned.

'How did she know where you lived? She can't have just popped up out of the blue. And what do you mean by 'help her out'?'

John was frustrated at what he felt was becoming an inquisition.

'Look Sully, she was having a fucking shit time and needed someone to help her. At the end of the day, yeah, I wanted to 'tap her'

104

again, as you so eloquently put it, but she needed somewhere to live and someone who wouldn't just treat her like shit.'

Sully held up both palms towards John, who accepted the peace offering and leaned across to pat his friend on the shoulder. Their interaction made him realise that no matter how long they had been separated by John's voluntary exile, a bond and the friendship nurtured throughout their school years together remained. Andy, the only smoker among the three who had all been hooked as teenagers, was fighting the urge to step outside for a cigarette, transfixed by the exchange and the revelation.

John opened up again, lowering his tone, as a foursome on a nearby table appeared intrigued by the occasionally heated exchanges during the discussion.

'I'm not proud of what I'm doing, but I think it's the only thing that keeps me sane. Rachel doesn't want to get married, or be in an everyday relationship and she doesn't want to have kids. If I leave Ellie it will devastate my daughter Vicky, at least right now, and I need to get away from the house some days, most days, actually. It is what it is, boys.'

'So? Do you still walk her home?' asked Sully, a mischievous smile encouraging John to divulge more information, rather than to antagonise him. John laughed and took the bait as it was intended.

'No Sully, I've gone one step better than that. You don't need to react to this, even if you're surprised, but I stayed in touch with Rachel over the years. Nothing regular, but we met up at a couple of conferences I attended. In fact, she walked me back to my hotel room on those occasions, if you know what I mean.

'When she called me looking for help, I was thinking of buying a flat in London, an income property that I was going to rent out. I thought it might be a place I could go and live if I did suddenly leave Ellie. It all just fell into place I suppose. I bought the flat, Rachel moved in and, well, that's about it. It isn't just sex. I have an emotional intimacy with her that's missing now between me and Ellie, which is completely fucked up because I've got that part totally the wrong way around. I see Rachel at least every time Fulham are at home.'

Having anticipated a bemused response, John explained his Craven Cottage alibi, his genius of deceit, as his business partner Dom called it. The trio debated the merits of marriage, fought back tearful emotions as they recalled the often-outrageous antics of their friend Stephen, who they were due to visit in hospital the following morning, and observed how Sully's beloved Birmingham City were in similarly dire straits to John's Fulham.

- - - - - - - - - -

John stood outside the Bull's Head, gazing across the busy main Stratford Road towards a row of shops and at a cosy restaurant with an Italian name that had changed multiple times during the past three decades.

'I took Siobhan on a date there once,' he told Andy, who slowly exhaled after a long pull taken on the cigarette he could no longer resist.

'Yeah, what happened with you and her? I mean, I remember what happened, but I thought you'd stay in touch. One minute it was Hall Green's own version of *Love Story* and then you were both gone. Sully was talking about you two earlier. He remembered he used to call you John and Yoko!'

John stole Andy's cigarette and took a deep drag himself. The forgotten rush of nicotine filling his lungs gave him a blurred buzz as he let smoke drift from his nostrils into the warm summer night air.

'It doesn't matter. It was a long time ago. We never stayed in touch after what happened. I did send her a letter telling her I was going to be a teenage dad and so that was the end of that, I suppose, even though it turned out to be a false alarm. She assumed I'd moved on, but I hadn't really. I know Stephen told her I was actually having a kid when I was in my early twenties. I wonder if she'll get here before last orders.'

Sully emerged from the pub, gasping from having climbed and descended the stairs to the toilets and began rifling inside Andy's inside jacket pocket for his pack of Embassy Number One king size filters as he spoke in his usual rapid fire manner.

'This place was better when the bog was on the same level as the lounge. Those stairs are a killer. Almost fifty pence you're burning each time you smoke one of these you know mate. I thought you were skint. So, what are you two plotting?'

Andy felt John had revealed enough already that evening and did not need to prompt Sully to dredge up John's romantic memories of a liaison at Pizzeria de Marco or whatever it was called these days. He decided to change the subject.

'Well, while we're alone out here, I think we should talk about you know what.'

John blew his latest mouthful of smoke directly into Andy's face, the harshness stinging his eyes.

'Fucking hell Andy, we agreed we'd never talk about that. I stood over there on the pavement thinking about it just before I came in here and that was bad enough. If nobody mentions it, it can't come back to haunt us. The bloke behind the bar recognised me tonight, which was a little unnerving, so you never know who might be waiting for us to slip up, even after all these years. Someone might know something.'

An apologetic silence hung over Andy as he cleared his throat and spat on the pavement. John was incensed as he hissed in a whisper.

'The four of us kicked the shit out of Matt Douglass then he disappeared and was never seen again. *The end*, Andy. What the fuck is there to talk about?'

Frustrated, John flicked the cigarette from between his thumb and middle finger to the floor, scraped his foot across the smouldering stick and stormed back inside the pub.

- - - - - - - - - -

By the time Sully and Andy returned to the small wooden table and three uncomfortable chairs that had been playing havoc with Sully's back, John had lined up a peace offering of three more pints of UBU and a compliment of Jack Daniel's chasers.

'Sorry lads, but this isn't an easy visit for me to make. Andy, I didn't mean to snap like that. I'm sorry.'

Andy didn't need to respond. He picked up his shot, nudged one each towards John and Sully and after another toast to Stephen, they forced back the Tennessee whiskey that burned as it raced down their throats.

There was a lapse in the conversation and while raising the latest pint to his lips Andy paused and returned the glass slowly and deliberately to the damp beer mat in front of him on the table. He shot a look at Sully and in turn at John, emitting an ironic laugh that intrigued them both, but sounded more concerned than humorous. He scratched his chin and searched for suitable words.

'You don't know, do you, John? You can't or you would have said something.'

Andy's question was confusing and too vague for either of his friends to understand.

'What did Craig tell you about what happened to Stephen? Did he tell you where he was found?'

John surveyed his alcohol-clouded mind, returning a blank expression and admitted he had only received minimal information from Craig Jones, who had called him the previous evening. He knew that Stephen had been beaten and was now in a coma. Come to think of it, that was all he knew.

Sully put his arm across in front of Andy who was about to speak and scanned the immediate area within the pub. The two couples in the nearby alcove were gone and the flashing lights and teasing promises of a fruit machine jangling at the opposite end of the bar occupied the nearest punter. Nobody remained within earshot and the pub manager was engaged in idle conversation while pulling a pint. Sully resumed the conversation on Andy's behalf. His words were deliberate and cutting as he whispered the revelation.

'They found him in the cut through that runs from the Stratford Road to the back of his house, John. It was in *exactly* the same place as, well, as Matt Douglass.'

John had stopped drinking his pint and was riveted by Sully's every word. His mouth felt dry despite the continuous consumption of liquid. His eyes pierced into Sully as he spoke.

'This, is why Andy is so freaked out. It's a fucking hell of a coincidence. Do you know what they found wrapped around his feet? A chair, John, a fucking rusty old chair that Craig told us the local coppers said looked like it had been there for donkey's years. Isn't that just a little concerning? A little too fucking close for comfort? What if they're combing that crime scene for evidence and all the new forensic gadgets they have unearth something from years ago? We'd be fucked John, fucked!'

John sat back in his seat and looked up to the ceiling, his mouth still gaping. It certainly seemed like one hell of a coincidence.

As he was poised to reply to this shocking disclosure, a figure beyond Sully's shoulder caught John's attention. He had not laid eyes on her since that fateful evening in August of 1986, but now she stood at the bar, sipping nervously from a tall-stemmed wine glass. She was undeniably as beautiful and as striking as she had been the first time he had met her.

Chapter Sixteen

'Hey! Have you forgotten? Those are my favourites!'

Siobhan Jones playfully smacked John Garland's hand, which he retracted sharply away from a shared paper package, allowing her to stab at as many overcooked and crispy chips as her wooden fork would allow. They shared a reminiscent smile.

'And since when have we used these things to eat? What's wrong with your fingers getting a little bit greasy like they used to?'

She tossed her fork to the ground and dug in with her digits. John laughed and shook his head. Some things never changed. Siobhan smiled back as she munched enthusiastically and half covering her mouth with a hand as she spoke before finishing the fried mouthful, tapped the wooden bench beneath them. She was more beautiful than ever, John thought.

'I haven't sat here for about thirty years and of course you can't have either.'

John conveniently had a mouth full of chips, so could avoid having to reply as he nodded. He didn't have the heart to confess to his Sunday evening fish feast of only a few hours earlier in that very spot. It would have spoiled their romantic reminiscent moment together. Their last playful exchange outside the former Jack's Fish and Chips Shop had occurred during much happier and comparatively innocent times. Now here they were, together again.

They had driven the short detour from the pub after Siobhan had offered John a lift to the budget hotel he had hastily booked before leaving London. In the Bull's Head, they had exchanged a jovial rapid-fire recollection of the summer of 1986, remembering Peacocks, the parties in Stephen's back garden, and miscellaneous immature teenage antics. The reunited foursome had stayed much later than expected at the pub as they delved into a catalogue of anecdotes from their youth. They had laughed cheerfully, but now John could sense sadness in Siobhan's deep brown eyes as she curled her auburn hair behind her ear, anticipating they were poised to break from their light-hearted exchange and chips consumption. She crumpled the empty white paper and stood up, shoving her rubbish into a nearby concrete bin that all but overflowed onto the pavement. Before John could speak, Siobhan beckoned him back to her car, which was parked around the corner; its amber lights flashing brightly as she remotely unlocked the doors. He reached out to hold her hand, desperate to rekindle the memories of a generation ago, but she pulled hers away, a look of disdain catching him by surprise.

As they sat in a briefly awkward silence, Siobhan paused as she slid the key into the car's ignition, choosing not to start the engine. John felt embarrassed at having made such a crude and poorly conceived move.

'Do you remember my mother, John?'

Confused by the tack of the conversation, John twisted back around to face Siobhan, his passenger's seatbelt retrieved from slightly behind his shoulder. He clicked the metal end into place near the centre console as Siobhan elaborated.

'I saw her at lunchtime today and I told her what had happened to Stephen and how some of his old friends were returning to Birmingham to, well, to say farewell, I suppose.'

For the first time since taking that devastating call from the hospital administrator, Siobhan could now confront Stephen's apparent fate in a controlled and sober manner. Her tears had flooded out at the Bull's Head at one point, emptying a reservoir of emotion that served as a catalyst for John, Sully and Andy to also address the grim reality they had avoided all night. So concerned was the manager at the sight of four previously buoyant characters suddenly plunged into apparent despair that he had brought each an after-hours nightcap in an act of mournful solidarity and told them to vacate the premises at their leisure.

Siobhan placed her hands at ten to two on the steering wheel and drummed each of her fingers slowly in a symmetrical rhythm. She stared straight ahead, her face expressionless.

'My mom had forgotten all about you, John. She isn't losing her senses or anything like that, but to her, you were just a brief intrusion, a hiccup that lasted a few weeks, back when I was a teenager. You interrupted my destiny, or whatever she might want to call it, with Craig. She remembers there being someone I dated briefly and trying to talk some sense into me in Ireland, but nothing more than that. No name. Nothing.'

John stared blankly at the dashboard in front of him, noticing a faded spilled tea or coffee stain and a series of scuffmarks that had damaged the cheap plastic interior. He had always considered himself more than just an inconsequential footnote in Siobhan's life. He was pricked by tinges of regret on a regular basis, often wondering how different his life might have been had he and Siobhan fought to maintain their relationship all those years ago. While journeying up from London, the discomfort of his hangover had been countered by an excited optimism that no matter how painful the return home to visit an ailing Stephen would be, it might provide a long overdue opportunity to perhaps rekindle the affections of his first love. Siobhan's words now swung like a wrecking ball into the foolish expectation he had built.

'The point is, we were young and definitely in love, but it's so long ago now that what happened between us doesn't really matter, in the grand scheme of things, does it? I mean, two eighteen-year-olds doing what all teenagers do when they're young and in love. It will always be a special time for me, but, well you know what I'm trying to say.'

John wished he didn't. He just listened.

'I can tell you why I didn't return from Ireland, which I know you're dying to ask, but, like I say, it really doesn't matter. I was only supposed to be there for a week or so, but ended up staying for months. You stayed in London. You were going to have a baby for god's sake! We just let it go, didn't we? We didn't fight hard enough to get back together.'

Siobhan could tell from John's sharp intake of breath that he was poised to reply, but cut him off. She laughed as she continued.

'You know I failed my A Levels, right? All of them! Everyone was so certain that my place at Liverpool was a foregone conclusion, but I knew I'd done badly. I just kept up the façade. Even when the results came through I kept them a secret, even from you. My mother was relentless on the ferry and on the drive to her sister's, probing and urging me to get back with Craig. It went on for hours, all the not so subtle comments. After a while, she was just nagging me. She had no idea what had happened to me that night at the Odeon.'

Siobhan's voice trailed off, her mood darkened. Seeking distraction, she started the engine.

'I slapped her!'

John omitted a sharp cough. His immediate reaction was one of genuine astonishment, which eased when he remembered how she certainly possessed a fiery streak that he always suspected might escalate when provoked.

113

'God, was she shocked! She didn't react; just stood there in disbelief. I broke down and told her everything. Well, almost everything. In between me sobbing and howling, I think she managed to decipher what had happened to me at the Odeon. I never gave her all the details. No name. She was incredible really. We've been closer than I ever imagined we could be, since then. If there was one good thing to come out of.'

Siobhan's reminiscing paused again. She collected a large breath and let out a deep sigh as if she had teetered back from the brink of exorcising her teenage nightmare of Matt Douglass. She sensed an acknowledgement from John as he stared at her, glancing away only when distracted by the noise of corrugated metal panels being pulled down to shutter the forefront of a now darkened chip shop.

'When you found out back then that I was staying in Ireland, I couldn't tell you the reasons. I couldn't talk to you about anything that had happened, even though I guessed you knew about it from Stephen. It was too painful.

'Now, and for a long time now, I just shrug off that night. It happened to a different person. You know how that feels, right? All those things that you experienced years ago, it was so long ago, they're just frail memories. They're not real any more. We're different people now. I can't relate to the eighteen-year-old Siobhan, or put tangible emotions to the events that took place.'

John rarely considered himself a good listener, usually eager to interject his thoughts and opinions, but on this rare occasion, he was nodding intently, his arms folded defensively across his chest in contemplative silence. He might have hankered after the relatively untroubled exploits of his past, but he knew exactly what Siobhan meant.

'That wanker disappeared. I've no idea what happened to him. I really don't care. At first I hoped he was dead, a predictable reaction I suppose. I was petrified I'd bump into him in the street if I came home, so Ireland was like a giant safety net for me. I definitely felt protected there.

'I pretended I didn't know who had assaulted me so my mom wouldn't call the police. If that happened to my daughter, well, I'd have to kill him. I had to beg mom not to tell Craig. He didn't need to know.

'With Liverpool out of the picture, I stayed in Enniscorthy, worked for my uncle's friend behind the bar in his pub and planned to come home eventually to retake my A Levels. I came home once it felt safe again, but there seemed no point in university any more and, well Craig and I, you know. Well, of course you know from talking to the lads. The rest, as they say, is history, but not much of one to be honest.'

Siobhan clapped her hands together sharply, pointing her fingers towards the road ahead.

'Shall we?'

John remained silent. He bit the inside of his cheek as he digested her words. They shared an accepting smile then edged towards each other, embracing not like former lovers, but as two mournful friends reunited unwittingly at a funeral. John held Siobhan affectionately, tenderly rubbing her back to console her and tracing soft strands of her hair where it fell on her shoulders. Earlier at the Bull's Head, while admiring the radiant woman she had become, he had imagined such closeness might rekindle the love from their teenage years, particularly given their respective turbulent marriages. Yet now, despite their physical closeness, he felt only sadness and regret, accepting that she would be appalled if he escalated the exchange.

As they hugged, John peered beyond Siobhan's shoulder spying an object laid out across the back seat of the idling Vauxhall Corsa. As they released each other, Siobhan wiping a lone tear from her cheek, he motioned subtly with his eyes to the rear of the car, where he had tossed his overnight bag. Intrigued, she shifted in her seat and half turned to look, letting out an ironic laugh as she caught site of a large umbrella she had placed there a few days earlier. It provided the required moment of comic relief to replenish her usually luminous smile and served as the perfect analogy to their lost love.

'You can't play golf with that, now, can you?'

- - - - - - - - - -

Andy Morris blew out his cheeks and shook his head, reluctantly accepting a freshly opened Budweiser beer, chinking his chilled bottle against the tall cold one held by Mike Sullivan.

'Sorry I only have this American crap Andy, but we should have one more before bedtime, don't you think?'

Andy pressed the bottle half-heartedly to his lips, while Sully chugged away before forcing two metal caps into a kitchen bin overflowing beyond its white plastic liner. Andy had lost track of the extent of their alcoholic consumption as a steady stream of pints and chasers had made their way from the Bull's Head bar to their table crammed with empties. He longed for the bed generously made up in the spare room of Sully's welcoming home, but dutifully teased at the final beer of the night as he propped himself up against the edge of the kitchen counter.

'Do you think he's getting the shag?'

Sully's suggestion that John and Siobhan might have rekindled their old romance only an hour or two since reuniting in the pub seemed highly unlikely to Andy.

'No, I don't think so. John might be a bit of a lad, but I doubt very much that Siobhan is going to take back up with him after all this time.'

Sully shrugged and downed another gulp of beer more substantial than Andy could manage at this point in the evening. Sully didn't reply, or protest, just wandered into the living room coveting his worn but comfortable armchair that offered a welcome respite from the awkwardness of the wooden chair that had niggled at his back at the Bull's Head. Andy followed, casually inspecting family portraits and inexpensive artwork that hung on a wall overdue a fresh commitment to more stylish wallpaper. He stood before a well-preserved map from the 1950s of the grid system of Manhattan's streets, picking off names of places he had heard but only ever dreamed of: Forty-Second Street, the Empire State Building, Central Park and Fifth Avenue. Sully reclined with a contented sigh, navigating his bottle from hand to mouth.

'Got that when we were over in New York on holiday, Christmas shopping, three years ago. It just took my fancy. An old map, not very expensive, but better than plonking one of those Statue of Liberty figures the missus wanted to buy on the mantelpiece. Place on the corner near the old Jack's chippy framed it for a reasonable price.'

Andy's obsessive-compulsive tendency prompted him to straighten the angle of the frame, which he had noticed was tilted slightly to the right. Then, caught up in a moment of curiosity and forgetting briefly that he was exploring someone else's home, he flipped the lid on an old tin canister that sat on the mantelpiece. Its hinges rusted and worn, the lid broke free from the small container and fell noisily as it landed on the concrete hearth surrounding the fireplace. Andy spied a small cigar-like shape that was wrapped carefully in a soft tissue paper and beside it an assortment of five- and ten-pound notes folded roughly on top of a selection of coins. Andy backed away from the fireplace apologetically, reaching down to retrieve the fallen lid. Sully leaped from his chair, snatched it from Andy's grasp and shut it tight on top of the tin canister that he obscured from view with a framed photo of his parents that also stood on the mantle.

'Jesus, Andy, that's personal. Don't go looking in there. Do you always go rummaging through people's things when you're staying at their house?'

Sully regretted reprimanding his old friend as soon as the words poured from his mouth and he slumped back into his seat, apologetic and embarrassed. Andy sat down cautiously on a sofa positioned opposite, which awkwardly matched the eclectic style of furniture arranged cosily between an oversized flat screen television and a large dresser housing china plates and special occasion glassware.

'I'm sorry, it's just.'

Sully failed to find sufficient words, but Andy nodded and pursed his lips, accepting that a night consumed by emotion and the prospect the following day of perhaps bidding farewell to their comatose companion was proving stressful for all concerned. He walked calmly back to the kitchen and returned to the front room with a peace offering of two more Buds. Sully laughed.

'We're really going to regret this in the morning, you know.'

- - - - - - - - - -

'What's in the box, Dad?'

John Garland usually delighted in lengthy chats with his daughter Vicky over FaceTime when away from home on business trips. His jaunts across the country and often further afield had been commonplace since before she was born and the mischievous grin of the one female in his life with whom he shared a love as unconditional as it was uncomplicated usually provided a welcome respite from the stresses of a busy day. On this occasion, cramped between the end of a foreign double bed and a bland wooden desk on an uncomfortable chair in a sanitised refurbished hotel room, his enthusiasm for anything other than sleep had worn uncharacteristically thin.

'I've told you before Vicky, if you're going to call from my office, please leave things alone that are on my desk. You know that's a box of personal stuff; nothing for you to see.'

Vicky shrugged apologetically and slid the tortoise-shaped Kerala wooden box back to its original resting place, positioned diagonally at the corner of John's large mahogany desk. Her father had returned home from his first visit to Asia when she was seven years old, carefully unwrapping the teak antique box edged in brass decoration that he had nurtured cautiously home from India from within layers of soft crinkling tissue paper. In excellent condition for an article believed to be almost one hundred and fifty years old, the expertly crafted artefact remained securely locked and the brass key that could reveal its secrets always seemed to be closely guarded upon John's person.

'Look Vicky, I'm really tired and it's been a difficult day. Tomorrow I'm going to see Stephen in hospital and my head is all over the place right now.'

Vicky traced a finger across the screen of her smart phone, as if pursuing an imaginary tear running down her father's cheek. She appreciated how upset he was based on the magnitude of the hangover he had been nursing when she had tiptoed around him at home that morning. Such drinking binges and the following day's consequences were usually triggered by tempestuous brawls with her mother. His distress over Stephen Taylor had tipped him towards the top of the scale by which she usually measured her parents' unhappiness.

John rocked back on the heels of the chair that dug into the thin grey carpet as Vicky replied with an over-emphasised thumbs-up sign that filled the screen of his phone as her digits closed in on her built-in camera.

'There is one thing though, love. I don't know how long I'll be up here. It'll probably be longer than I'd planned. I'll aim to be home for your party on Friday, but if something happens, I can't promise.'

John landed the chair back on its front legs with a thump, imagining the guest occupying the room below might have glanced towards the ceiling, poised to reach for the phone to contact hotel reception and register a complaint. The Saracen's Head Premier Inn assured all occupants an untroubled comfortable night's sleep at the boastful promise of providing a full refund if an inconsiderate fellow guest should break that guarantee. John had dutifully removed his shoes when entering his room having opened and closed all doors on his floor as gently and thoughtfully as he could manage under the influence of several unsteadying pints of ale.

'I know, Dad. Mom already said she thought you might have to stay until at least the weekend. I understand.'

Vicky leaned forward and kissed the screen goodnight. John grinned a lopsided smile as the image of his daughter evaporated. He put down his phone and eased himself onto the large white expanse of a feathered duvet and gradually half-undressed as he stretched and reached for the rocker switch on the bedside lamp that plunged his room into darkness.

He felt guilty at having genuinely enjoyed the long-overdue reunion with friends he soberly appreciated should never have been allowed to drift out of his life so casually. He and Sully should have remained best friends forever. Andy could probably have been coaxed from his campsite cocoon to split more time between the seaside and his old stomping ground with John's interference over the years. And then there was Siobhan. She remained John's biggest regret of all.

He stared at the silhouette outlines of the room's economically installed furniture that his adjusted eyes could now trace in the darkness. He listened to cars zipping by on the Stratford Road, the noise of their engines muffled by double-glazed windows and thick draped curtains. John thought of Stephen Taylor, the closest of his comrades who also lay on his back in an unfamiliar sanitary room, but without the mental capacity to contemplate such regret. That tear Vicky had imagined rolling from the corner of her father's eye welled and slowly traced his cheek to dampen the cotton pillowcase that absorbed the sadness overwhelming John as he drifted off to sleep.

119

Chapter Seventeen

'Do you lot ever buy your own fags, or just bum them off other people?'

Andy Morris turned his Embassy Number One packet upside down to illustrate and protest that his non-smoking friends Mike Sullivan and John Garland had again taken the last of his cigarettes. Falling flecks of loose tobacco were swept up by the breeze and swirled along a stark alleyway between two buildings where the trio stood beside a hospital sign that clearly stated *No Smoking in This Area*. Andy felt as though they were back at school, when they used to craftily share one cigarette, their whereabouts carefully concealed. Painfully absent from the gang of four reunion was Stephen Taylor. His lungs were being force fed oxygen, or some form of life-preserving substance, while they filled theirs with medicinally self-prescribed nicotine.

Andy's complaint that he, the most financially challenged of the three, was supplementing their apparent return to a habit both John and Sully had kicked as far back as their early twenties, provided brief light relief from the painful and distressing reality they had just discovered the on other side of the hospital wall all were slumped against. John tucked a twice-folded twenty-pound note inside Andy's shirt pocket, waving away his inevitable protestations. Two nurses hurried past, smiling sympathetically, acknowledging a fresh group of mourners they had become accustomed to witnessing, congregated in a private sanctuary in close proximity to the ominous intensive care entrance.

'He's not going to make it, is he?'

Sully's grim assessment as he took a long and defeated pull of smoke was met with blank stares. Neither John nor Andy wanted to admit that he was right and that their childhood friend Stephen indeed appeared to be propping death's door open, likely at any time to have it close shut without much warning. Barely recognisable as the flamboyant life and soul of the party who had blossomed in recent years, shedding the cocoon of a painfully shy and cautious youth, his near lifeless body was now a soulless sight. A machine beeped monotonously, a fluctuating digital display monitoring his heart rate rose and fell erratically and the sound of assisted breathing broke the morbid silence of an otherwise tranquil room.

Andy had spent only a few minutes by Stephen's bedside before racing outside to find solitude in the makeshift grieving area, where he could privately pour out his emotions. Tall and lean, he crouched awkwardly beside the wall, his knees buckled, his head cradled by cupped hands filling unashamedly with tears.

Sully had allowed muted sobs to lightly dampen a wad of Kleenex tissues as he surveyed tubes and wires and needles poking unceremoniously from Stephen's helpless body. John just stared at his old friend, while comforting the other. He was more consumed by rage and anger than the distress that overwhelmed Andy and Sully. Their childhood comrade had been mercilessly and senselessly beaten into this lifeless state for no apparent reason whatsoever.

John recalled the disturbing facts Andy had shared with him the previous night; that Stephen had been assaulted in the exact same cut through where tall whispering trees lining the wasteland had witnessed the four of them viciously attack Matt Douglass in 1986.

'That was a different situation and we had good reason,' he convinced himself, justifying their act of retribution. John fought to repress a vivid flashback he had banished since that fateful night: his black leather boot connecting sickeningly below Matt Douglass's chin, snapping his head back violently, as he delivered the final blow. The memory of the piercing cracking sound that tore through the silent wasteland as Matt's neck broke and his spine splintered now caused John to grip his fists so tightly that his fingernails dug into his palms, briefly leaving imprints that stung as she shook his hands and his mind loose.

Flicking his smouldering cigarette butt to the grey gravel below his feet, John now wandered slowly back towards a hospital entrance devoid of activity apart from a flustered looking male visitor clutching a bunch of hurriedly purchased flowers in one hand and fumbling a ringing mobile phone with the other. John waited patiently for Sully to follow, but Andy trailed behind indecisively.

'I can't lads, I just can't. I've said my goodbyes and I want to remember him as he was, not like this. Not with all those tubes. I might come to see him again later in the week, but for now…'

His trembling tone tailed off and neither John nor Sully voiced any displeasure at Andy's decision as they wandered almost aimlessly through the automatically opening doors to again stand forlorn over a motionless, lifeless body.

- - - - - - - - - -

Andy sat on the bonnet of Sully's sensible family saloon puffing on a fresh supply of cigarettes purchased from a corner shop across the busy street outside the hospital, his heels kicking against the rubber rims of the front driver's side tyre. He blew smoke aimlessly into the air, barely noticing the blur of cars passing by on the adjacent main road. He focused on John and Sully as they approached.

'Any news?'

Andy's question was met with a solemn shrug of the shoulders and a resigned shake of the head. John and Sully had conspired to shield Andy from the harsh truth shared by Stephen's doctor that he was not expected to wake from his coma.

Sully drove in silence, his hands and feet operating on autopilot as he navigated a route to his favourite city centre restaurant. He hoped they could stomach lunch. The drinking bout of the previous night had fashioned a dull hangover that still pounded their heads. John massaged each temple with his middle fingers, his eyes closed as visions of a comatose Stephen blurred and merged with those of a dead Matt Douglass, lying broken in the dirt all those years before. He was on the brink of letting out a frustrated scream when Andy interrupted his thoughts.

'Hey Sully, I wouldn't mind taking a walk around Broad Street and by Symphony Hall after lunch if that's ok. I haven't seen some of the changes they've made up there, like the new library and, of course, John hasn't either.'

Sully's eyes met Andy's in the rear-view mirror and he nodded affirmatively, happy to oblige, but overcome by grief for his dying friend.

Chapter Eighteen

John Garland was pleasantly surprised to discover at first glance that Gas Street appeared to have been impervious to the overwhelming wave of reconstruction that had morphed the centre of the city he once called home into a foreign landscape. He gazed upon the still partly preserved side road from the corner of a comparatively exotic Broad Street, which championed clubs, bars, strip joints and restaurants and the world-renowned Symphony Hall concert venue in place of the once crumbling Bingley Hall, the boarded up Rum Runner club and dingy all-night greasy spoon cafés that he remembered. John considered Birmingham's twenty-first century transformation a welcome departure from the post-war concrete monolithic architecture imprinted on his youthful memory, but he delighted in stumbling across this relatively untouched idyllic relic from his past.

Sully was acting as tour guide for his two out of town visitors as they walked off a hearty pub lunch and fought to suppress the stark reality of Stephen Taylor lying comatose in a forlorn hospital bed. They had passed time between vantage points of a rooftop café and the observation deck of the new Birmingham Library, surveying a sprawl of rerouted streets and new development that illustrated the city's appeal as a pleasant alternative to individuals and businesses relocating from expensive real estate in London and the south.

'It hasn't changed much down here, apart from the canals being spruced up a bit, of course. That nightclub down there is derelict and they've embraced hip inner city living over there. But for the most part, it all looks the same.'

Back in 1986, all three of them and Stephen had spent countless evenings and weekends working a part time job in an office on Gas Street. They would painstakingly cold-call potential timeshare customers from sparse office space at number twenty-one, earning a paltry basic wage supplemented only when they secured a definite sales lead. They had dubbed their workplace Silver's after the flamboyant owner of the fledgling business, a local entrepreneur named Tony Silver, who was rarely in attendance to supervise their shoddy work. They had caught the timeshare boom of the eighties at its peak and became adept at convincing yuppies and middle class earners with a disposable income to set sail for destinations that sounded as exotic as they were unfamiliar to the sales force. The nice little earner, as the era's popular wheeler-dealer Arthur Daley, from the television show *Minder* might have described the initiative, ended abruptly when John was caught abusing the trust that had furnished each of them with a personal key to the premises. He and Siobhan would often sneak into the offices after hours and take advantage of the seclusion and a large comfortable love seat in the private office suite at Silver's. One night, the proprietor made similar plans himself, having met a willing partner at the Opposite Lock nightclub at the end of the street, and was displeased to discover his romantic retreat unexpectedly and brazenly occupied. John's key was confiscated that night and the irate Silver sent blunt letters to Stephen, Sully and Andy, also terminating their employment and ordering them to return their keys by mail.

John ran a reminiscent hand appreciatively along a stately old redbrick wall, its original structure preserved up to the point where it reached a covered archway that led to a painstakingly restored cobbled ramp, angled down to the narrow towpath beside a canal and the rear of their former workplace. The colourful Mailbox upmarket shopping and office development, with its futuristic 16-storey Cube clad in glazed and gold anodised aluminium panels now loomed large on an unfamiliar skyline, but John's indelible teenage memories still came flooding back.

'Do you remember that winter when this canal froze completely? What were the names of those bands that rehearsed in the empty offices at Silver's some nights? We had a crazy game of football here with them once. Except Stephen of course because he was convinced he'd fall through the ice and freeze to death!'

Andy remembered. Casting his mind back to such carefree times, when slipping and sliding haphazardly across the ice, kicking an improvised ball in the form of a Coke can, provided a pleasant distraction from the still vivid memory of that morning's morbid hospital visit. He could visualise Stephen, cold and complaining on the safe-haven of terra firma voicing his concern at the frozen skirmish that ended only when both sides were drained of energy, or their feet became numb from the ice that pierced a chill through their boots. Soon, he imagined, Stephen would be cold again, lying on a slab, only no longer afforded the option to complain.

'One of those bands was These Tender Virtues. Their singer Pete Williams played bass in Dexys Midnight Runners before that.

126

Whenever we staggered into that greasy spoon all night café, The Tow Rope, back there on Broad Street after a gig, he always seemed to be in there. He's still gigging now, you know. The other was Major Hero. If you remember, Craig spent most of his first few weeks on the beat trying to catch them putting up posters on bus stops and lamp posts all over Hall Green. I don't think he ever nicked them.'

The old friends returned to modern day Gas Street, which was relatively deserted compared with the once grimy towpath that now welcomed tourists and lunchtime drinkers, spilling onto a canal-side patio from the Tap and Spile pub.

'Speak of the devil!'

Sully pointed towards the old Silver's office building of their youth.

'Pete Williams? Where?'

'No, Andy, you pillock! Craig. Craig the copper.'

The trio ambled along the pavement, fascinated as they watched a uniformed police officer unravelling a spool of blue and white plastic tape that cordoned off the entrance to what was once Silver's as he stretched it from an old black-painted wrought iron fence, around a lamppost and across to the fence on the opposite side of two heavy red doors. They observed how police cars were now parked across either end of Gas Street, their blue lights flashing a warning for vehicles to seek an alternative route. As they approached the intriguing scene, Andy commented on the noticeable cracks in the building's white exterior walls that zigzagged downwards towards the tops of the four windows of their former office space. Sully provided a likely explanation.

'Well it's a listed building if you remember, preservation orders and all that. It's probably a pain in the arse to do any work on this place. That's why it looks like it's barely been touched since we were last here.'

They paused at the tape, just as Detective Inspector Craig Jones hurried back out, heading towards an anonymous black BMW identified by its conspicuousness as an unmarked police vehicle, its engine running.

'Oy! Whatever's happened, he did it!'

A juvenile smirk on his face, Sully was waving frantically with one hand and pointing accusingly at John with the other, as he caught Craig's attention. Startled and somewhat confused at the unexpected spectacle of three relics from his past hollering from the edge of a crime scene, Craig stopped and stared back at them. John took an agitated swipe at Sully's hand as Craig briefly peered his head inside the passenger's side window of the car to speak to the driver and then turned to approach the three unlikely observers.

'Well, well, well. What do we have here then? If it isn't the three musketeers.'

Craig stopped short of inquiring as to the sobering whereabouts of their traditional partner in crime D'Artagnan as he appreciated the inappropriate reference, given Stephen Taylor's current sorry state. His reaction to their presence betrayed an awkward mix of surprise to see old acquaintances, his sadness over Stephen's injuries and an agitation at the unwelcome sight of John Garland. He shook the hands of all three, staring uncomfortably as he made eye contact with John for the first time in some thirty years.

'Glad you could make it up here, for Stephen.'

John nodded in agreement and pursed his lips, sensing the awkwardness between them.

'Look lads, I can't hang around, but I'm really sorry about what happened to Stephen. I've asked someone I know who is investigating to keep me informed. If I hear anything, I'll let you know. Siobhan's visiting him again this afternoon, I think.'

Andy thanked Craig, relaying details of their earlier visit to intensive care, then gestured towards the red doors that were now blocked by a motionless uniformed officer standing guard outside.

'What's going on here, Craig? Looks serious.'

Craig blew out his cheeks, held his hands out and raised his eyebrows. He bent down to make eye contact with the waiting driver of the sleek BMW, its interior hidden by tinted windows. He tapped his watch with two fingers to indicate the likely longevity of his brief delay.

'I can't tell you a lot really and to be honest, we don't know a whole lot right now, but it looks like there's a body in there.'

Craig's revelation provoked a mix of intrigued and impressed facial expressions, all eager to learn more. The silence encouraged Craig to disclose further details.

'There's an old concrete slab down in the basement, been there for years, covered by tatty carpet and old metal shelving in a room that was once used for storage. Anyway, some old fella, you knew him, didn't you, Tony Silver? He sold the place a while back and the current owners started some refurbishment recently. They were hacking away some of the concrete so they could access the sewer line and put toilets down there. A couple of hours in with a jackhammer and they came across a load of old bones, wrapped in what look like old blankets, or something. We've got our team in there now, extracting a skeleton it seems. Anyway, I've already told you too much.'

Craig put a finger to his hushed lips, requesting confidentiality. Sully immediately shot back a salute perfected during his brief stint as a boy scout.

'All right, I can't keep my driver waiting any longer. I'll probably see you lads down the pub then. Hopefully 'Bones' won't keep me here all night.'

- - - - - - - - - -

Finally, he was alone. He banged both fists on the surface before him, frustrated by the day's harrowing events, causing a beer bottle to shake and almost topple before he grabbed its long glass neck. He reclined, sipped slowly and closed his eyes as he swallowed, seeking to calm his agitated mood.

His concentration was broken a few minutes later by the headlines of the local evening news. He sought out the remote control and raised the volume, intrigued by the scene he had witnessed on Gas Street, which now provided the backdrop for a stern-faced reporter who turned to point at an office building a short distance beyond her shoulder. She spoke purposefully into a foam-capped microphone, exaggerating the grisly discovery of a skeleton unearthed within the foundations of the building in question. The television crew had established a base camp at the Broad Street end of the barricaded side road and provided almost identical periodic live updates to its audience, which were all delivered with equal zeal. A zoom lens captured the image of a temporary polythene incident room, its tent edges flapping in the light breeze, confined within the extended cordon of blue and white police tape. Detective Inspector Craig Jones had politely declined to answer questions, instead reading a benign prepared statement when reluctantly placed in front of the camera. He did admit that dental records would soon be checked to determine the identity of the unfortunate soul, whom it was believed was a male victim, though his age and the length of time he had been entombed was, so far, unconfirmed.

One eager media outlet ran a news ticker across the foot of the television screen proclaiming it 'The Silver Skeleton' after hurriedly inaccurate reports had suggested the office block's former owner had met a grizzly demise. The retired businessman was then unearthed by a rival channel, found living in a retirement home in Worthing on the south coast. From a comfortable wicker chair perched on a second-floor balcony overlooking the English Channel, the ageing Mr Silver confirmed he had cooperated fully, though as far as he was concerned irrelevantly, with authorities delving into his former ownership of the cordoned off property. He added with a smile that reports of his death had been greatly exaggerated.

The news channel switched its attention to the comparatively trivial matter of the ongoing mixed fortunes of the city's local football teams, while promising to keep its viewers abreast of breaking news from Gas Street, of which there appeared to be precious little.

The concerned viewer mulled over the discovery of the skeleton whose identity was no mystery. He sat calm and relaxed, remembering every miniscule detail from the killing and the removal of the body, to the burial and the disposal of all incriminating evidence. They were memories that had been barricaded in his subconscious for decades. He grimaced as he spoke to himself, lamenting the unexpected renovations on Gas Street.

'It's a listed building; they shouldn't be allowed to tamper with the foundations. He was supposed to be buried forever. How can this be happening?

'And why the hell did I have to take a trophy?'

Chapter Nineteen

Summer 1986

'This stuff tastes like piss.'

John Garland held a tall pint glass up to the glare of a spotlight inset into a false ceiling and surveyed the offending amber serving of Davenports Continental Lager. Huddling around a table in a quiet corner of a virtually deserted Moor Green Football Club members bar on a slow Sunday night ensured a confidential conversation would not be overheard by curious eavesdroppers as it surely would be by friends and familiar faces in the nearby Bull's Head. The only other drinkers present were two fixtures at the bar, sixty-something regulars chatting with the steward and his wife, who was trimming the edges of her cheaply manicured nails delicately with her teeth as she listened intently to the customers. Perched on tall stools, they seemed to be recounting every pass, shot, tackle and goal from the previous day's football match.

The price the secretive group across the room paid for privacy was the cheap beer all agreed failed miserably to satisfy their palates, though the quality of alcohol on offer was the least of their concerns.

'So, you're sure he's gone? No sign of a body or anything?'

John probed at Stephen Taylor's revelation that Matt Douglass no longer laid dead or dying on the path that provided a shortcut between the Stratford Road and Stonor Croft, where they had administered a severe beating two nights earlier and killed him, as far as they were concerned. Stephen nodded, causing Andy Morris to slump slowly against the back support of his wooden chair, a combination of confusion and a sense of relief etched across his face. None of them had slept more than a disturbed catnap's duration for almost the past 48 hours and had avoided contact with each other until now. The weary strain told on their frightened faces. The palpable smog of fear that had engulfed every waking moment of each of the four friends since they had run in panic away from the scene of the assault seemed to be lifting at the realisation that a dead body had not been discovered in the leafy cut through, in stark contrast to their expectations. Andy prayed that the petrifying prospect of a lifelong prison sentence was diminishing as Stephen continued.

'My mom's bedroom overlooks the wasteland and the garages and you can see the cut through from there too, but I couldn't go in there to look. I would have woken her up if I had. I just stood in the kitchen, trying to get mud and blood off my clothes, waiting to hear police cars or something. I expected it to be like when Craig and that other copper were swarming around looking for the mannequin murderer a few weeks ago, but nothing happened. I curled up on the settee, but I couldn't sleep. I don't think I'm ever going to be able to sleep.'

The others nodded in silence.

'But he's gone all right. It took me a while to work up the nerve, but I went and looked for myself yesterday. I thought about grabbing that old chair, you know, to get rid of any evidence, but I just shoved it under some bushes with my foot when I walked past. If nobody saw us, and he's crawled off home or somewhere, we're in the clear. Plus, it pissed down with rain all night afterwards, so there's no obvious traces of blood anywhere. You wouldn't know anything out of the ordinary had happened there by looking at it.'

Andy laughed, his hands shaking as he used both to hold his pint and sip cautiously while hanging on Stephen's every syllable before managing to speak for the first time since they had sat cautiously at the table.

'When the three of us were hiding in the graveyard, I was certain we'd killed him. I mean. I can't even; that noise when his head snapped back. And now he's gone. Not there. Not dead. You're right. We're in the clear!'

John, whose original suggestion that they had merely ruthlessly assaulted Matt had infuriated Sully after the trio had scarpered from the scene, was more guarded as he muted the apparent celebration.

'Hold on a minute, Andy. Until we see Matt, on the bus, or in the pub or somewhere, we have to be careful. We need to keep this between the four of us and nobody else. We can't go around telling people we taught him a lesson. What that bastard did to Siobhan makes me hope he is dead, but we can't make any assumptions.'

John was right. Even if Matt had crawled the relatively short distance home and was now recuperating in bed, or his severe injuries were being treated in an emergency room, they needed to avoid detection. The punishment for actual or grievously bodily harm might

134

not measure as severely on the scale as the sentence for murder, but it remained a petrifying concern.

Sully wandered slowly back in the direction of the bar, almost reluctantly ordering four more pints as the steward's wife craned her neck to remain engaged in conversation while she poured. He returned balancing the fresh glass pots on a rusting tin tray, with two packets of pork scratchings stuffed into his jacket pocket. He surveyed three faces that stared back, soliciting his opinion.

'It doesn't make sense to me, but if he's gone, he's gone. And as John says, we need to remain cautious and keep silent about this. What about alibis? What do we have?'

Andy confirmed he had been able to sneak into his house through the back door, which was routinely left unlocked, without waking his light-sleeping father. As John had demanded, Andy had checked the Radio Times and silently switched on the television in the living room that crackled with static as it aired the final half an hour of a Clint Eastwood cop movie. He had watched the film a few years earlier, so could lie with confidence that he had followed its plot from beginning to end and then fallen into a tortured sleep on the sofa.

'Me too,' chimed in Sully. 'I caught the end of that as well. That Dirty Harry's a mean bastard, isn't he! My mom came down and made me a sandwich as she saw there was a light on and I said I was hungry. She hadn't heard me come in. I ate that and then went up to my room.

'I almost ran into a spot of bother by the Kentucky on the way back. Just a few lads pissed up and looking for a fight, but I crossed over the road to avoid them. I didn't know them and I'm sure they'd have forgotten seeing me by the time they woke up with a hangover.'

John noted the irony of Sully slipping away from a possible confrontation less than an hour after he had helped administer a vicious kicking that might have resulted in murder. Their rage and brutal reaction had been one of passion, of pure hatred and revenge for an unforgivable assault as far as John was concerned and retribution for countless years of bullying and intimidating Stephen. They weren't a danger to society, killers likely to reoffend. They had snapped. Their tirade was brief and impulsive. Now, a bewildering blend of remorse and pure fear for their precarious fate gripped each of them, even if Matt, or his corpse, had vanished without explanation. John sighed as he recalled how the assault on his girlfriend had been the catalyst for their actions.

'I didn't go straight home as planned.'

John's three friends paused. Andy shook his head in anticipation of their innocence being shattered by John veering off script from the agreed course of action.

'I just couldn't. I had to go and try to see Siobhan.'

Frustrated through they might have been, the others appreciated John's need to console his distraught girlfriend.

'I tried throwing a few small stones at her bedroom window, but it was no use. The wind and then the torrential rain that came down were noisy and what I was doing probably just sounded like the weather. I couldn't ring the doorbell, or call the house. I'm sure someone else would have answered the phone and not been too pleased at me ringing at almost two in the morning. They were getting up at five to go to Ireland.

'I got soaked when it absolutely pissed down. I threw my clothes in the washing machine because my mom and dad are away. Then I took a shower because, well, I just felt dirty. We should have thought of this before, but if any of you need to come over to mine and wash your clothes, you can, no problem.

'I suppose one good thing is that taxi you took to Siobhan's, Stephen. There's your alibi. It's not perfect, but I think we might well be in the clear.'

They sat there in silence, all mentally and physically exhausted from sleep deprivation and the threat of being brought unceremoniously to justice, which hung over them like a guillotine. The two regulars at the bar were now trying their luck on a flashing fruit machine that teased the promise of a three-figure jackpot to those who gambled. John looked at his watch and then deliberately at Stephen, Sully and Andy, each in turn, confirming he held their attention.

'We have to agree that if nothing else happens and life goes back to normal we're never going to talk about this again; no matter what the circumstances. Not now and not when we're thirty or fifty or eighty years old. No speculating if just two of us are at home watching telly, or if we're in the pub and nobody else is around. No telling future wives or girlfriends or whatever. No wondering how Matt got home or to a hospital, or wherever he ended up. No talk that could incriminate any one of us. If things change, we can talk in private, but if a dead body isn't going to turn up and start a murder investigation then we should just never talk about it again.'

Three heads nodded silently in agreement.

'Right, we should go somewhere else to grab another pint. Just being in here makes us look suspicious. We should show our faces in the Bull, make it look like we're just going about our business as usual and not stewing or worrying over something. If we're missing from the pub, or we're there all gloomy and miserable, someone will suss that something's not right. That makes sense to me anyway. And besides, I can't stomach any more of this piss.'

Chapter Twenty

Two nights earlier

Matt Douglass was a dead weight. His toned frame tipped the scales at around 16 stone, but seemed much heavier. His eyes were glazed and lifeless. Blood that had poured from his nose, mouth and a deep wound to his head had matted into his thick bleached blonde spiky hair. His torn clothes exposed severe bruising where he had been battered and beaten. He was congealed, sticky and tacky to the touch. His head flopped back and forth like a ragdoll, barely connected to his neck it seemed. He was a dead weight indeed.

A line of mature oak trees that bordered the nearby main road stood like a column of sentries dutifully guarding the brutally murdered body. The carcass lay abandoned below them, begging to be discovered. These trees had born witness to a murder less than an hour earlier and like a long line of informants, impatient to bring the guilty to swift justice, seemed to be whispering the names of the perpetrators in the wind for all to hear as they swayed. The looming silhouette of a white pebble-dashed housing estate on the far side of the adjoining wasteland stood lifeless apart from the occasional sound of a dog sending warning barks to phantom intruders.

Two figures, operating in haste while the short period of late summer darkness still preserved their anonymity, had slipped stealthily between the whispering trees and bushes. One grasped Matt Douglass, or the body formerly known as Matt Douglass, by a protruding ankle and attempted without success to yank him callously from the spot where he had been beaten to death.

'Wait,' said a hushed voice. 'Don't rush. If we take a leg each we'll be able to drag him.'

Slowed by the unpredictable dirt path that dissected the bushes on the wasteland and led to the perfect examples of semi-detached 1930s architecture in the near distance, they began to haul his carcass. Matt Douglass lived there. Or he used to. Dragging the corpse just a measure of a few feet in one coordinated motion was exhausting and infuriating. An arm would occasionally seem to reach deliberately into the bushes and become lodged in the nettles, hell bent on impeding their progress. Jeans rolled up at the ankles provided enough material to grab by the handful and haul, but as one body snatcher pulled and made up ground, the other would slip or lose grip and the corpse would twist through ninety degrees and lie across the path, facing in the wrong direction.

They worked in near silence, pointing and motioning, talking only at a minimum. One directed; the other followed. Staggering, tripping and stumbling, they eventually reached a cookie-cutter row of brick-built garages located at the rear of the houses of Stonor Croft, unseen by curious eyes, they were certain.

The silver metal side buckles on the boots attached to Matt's flailing legs scraped against a strip of concrete over the final few yards of dragging his lifeless body, which landed with a dull thud. They were now truly sapped of the adrenaline that had provided the fuel and capacity to heave 16 stones of totally dead weight.

The white t-shirt Matt had been wearing, the sleeves cut off to reveal the biceps he had proudly and resolutely toned at the gym, was now a discoloured mess of rich brown dirt and red bloodstains, mixed with green grass streaks from where he had been dragged relentlessly. The torn and misshapen material had ridden up over the head of the corpse, exposing bruises and boot marks from the beating that had been grievously delivered. When the t-shirt was pulled back down to cover the body, Matt's bloodstained head rolled back and two lifeless eyes stared hauntingly at the assailants, causing them to reel back in terror.

'He's dead. Just remember, he's dead and let's get him away from here.'

Now, there was a problem they had not anticipated. One beyond their control. There was no mistaking a weaving trail through the grass and dirt that betrayed their route taken from the cut through to the garages. An intermittent spattering of blood scarred the path and wasteland back to the spot where the killing had occurred, but there was no time to worry about a Saturday morning stroller questioning its origin and making an alarming assumption before alerting the authorities. The priority remained moving the body.

Matt Douglass housed a Ford Escort Mark II in the family garage behind two creaking old doors stained multiple times with creosote that splintered to the touch and barely hung from their rusty hinges. A bulky padlock securing the structure was opened by a key among several found on a ring stuffed into the deceased's pocket.

Attached to the ring was a tasteless key fob, depicting a cartoon bird, its chest puffed out arrogantly, overlaid with the words 'Bionic Cock.' The solid metal loop of the lock clicked and popped up and was removed slowly and quietly, without disturbing the slumbering locals. In stark contrast, the two garage doors screamed loudly as they opened. The creaking and squealing of the decades old hinges seemed to be calling out to Rose Douglass, who slept in the back bedroom of a nearby house, urging her to peer out of the window and catch her son's killers red handed.

Matt's old Escort was rusty red in colour and typical of cars local boy racers restored passionately during weekends and evenings. It bore a tacky spoiler, go-faster stripes and hubcaps expropriated from more expensive cars to camouflage its deficiencies. The driver's side door was unlocked and opened almost silently. When turned slowly, the ignition key made only a quiet click, releasing the steering lock.

'No, wait! Don't start it!'

Starting the car in the garage would amplify the engine noise, so it made more sense to push the Escort slowly to the spot where the dead body lay lifeless, waiting to continue its clandestine journey. Pushing the car was a challenge, but no more so than dragging Matt Douglass through the bramble and across the wasteland had been. After a strained start, the rusty old vehicle eventually rolled slowly and silently and came to a halt after some frantic pumping on the brakes, which were less responsive than they would have been with the engine engaged.

A brief scan of the inside of the boot revealed only a midsized suitcase and a can of motor oil. The moderately heavy suitcase, a bland light brown in colour and worn around the edges, was thrown onto the back seat and the door closed more noisily than was comfortable. Almost frantically now, Matt Douglass needed to be leveraged into the car.

And then, without warning, it rained. A torrential downpour. The tail end of Hurricane Charley, which had battered Ireland, parts of Wales and the south coast, was migrating north and was suddenly flooding the West Midlands. A sea of swirling rain crashed down in waves, drenching everything in its path.

A futile first attempt to lift an increasingly saturated dead body failed spectacularly as it slipped from their grasp and slumped lifeless onto the ground. The car's loose exhaust pipe clanged as it was struck by a flailing arm, the noise echoing as it bounced mercilessly between

141

the garages and houses. At the second attempt, each bore Matt's dead weight below impressively wide shoulders, using his armpit hair to provide grip, straining as they lifted him at an increasing angle. Once leveraged past about forty-five degrees the body started to slip again, the relentless rain and slippery skin impeding their progress. Both instinctively and unceremoniously shoved him towards the car and he flopped forward, but this time did not collapse back down to the concrete. The top half of deceased Matt Douglass instead slouched into the boot, his head butting its large metal hinges with a dull thud as he fell, and came to rest in a convenient kneeling position. His solid legs, now even heavier since his denim jeans had soaked up rain like a sponge, could be lifted, one at a time, and his awkward corpse twisted and was finally stuffed crudely into the space that could barely accommodate his bulk. The boot clicked closed quietly.

'Fucking hell, I'm soaked. Quick, we've got to get out of here now! Get in the car.'

A full frantic turn of the ignition key failed to provoke a response. No spark, no engine noise, nothing. The Ford Escort was lifeless. A second attempt and a third followed, but again there was no reaction between starter motor and engine. Nothing.

'Bollocks!'

In a moment of pure panic, a desperately clenched fist pounded the steering wheel repeatedly and frantically.

'Bollocks! We can't do anything else. We can't leave the body here in the car. We can't move it. Shit!'

There seemed nothing to do other than sit back and give up. Breathless, sodden, physically knackered from dragging a dead weight for hundreds of yards, and mentally drained from the stress of jumping nervously at every sound that amplified in the early hours, conceding defeat felt perversely satisfying. Someone would likely knock on the car window to inquire as to what was happening, although not until the torrential rain that continued to bounce several inches off the roadside had subsided. Perhaps they could conceal their presence as lovers seeking a secluded spot for a secret liaison. Perhaps Matt's mother would see her son's car parked unexpectedly outside the garage and come calling. 'Oh yes, Mrs Douglass, I have seen Matt. He's in the boot having a nap.'

Surely it was worth another try, but still the ignition failed to respond. They looked at each other blankly. They were finished.

A river of bucketing hurricane rain was still cascading past the lifeless parked car. It streamed along the strip of tarmac and down the slope that led from the row of garages to Stonor Croft.

Down the slope! That was it!

The handbrake handle had been jerked up at an angle far beyond the usual holding place such was the looseness of the cable that ran beneath the car. Pulling it up half an inch further and pressing the small button on the end released the handbrake. The Escort began to roll, slowly at first and then at a quickened pace, following the course of the flash-flooding rain.

'Put the gears into first. No, second! Second gear, not first.'

The car rolled beyond the row of garages, down the moderate slope that was sufficient to carry the vehicle forwards, towards the entrance to Stonor Croft and then after a sharp right turn, in the direction of the main road beyond. It was now or never. Turn the key, gradually lift the clutch and tease the accelerator pedal.

'Come on!'

The car jerked awkwardly forwards and then back again, threatening to come to life. The engine spluttered, but then nothing. Another turn of the key and frantic massaging of the clutch and accelerator pedals and suddenly the ignition caught and the engine kicked in and revved loudly. The abrupt burst of power propelled the car towards the bend and it took a determined grip and turn of the steering wheel to right the Escort, swerve onto the wrong side of the empty road and skim the curb before gaining control and aiming for the main road.

'Where the fuck are the lights?'

After a brief blast of a pathetic horn caused by two pairs of hands fumbling around on the steering column and dashboard in search of the headlights switch, and changing the speed of the windscreen wipers from slow to intermittent to unnecessarily fast, a dim yellow glare eventually illuminated the shiny wet road ahead.

The torrential rain was making driving difficult, but the upside was that surely by now it would have washed away all signs of Matt Douglass having been beaten to death. There would be no indelible record of his lifeless body being dragged across the wasteland. No bloody trail, no incriminating evidence. The forces of nature were removing the once tell-tale traces of blood and cleansing the guilt of four teenage killers. All was suddenly well with the world.

'Oh shit! The chair! The fucking chair!'

143

The farcical wrestling prop that had delivered the first antagonised blows needed to be removed and disposed of in a canal, as planned.

'Shit! Go back and get it.'

'No! We can't go back and get it. There isn't time.'

Recovering the chair would require returning to park conspicuously beside the garages and twice running across the open patch of grass with the added danger that the cold and temperamental engine might stall.

'Shit!'

They had Matt Douglass, lifeless and crudely stuffed into the boot of his own car. They also had a chair, arguably the murder weapon and a crucial piece of evidence, sitting there among the bushes, waiting, perhaps begging, to be discovered.

Chapter Twenty-One

'Maybe we should have thrown the body in there.'

The curled edges of a dog-eared lining torn hurriedly from the boot of the improvised Ford Escort hearse that had transported Matt Douglass to his final resting place disappeared from view. The pace of the plunging weary grey material towards the bottom of the Gas Street Basin canal quickened as a worn brown suitcase and can of motor oil joined the dive with a light splash. A car jack and iron bar, added to two weeks' worth of clothes Matt had packed for his pending visit to London in search of employment, added sufficient weight to the sinking objects to ensure they vanished quickly from view.

'Well it's too late now, isn't it? Anyway, a body might sink but then I think it'd fill with air and float up, wouldn't it? I'm not sure, but if it did, they'd find him in no time at all and then we'd be in deep shit. The basement was the best option.'

They had buried the corpse only a matter of minutes earlier in a gaping cavity in the disused basement of their former boss Tony Silver's offices that was primed to welcome a slop of freshly poured concrete the following morning. The intermittent work selling time shares that they had performed at the city centre location throughout recent months granted convenient access. The recently deceased Matt Douglass had been dragged crudely and hurriedly into the relative seclusion of the office hallway and propped up in a lifeless sitting position atop the basement stairs. As he came to rest, he had expelled an alarming final breath, an unexpected release of gas trapped previously in his lungs that sounded like a wounded groan. Terrified for a moment, both froze, incredulous that a body already stiffening due to rigor mortis appeared to be breathing.

'It's ok! I remember my mom sitting with my aunt not long after she'd died at home in bed. She told me she almost jumped out of her skin when my aunt suddenly sighed. Dead bodies do this, honestly.'

Relieved to be vacating the ghostly office, one of them had quickly returned to the red Ford Escort that was parked outside, its previously temperamental engine left running as a precaution. The other had wrapped the hulking corpse in tattered old blankets brought to the scene of the burial for just such a purpose. The discarded moth-eaten grey garments had been piled in a corner and gathering dust in a grimy garden shed for decades. They were now mummifying the lifeless carcass that had been swaddled as meticulously as an infant child might be carefully protected against the onset of a winter chill. Once rolled into a pit some three-feet deep, consigned to his final resting place beside miscellaneous rubble, Matt Douglass was concealed by three splintered wooden pallets, which had previously rested in the basement cavity. The scene looked exactly as it had before their intrusion. When a local crew of construction workers arrived to perform a morning's foreign earner in just a few hours' time, they would be none the wiser as to the contents of the vat they were contracted to wallow in soft cement. Matt Douglass would be consigned to a sloppy grave, buried forever beneath an impervious slab of concrete.

Having finally sunk all further traces of the murdered teenage bully's belongings in the depths of the silent canal, the two shadowed figures now hurried up a crumbling ramp and through an equally unkempt old brick archway, leaving behind a grimy towpath and a polluted watery grave. They planned to abandon the car more strategically than its random disposal suggested. Driving unseen down Gas Street, passing a nightclub emptied of Friday night revellers, they navigated a tangle of back streets lined with dilapidated brick buildings and darkened warehouses. They crossed a spur of the neglected canal on Granville Street, skirted Commercial Street and turned into Washington Street. Coming to a halt within the faded white lines of an expired parking meter bay, about a hundred yards from the Birmingham City Mission that provided a temporary home to the city's destitute population, they eagerly vacated the car. An oily rag that had been employed to wipe away every possible betrayal of fingerprints and a pair of precautionary leather gloves were stuffed through the grate of a large curb side metal drain and disappeared, engulfed by the sewer pipe below. By morning at least, they expected a vagrant unable to claim a bed for the night at the Mission would notice the passenger seat door of the Escort left deliberately ajar and take full advantage of a comfortable location preferable to sleeping rough on the pavement or a park bench. They banked on an eager traffic warden ticketing the illegally parked vehicle, which would eventually be towed and impounded. Its rightful owner would be informed of an unexpected and long-overdue retrieval of a barely recognizable car stolen several months earlier by a person unknown, whose identity they knew was Matt Douglass.

- - - - - - - - - -

The cheap white plastic spoon could almost stand up unassisted in a chipped old pottery mug, such was the soupy consistency of a steaming black liquid masquerading as coffee in the Tow Rope all night café. Two solid lumps of sugar dissolved eventually when stirred. Three strips of mildly burned bacon, a limp sausage and a crispy fried egg swam on a plate of grease, ready to be mopped up by two rounds of blackened and buttered toast. One patron tucked in heartily as the other picked cautiously at the dubious feast, whispering carefully while leaning across a table almost as grimy as the crockery it supported.

'How did you know there was going to be fresh concrete poured in the basement? And what on earth took you so long burying him?'

Nobody had overheard the potentially incriminating questions. The sparse population of the deadbeat café kept their own company, either staring blankly out at a deserted Broad Street gradually illuminated as dawn cracked open a new day, or thumbing through the well-worn pages of the previous day's tabloid newspapers.

'A few weeks ago, I told Silver we were going to see The Smiths and he mentioned he quite fancied that himself. At first, he asked me to get him a ticket, but then realised it was the same day he was off to Spain to his timeshare for a couple of weeks. He told me not to go to the office to hang around like we sometimes did after gigs in town because he was having concrete poured to fill that great big hole in the basement floor. He didn't want us to accidentally make a mess once it had been prepared. He told me the concrete would be poured on Saturday morning, dumping a load on top of our contribution to the new foundations. Silver might have booted us out since I spoke with him, but I've still got all the keys we were supposed to put in the post.'

That made sense. More sense in fact than attempting to digest the early-hours breakfast that oozed fat when impaled with a tarnished stainless steel fork, but both were ravenously hungry. Moving, dragging and disposing of a dead body had created quite the appetite.

The black hands of a cheap plastic clock, its once white face severely discoloured from untold years of absorbing kitchen fumes and

147

cigarette smoke stains, clicked silently beyond four-thirty in the morning. Foraging in pockets for coins of varying sizes and denominations, the pair collated funds enough to buy two teas, which they hoped would taste less offensive than the stale coffee, which had sat stewing on a hot plate in its black-handled glass Cona pot since long before their arrival. They sipped in muted approval at the tea that provided a welcome milder brew than the dank coffee and waited for the first signs of sunlight to reflect off the large smudged windows that fronted the café. Two tired faces reflecting in the glass betrayed the secret of an endless night, without so much as an ounce of sleep, spent carefully camouflaging a vicious murder. Matt Douglass was dead and buried, quite literally, and neither had reason to suspect any further incriminating evidence remained to tie them to the crime, other than the object that had set in motion the night's chain of events.

'I can't fucking believe we left that chair behind. It's really bugging me. It's the one thing, the only thing that we missed. I'd feel a lot better if that was at the bottom of the canal as well.'

They debated finding a way to return to the scene of the crime to retrieve the unlikely murder weapon, but agreed that the relentless torrential rain that had saturated and washed clean the cut through and their successful removal of the body now negated such actions. They concurred that creating as much distance between them and the only lingering physical evidence of the night's events was paramount.

'We can't tell the others about this; the fewer people that know about the final resting place, the better. I'll take it to my grave. We must pretend the last thing we knew; Matt was lying in the cut through. Keep it as simple as that and I think we'll be fine.'

The guilty pair sat in contemplative silence sipping their tea until the sugar that stubbornly refused to dissolve emerged from beneath the sweet dregs. The first sunlight of an Indian summer Saturday began to glisten off an otherwise dreary Broad Street as the harsh reality of the night's vicious murder flooded their thoughts.

'I still can't quite believe it. Ten hours ago, I was on the bus, going to see The Smiths. We'd all looked forward to that gig for so long. It was bloody great too, but I haven't really thought about it until now. I can still see Morrissey up there on stage. I can still see Matt Douglass too, in the crowd, sneering at us and then lying dead in the dirt, beaten to death.'

Chapter Twenty-Two

One week later

John Garland watched impatiently as the young glass collector behind the bar at the Bull's Head placed pint pots on top of spinning bristle brushes as jets of warm water whisked away dregs of beer foam. The four lagers he had ordered while cramped awkwardly among an over-capacity Friday night crowd would be poured into them soon enough. With clean glasses in short supply, the process warmed already tepid beverages, but he and his friends would still down the beer without complaint. John tried politely to avoid entering a conversation with an eccentric regular known affectionately as Barry Questions, who had earned his nickname through an odd habit of posing queries throughout a conversation and then answering them himself. John caught his eye at precisely the wrong moment.

'My mate asked, do I mind drinking from those warm glasses? Of course I do, I told him. Are they safe, what with all those chemicals? Well they must be or they wouldn't use them, would they? Am I still going to drink my pint? You bet I am, mate!'

John smiled civilly, noting a third glass had finally been washed and was filling up gradually with Carling Black Label, leaving him just one measure short of escaping Barry's bizarre banter.

'You know why it's so packed in here tonight? It's all those school kids getting their last few weekends in at home before they go off to university. Are they scroungers who should get a job instead of that studying lark? Of course they are. Is it like this every Friday through the summer? Well I suppose it is, but if the weather was better we could spill out onto the car park.'

John grabbed the two settled pints and pivoting on his heels, now blatantly ignored babbling Barry, turning his back as he stretched to hand the drinks over to Sully, while visibly agitated at the inconvenience of being served so slowly. The enquiring voice continued to assault his ear.

'Is unemployment going to improve, or will one in ten become two in ten? I think it probably will and UB40 will have to write another song. Will that Matt Douglass find a job? Well, he's probably got more of a chance down in old London town than he has up here.'

John dropped the latest pint of lager he had retrieved from the bar. The glass shattered with a loud bang as it met the wooden edging that circled the carpet fitted to the remainder of the lounge. As those in the immediate vicinity hopped away instantly, cursing the liquid that splashed and lapped at into their trouser legs, a mocking cheer went up around the pub as it always did in response to a broken beer glass and a wasted pint. John moaned as he glanced towards the bar, mouthing 'sorry' to the glass washer, who handed another warm pot to the barman. He in turn presented a palm to request payment for a replacement pint. John whispered to the eccentric drinker as he fumbled in his pocket for sufficient change.

'What did you say Barry, about Matt Douglass? And please just tell me without a load of questions.'

Puzzled, Barry replied, his voice mercifully quieter than before.

'You know that kid who's a bouncer in town? Matt Douglass; comes in here sometimes. How's he going to find a job, the state of things today? Go to The Smoke, that's how. When's he off there then? Bright and early last Saturday morning, he told a mate of mine who fixed the starter motor on his car for him. Would you take your car down there though? I'd have thought the coach was a much better bet and cheaper too.'

John patted Barry on the shoulder before declining the few small coins of change from the pound note handed over to fund his substitute beer, feeling obliged to pay in part for the broken glass, which was now being swept from the beer-soaked floor. He elbowed his way between bodies and re-joined Stephen, Sully and Andy who stood in a corner of the pub thankfully less congested than the bar area. Sully mocked his friend.

'Slippery things those glasses, hey? What a fucking performance! You should have ordered a double round I suppose, to steer clear of that madness again for a while, not to mention avoiding your mate Barry Questions.'

John accepted the ridicule he had anticipated and lowered his voice as he leaned in towards the circle of friends.

'You know what Barry told me?'

Sully leaned back and laughed raucously.

'He's worn off on you, mate. Ladies and gentlemen, I give you Johnny Questions, brother of Barry!'

John tried to laugh, but was frustrated with Sully. He peered across the busy pub in the direction of the door that led outside to the toilets and a car park misted by drizzling summer rain. He decided against suggesting they seek refuge out there in a quieter spot where he could share the news he had learned of Matt Douglass.

'Forget it mate, I'll tell you later.'

- - - - - - - - - -

'Alright boys and girls, and by that, I mean those of you who are underage and can't prove you're old enough to be drinking in here. Our good friends from the local constabulary have just left the Robin Hood and will be gracing us with their presence shortly. So, you lot, out! Now!'

The walls of the Bull's Head seemed to heave a sigh of relief as almost a third of the Friday night crowd that had packed into every corner, alcove and square foot of standing space hurriedly supped up their beers and dashed for the exit. Behind them, they left a wealth of emptied pint pots that would soon strain the capacity of the bristled brushes behind the bar. No sooner had the last stragglers vacated the premises via the front door than two uniformed police officers sauntered slowly in through the side entrance, tipping their hats at the remaining drinkers.

'Evening officers,' welcomed the landlord, whose booming announcement had decimated the attendance in his pub a few minutes earlier. 'Can I pour you both a half, or not while you're on duty?'

The friendly visit, which occurred every three or four weeks, with prior-warning phoned through from a neighbouring pub that had just bode farewell to the boys in blue, was a harmless game of cat and mouse. The landlord knew he was serving underage drinkers, but provided all remained within the boundaries of acceptable behaviour, he gladly turned a blind eye in the name of boosting the night's takings. The policemen often passed the teenagers they knew had just been turfed out of one local pub, trekking in the direction of the neighbouring establishment they had just culled. Nobody lost their license, nobody got frogmarched back to mom and dad smelling of snakebite and cigarettes and public order was preserved, at least in theory. Once the roaming constables had either declined a jar or sipped half a lager at the bar, the landlord of the Bull's Head would then telephone an alert to the Three Horseshoes less than a mile further down the Stratford Road, continuing the charade and triggering another departure of young boozers. The 'Shoes was traditionally the last stop on the chain before the officers returned to the police station. Local legend claimed that only once had two coppers mistakenly ventured on to the Hall Green border with Sparkhill and with similar intent, darkened the doors of the College Arms pub, where a renowned local family with alleged underworld ties reprimanded them for straying onto their patch with a combination of cricket bats and iron bars.

Safe in the knowledge that each carried photocopies of their birth certificates out of habit in their jeans back pockets to prove their age, John, Stephen, Sully and Andy ignored what had become a familiar farce. This was the first night they had truly felt comfortable sipping pints in public since the traumatic events of a week earlier. None of the potential recriminations they feared had come to fruition. There was still no body and they were not under suspicion.

Sully nudged John and motioned towards Andy, who was transfixed by the scene at the bar, rigid with fear, his hands shaking slightly, causing his glass to rattle on the surface of the tall wooden table. John steadied the pint, while Sully turned to see one of the barmen pointing in their direction.

'They know!' whispered Andy in a mild panic. 'They fucking know!'

John strode purposefully, almost confrontationally, blocking the path of one officer before he could wander from the bar to where the four friends stood as Sully convinced a now distraught Andy that there was no cause for concern.

It was Craig Jones.

'You need to see my birth certificate, PC Plod? We're all eighteen you know.'

John stood barely an inch shorter than Craig, who sneered at the rival who had stolen the affections of his girlfriend Siobhan just a few weeks earlier. The pair had not crossed paths since, but now met almost nose to nose in an aggressive pose that caught the attention of intrigued drinkers at the bar. Their overdue exchange was as unsavoury as anticipated.

'I heard you don't have a birth certificate, mate. Just an apology note from Durex.'

'We could step outside if you weren't hiding behind that uniform.'

PC Wayne Edmonds intervened, almost lifting Craig by the collar as he scowled at his partner, reprimanding him as his outstretched arm created a space that allowed him to step in between them. He poked at John's chest with a stern middle finger that felt as though it left a bruise with every jab.

'I was asking the gaffer where you were and was going to have a laugh with you about the dummy you and your idiot friends hung from a lamp post a few weeks back. I can see the funny side of it now, but if you're going to be an arsehole, I can regard it as a crime instead. Okay? I'll be keeping my eye on you, son.'

John nodded remorsefully, retaining eye contact with PC Edmonds rather than exchange another potentially volatile glance with Craig.

'Come on you, the Horseshoes next. Then we're done for the night.'

The landlord waved away John's shrug of an apology as he picked up the phone to provide the Horseshoes with the customary advance warning as the local constabulary slipped beyond the heavy wooden front door of the Bull's Head. John returned to the table.

'I thought that…'

'I know what you thought Andy, but stop bloody worrying. That fucking wanker; thinks he's so tough in that uniform with his bum boy fighting his battles for him. Anyway, now that it's finally quiet in here, I have something I need to tell you all. It's about Matt Douglass.'

John had their attention now. All three were silent again and Andy's mood darkened as he exhibited the emotions that had gripped him when Craig had approached them from the bar.

'But you said we should never talk about it!'

John steadied his friend with a calming hand on the shoulder and replied in a soft assuring tone.

'It's okay; really, it's okay. I was trying to tell you all when I came back from the bar earlier. Barry Questions told me Matt was going to London the day after the Smiths gig to look for work. So that's why he hasn't shown up. He was driving that crap old car of his down to London. I guess he wasn't hurt as badly as we thought and he must have just left.'

Stephen urgently contributed an important component to the conversation.

'I saw him! Not the morning after, but on that Friday afternoon, before the Smiths gig, when I was on my way out. He carried a suitcase out to the garage where he kept his car. I waited in the alleyway between our houses because, well, I wanted to avoid him. He topped up the engine oil and then I saw him put the suitcase in the boot of his car. That must have been for the trip to London.'

John held up his glass and motioned to the others to follow suit. Sully swirled the dregs of the pint that barely coated the bottom of his pot. They chinked them together to drink to John's toast.

'To never having to mention this shit again.'

As they drank, John suddenly and without warning coughed up his beer, managing to cover his mouth as he performed a combination of swallowing urgently while choking briefly to avoid spraying those opposite him with liquid. He coughed a couple more times and composed himself, allowing Sully to take his glass from him, while Andy patted his back urgently.

An unexpected and sudden pinch to his backside had been quite a shock, causing him to almost drop a second pint of beer. He turned around to see the provocative smile of Rachel Turner as she sauntered towards the bar, waving playfully as she winked at him. Then Rachel caught the eye of a smitten male member of the bar staff willing to serve her without first asking for proof of her age, which was below the required minimum. Sully laughed as John coughed one final time and took a soothing sip of beer.

'Good job she wasn't in here earlier or Starsky and Hutch would have chased her out. Not even seventeen yet, is she? Can't complain though, can we? She always brings a couple of friends along to join our merry band of brothers. We should pull up some chairs and get them to sit with us in that corner over there.'

- - - - - - - - - -

Andy reeled away in mock celebration as a beaten and battered Coke can flew between Sully's legs into the bus shelter, where it clattered against the metal panelling with a brief tinny echo.

'The goal that sends Birmingham City down to where they belong; the fourth division!'

Sully stamped on the can, flattening the aluminium to end their impromptu game of football.

Stephen emerged from behind them, exiting Jack's Fish & Chips Shop juggling a wrapped white packet of chips hot to the touch, its contents having been lifted from the fryer only moments earlier. The trio sat down on a nearby bench and unwrapped the stodgy supper that scolded the ends of eager grabbing fingers. Sully inhaled urgent gasps of cool air as the chips burned his mouth as he spoke.

'I was sure Rachel's two friends were going to come to the chippy with us. That blonde girl, Alison, she's gorgeous. She was chatting away in the pub, even saying she might want to go down the Blues one Saturday, but then she buggered off with that lad who works at the bank. I suppose he did buy her a drink though. I'm skint, so I couldn't. Maybe I should come to one of those poof pubs with you Stephen and see if I have more luck, find me an iron.'

Andy interrupted, noticing Stephen wince at Sully's comment. Ever since Stephen had confided his sexuality among his closest friends, Sully seemed to have employed derogatory remarks as a mechanism to deal with the reality that he was struggling to cope with his friend's homosexuality. The regular pokes at Stephen's now relatively openly gay lifestyle embarrassed Andy, while they clearly aggravated the brunt of the thoughtless comments.

'Hey, that was nice of John to walk Rachel home,' observed Andy. 'After all, she lives in completely the opposite direction to his house, so he has a long walk to get home afterwards. When she first came in the pub, I thought it was Siobhan for a minute. I'd never noticed before how much they look like each other.'

Sully just stared at Andy; his gawp of disbelief mocking the observation. Andy was puzzled.

'What? Don't you agree?'

'Yeah, sure, she looks a lot like Siobhan, but Andy, are you serious? Don't you know why John walks Rachel home? Admittedly this is the first time since he's been seeing Siobhan, but for probably six months now, he's been doing that, ever since Rachel first came to the Bull.'

Andy's blank expression remained.

'Wow, I thought you knew! Ok, so that Rachel is a lovely girl, isn't she? Very pretty, I think you'd agree? Well, the first time she came to the pub, John was chatting away to her and fancied his chances. He knew she was a couple of years younger because we'd seen her at school. Anyway, I know he expected a good snog at the front door when he walked her home, but nothing much more. Better than that, much better in fact, she thanked him for traipsing all the way back to her place by following up a good old game of tonsil hockey and a grind by kneeling in front of him in the porch and unzipping him, if you get my drift. Ever since then, he's been only too willing to walk the lovely Rachel home.'

Sully laughed loudly before stuffing a final handful of cooled chips into his mouth and screwing up the emptied paper. He volleyed the sphere into the bus shelter, claiming a last-gasp equaliser to dramatically save Birmingham City from relegation. Andy looked for confirmation from Stephen, who shrugged, unimpressed by the retelling of old news. Andy's eyebrows raised at the revelation, then he frowned at the memory of only a week ago when John's fury had spurred the severe beating of Matt Douglass, so enraged was he at the assault of the supposed love of his life. Andy rose from the bench and trudged towards home, disappointed at his friend.

'Well, I guess he's got over poor Siobhan pretty bloody quickly then.'

'Today was the first day I didn't wake up really thinking about it.'

John Garland and Stephen Taylor nodded in appreciation. They too had woken every morning during the past week, gripped by the same tortuous start to each day that mercilessly continued to haunt Andy Morris. The serene transition from a night's sleep to consciousness generally lasted barely a few seconds before his stomach tied tight in a knot and his every thought was consumed by the vision of Matt Douglass lying lifeless, caked in his own blood and other bodily fluids. Andy would roll agitated onto his back, stare at the bedroom ceiling and massage his temples, kneading the sides of his head with his fingertips, eyes shut tight, fighting to banish the potential for a life of incarceration from his mind. No matter what the distraction throughout the day, his thoughts would always be jerked unceremoniously back to the constant undertone of guilt and fear that seemed to devour his every waking hour. He supposed his three friends suffered a similar torment.

'I know we agreed not to talk about it, but since you told us what Barry Questions had said, well, I haven't felt as worried. That was four days ago and I suppose I've just assumed that bastard is in London and not, well, not dead!'

Andy laughed, almost relieved. John was poised to share a similar emotion when the doorbell, which played *Le Marseillaise* at an annoying decibel, rang out in the hallway.

'What is it with your parents' John? Are they frogs? That French tune is really bloody annoying.'

John waved away Stephen's displeasure. His father had installed a device that offered a multitude of national anthems that would ring out either randomly or specifically by country at the press of the doorbell. The previous week, almost as if navigating a musical tour of the continent, it had been the patriotic tune of Belgium *La Brabançonne* that alerted the Garland family to the onset of visitors before the latest Gallic melody was preferred.

Mike Sullivan was the expected guest waiting beyond the front door and wore a frown of concern. He thrust a folded copy of the Birmingham Evening Mail purposely into John's chest and strode into the living room without muttering so much as a friendly hello. Stephen and Andy were arguing over which side of the eponymous first Smiths album should be rotating on the turntable as they wiled away time before leaving to watch their local football club Moor Green in midweek action. Sully entered, falling into a worn red armchair, exhaling in frustration as he landed. John followed him into the room, scanning the pages of the newspaper.

'Oh Jesus. This?'

John held the newspaper aloft to expose a story relatively buried on page eight. Stephen and Andy shifted forwards on the sofa, both eager to view the news that was generating so much interest and an apparent measure of concern. Andy spied the newspaper and then slumped back, massaging his temples again, muttering in despair.

'No, no, no! I knew it felt too good to be true. Missing! How can that fucking wanker be missing?'

The Birmingham Evening Mail editors had earned a reputation for devoting alarmist headlines to even the most benign story and this short almost apologetic article ran beneath dramatic large black capital letters that leaped out from the page. John crouched beside Stephen and Andy and they all hurriedly read the article.

MIDLANDS MOTHER DISTRAUGHT OVER MISSING SON
By Steve Sharma

A distraught mother, who is worried her son has been missing since failing to return home from a night out in the city centre ten days ago, has hit out at local police she claims are not taking her concerns seriously.

Pensioner Rosemary Douglass, 62, of Stonor Croft, Hall Green, reported her son Matthew Douglass, 18, missing on Monday when he failed to contact her from London. The nightclub doorman, who is a familiar face to club goers at The Dome on Bristol Street, planned to leave for the capital to begin job-hunting on the morning of Saturday, August 30.

Mrs Douglass, a widow, is concerned that her only child did not return from watching pop group The Smiths live in concert at the Birmingham Odeon the previous evening and was distressed when she spoke exclusively to the Evening Mail.

"Matt's car has gone from the garage, so he could have driven down to London as planned, but he hasn't called me like he promised

158

to once he got there. I'm really worried, but the police don't seem to care about my boy."

A West Midlands Police spokesman confirmed the filing of a missing person report and that officers have contacted their counterparts in London. He declined to comment further on the ongoing inquiry.

"They didn't take me seriously," added a tearful Mrs Douglass. "He'd put his suitcase in the car, ready to leave, but he'd left a parcel he was supposed to deliver to someone in his bedroom. Something doesn't feel right to me. He's all I have, but the police don't care."

Staff at the Birmingham Odeon on New Street confirmed seeing Mr Douglass at the concert, but his whereabouts since the evening of August 29 remain a mystery.

Andy returned to his slumped position of despair. Stephen looked up, staring blankly at Sully, whose expression was as exasperated as it had been since he arrived. John picked up the newspaper and tossed it with complete disregard in the general direction of a small wicker waste paper basket.

'So what? So fucking what! Where is Matt Douglass? Who knows? And in the case of the wooden tops - who by the way know that he's a nasty bastard with some previous and some dubious friends - who fucking cares? I'll bet if Craig the copper was here right now, he'd tell us they're not investigating and they're actually glad, just like we are, that he's off our streets. Rosemary Douglass is a fucking slag who can piss off.'

The others were momentarily stunned by the severity of John's outburst. Sully stood up from the sofa and paced around the room, poised to speak as he waved his finger in the air authoritatively while searching for the right words to convey his thoughts.

'You know, you're right, John. No, you really are right. I mean, think of the different scenarios for a minute.

'One, Matt Douglass is dead; right where we left him, but what happened then? Somebody would have found his body, even if he'd crawled under a bush nearby and then died. The smell would have alerted someone. People walk along that path every day. There aren't any wild animals that could have eaten his body. What? A fox, a badger, a small army of squirrels?'

The consideration raised a smile and a chuckle from around the room as Sully's deduction gathered pace.

'Two, he was kicked to fuck by us and then dragged his miserable carcass to his car and drove off to London as planned. He might have crashed the car be hidden in a ditch somewhere or he might have stopped and be lying dead from his injuries somewhere else. Either way, that doesn't leave us in the shit. And again, surely someone would have found him.

'Three, he made it to London and he's still there. The tosser just hasn't bothered to call the old lady and he's fine apart from a few bumps and bruises. Again, and I'm sure this is what my mate here is thinking, either way, it doesn't come back to us.'

John draped an arm around Sully, almost in an act of triumph as both sought agreement from their friends. More than any of them, it seemed, Andy wanted to believe. He retrieved the discarded rag and scanned the story a second time. He prodded his finger against the newsprint.

'Wait, wait, what about this part? The parcel he left behind. He would have gone into the house to get that, surely.'

John was poised to shoot down the issue when Sully beat him to it.

'Same answer Andy: So what? Maybe that means he did crawl off and die and he didn't make it back to the house, but he would have been found if that was the case. We know he was pissed up, so maybe he forgot to get the dubious-sounding package and some of his criminal mates have done him in as punishment. Or, as I've mentioned before, maybe he just hasn't been arsed to call his Mom.'

The four friends continued to debate the likely fate of the missing son of Mrs Douglass. As the closing bars of *Suffer Little Children*, the final track on The Smiths' debut album faded out, they concluded that each would again be able to wake daily in a relaxed state, believing Matt was neither dead nor missing. He was indeed most likely in London, choosing not to phone home. If their assumptions were correct, there was little cause for concern. If there was no body, no crime, no investigation, their vicious assault would go unpunished.

Stephen cringed and laughed as a cuckoo chimed in the seven o'clock hour. He supposed Mr Garland must have been lured more than once to a kitschy shop selling tasteless clocks and doorbells and perhaps other novelty items as-yet undiscovered around the house. The

160

realisation that a half an hour countdown to kick off at their local football club had just begun sprung Sully from the sofa. On the Sunday night when the four friends had first reconvened to covertly recall their crime, he had seen a poster in the Moor Green clubhouse advertising the match. A two-for-one entry price and a beer promotion to drum up a crowd for the midweek visit of Bridgnorth Town in the oddly-named Beazer Homes Midland Division, some half a dozen levels below the local professional clubs' standard, had successfully recruited four new converts.

'Come on Stevie, I know you don't want to go, but it makes a nice change from The Bull, even if the beer does taste like piss. We can watch from the bar if you like. Think of all those men running around in tights shorts. Twenty-two of them, mate!'

- - - - - - - - - -

John had just patted his jeans pocket to confirm he was carrying a key to the front door Yale lock that clicked closed behind him, when the telephone in the vacated hallway rang, its loud tone muffled but still clearly audible. Sully and Andy had already wandered to the end of the driveway, eager to leave, while Stephen lagged slightly behind.

'Ignore it mate, or we'll miss the start of the match.'

John hesitated then fumbled for the key to hurriedly unlock the door.

'You go on, I'll catch you up.'

It might be her, he thought. He hoped. Siobhan had failed to call since leaving for Ireland with her family ten days earlier. John could not initiate contact since her aunt in Enniscorthy refused to own a telephone. A pay phone down the street was the family's only means of communication and even then, only for outgoing calls.

Perhaps she was too embarrassed to call, knowing Stephen would have confided in John the secret of her traumatic assault at the hands of Matt Douglass. Perhaps she simply needed time alone to convalesce, but John wanted to be there for her to aid her recovery. He loved her. It was as simple as that. Even though she was due to return to Birmingham the following day, John vigilantly answered every ring of the telephone, hoping, just as he had every day since her departure, that it might be Siobhan calling.

It never was.

Once she returned, they would have only three days together before he journeyed to London to begin his university studies. John had tried unsuccessfully to delay his travel arrangements to afford them more time, but neither the National Express coach service nor the university were flexible enough to accommodate his request without imposing a financial penalty he could ill afford. He had ordered flowers to be delivered upon her arrival back home, spent too great a percentage of the wages from his summer job on an expensive necklace holding a silver heart engraved with their initials, and had a table booked at their favourite intimate restaurant to celebrate the reunion.

John reached the phone before the tone tailed off and uttered a hopeful hello.

- - - - - - - - - -

'You've missed a cracking first half mate. The Moors were down an early goal, but came back and now they're 3-1 up. Fantastic second goal by that tricky winger, Phil Davies; he should be playing league football. The keeper never stood a chance. Me and Andy are off to the tea bar. Coming? Hey, where's John?'

Sully was so engrossed in reliving the first half action, which Stephen had heard whistled to an interval as he arrived that he walked on without waiting for an explanation for John's absence. The trio paused at a metal barrier pulled down across a concrete walkway behind the goal that allowed both teams to exit the pitch. Slaps on the backs of sweaty light blue shirts, mostly delivered by awed young kids, slowed the retreat of the players to the dressing room where the Moor Green team talk would surely be of a positive nature since the balance of the game had swung firmly in their favour. Sully and Andy clapped enthusiastically in appreciation of the first forty-five minutes of entertainment, each saving a congratulatory phrase for when the impressive Davies passed them.

'The first ten minutes, a couple of defenders were trying to kick lumps out of him, but he's been too quick and tricky for them all half. Scored one, made one and was fouled for the penalty the centre forward tucked away. I'm telling you, Blues should have their scouts take a look at him. He's better than half the muppets I usually watch down at St Andrews.'

A breeze of grilling burgers and onions wafted from the hole in the wall tea bar and only once they had joined the end of a short line of customers did Sully again inquire after John.

'He's stayed at home,' Stephen explained. 'I thought I'd come up and see you two to let you know. I'm not really bothered about the match.

'That was Siobhan's cousin when the phone rang. He had some bad news for John. He told him that Siobhan is staying in Ireland. Indefinitely.'

The finality of the word surprised Sully and he fumbled through ordering three teas, all with milk and one with three sugars, confusing the sweet dosage that resulted in three beverages, each with one sugar.

'Bloody hell! What does that mean? She's never coming back? John must be gutted.'

'He's pissed off alright. Her cousin said that Siobhan wouldn't call for some reason and that her mom didn't want her to talk to John because apparently, she's all fired up about wanting to get Siobhan back with Craig. Sounds like a right mess. Keep this to yourselves, but Siobhan's even giving up her place at Liverpool. Her cousin mentioned she was upset about something. I doubt he knows what happened at the Smiths gig, but she must have told them something. And now Siobhan's mom and dad are coming home and leaving her with family in Ireland.'

Sully sipped at his tea, blowing first to cool the hot liquid. He banged his spare hand repeatedly against one of the peeling wooden advertising hoardings that surrounded the pitch to signal his support for a confident-looking Moor Green team as their players ran out for the second half.

'John leaves for London at the weekend. He was frustrated enough that he'd only have a few days with Siobhan and now he won't get to see her at all. No wonder he's pissed off.'

Andy led the way around the corner of the pitch to the side to seek a vantage point from which they could again marvel at the skills of their new favourite player. He leaned on a metal barrier, pouring away the sugary tea, creating a steaming puddle on the dirt beside him before crushing the Styrofoam cup beneath his shoe.

'Well, yeah, I'm sure he's upset and I feel sorry for him. But to be fair, a few nights ago he was missing his beloved girlfriend so much, he had to go and get a blow job from that young tart Rachel.'

The Murphy home was shrouded in darkness apart from a glow that illuminated an ageing set of curtains drawn to conceal the living room of a neat council house unmistakably vacated by a family away on holiday. The half-closed blinds of the upstairs rooms, a large metal dustbin still prostrate since a storm of more than a week earlier and the predictable timing of a security switch controlling a lamp in the lounge all betrayed the status of an empty dwelling to even the most casual of observers.

John Garland sat suspiciously on a three-feet high brick wall bordering a small front lawn that urgently required the attention of a mower and fumbled at mortar that crumbled in his fingers almost to the touch. He flicked a stone from the pavement to the kerb with his foot and let out a defeated sigh. He couldn't explain, even to himself, why he was sitting there. Siobhan was still hundreds of miles away, indefinitely he had been told, but somehow, gazing up at the bedroom window he had peppered with small stones ten days earlier seemed to make him feel closer to her.

John felt an urge to kick down the front door and hurriedly burgle a handful of items of worth and run from the scene. He would take a perverse satisfaction from Mrs Murphy championing her knight in shining armour PC Craig Jones to solve the crime, only for her favoured future son-in-law to fail to deliver. The apparent golden boy would be exposed as a fraud, John thought. A lace curtain twitched across the street and rather than elevate suspicion, John slouched from the wall and paced slowly towards home. If he introduced some urgency into his step, he figured he might reach Jack's before the chip fryers were powered down for the night.

- - - - - - - - - -

'Yeah, one of my customers told me it finished three-one. Moors had a bunch of chances second half, but were cruising by then apparently. A couple more decent players and I think they might be a fair bet for promotion next season. Good game and a good crowd, they said. Those posters I put in the window each week must work.'

Jack was as enthusiastic about the local football team whose match ball he sponsored occasionally, as he was liberal in applying a generous layering of salt and vinegar to each bag of chips he served. John turned down the offer of a pickled egg to accompany his chips as Jack smiled, having no doubt remembered John's presence when Sully had consumed and regurgitated several of the hideous objects a few weeks earlier.

Outside, kicking his heels beneath the bench, John sat where his friends and more recently Siobhan had joined him countless times before. Due to his departure for London at the weekend, he wondered when he might next grace the worn wooden slats. The local football crowd had long since dwindled and John was in no hurry to return home as he surveyed patrons of the Bull's Head and the Robin Hood sauntering or staggering their way home. The traffic eventually slowed to the passing of only an occasional car. By now, he had been a lone spectator outside Jack's for more than an hour since closing, but the idea of continuing his walk home held little appeal.

John watched a black Mini Metro cruise slowly from as far as he could see in the direction of the Stratford Road, off in the distance, and he traced its gradual route around the small nearby traffic island and along the adjacent dual carriageway. Only when the car paused indecisively at the kerb, parking awkwardly, engine still running, did John truly take notice. The passenger side door opened and a figure he recognised stepped out, closing the door purposefully before rapping his knuckles on the roof to signal the driver to continue. It was Craig Jones, out of uniform and striding purposefully across the road towards John and the bench. Instinctively, John stood up, assuming a pose as confrontational as that of the nemesis heading straight for him.

'I'm not in uniform now, if you want to take a pop, you wanker.'

John was surprised by the immediacy of Craig's anger. He had anticipated conflict almost since he had stolen Siobhan's affections weeks earlier, but imagined there would be a bout of posturing and a volley of threats before any physical exchanges. Craig shoved John backwards, planting the base of both palms firmly into either side of his chest. Struggling to maintain his balance, John reeled into the entrance of a bus shelter, its main window shattered some time the previous evening into what appeared to be a million frosty pieces, but still intact due to its safety glass design. John imagined for a moment that the rage he saw pouring from Craig as he snarled through gritted

166

teeth must be like the fury that had consumed him when he led the charge to beat Matt Douglass lifeless. Before John could steady his feet, Craig drove two angrily clenched fists low and hard below John's ribs, the full force of his body behind the blow lifting John off his feet. John crashed loudly and painfully through falling shards of splintered bus shelter glass, propelled through the flimsy damaged obstruction into the gutter, where he squirmed on his back. The crown of his head throbbed from colliding with the tarmac. In a possessed frenzy, Craig climbed through the hole in the shelter, broken glass crunching beneath his dutifully polished black shoes and he kicked John mercilessly in the area of his hip. Craig bent down, grabbed John's head coarsely by the hair and landed a cruel punch to the side of his face. A second punch followed and a third before Craig discarded John's head and spat in his face.

Noisily, a car screeched to a halt beside John as he rolled in the gutter, while Craig stepped back to survey the assault.

'Bloody hell mate, are you ok? Get in! Just get in the car!'

John didn't know the passing Good Samaritan, or care to inquire as to the reason for his welcome interruption. Dazed and disoriented, he willingly clambered into the passenger seat, the door thrust open by the driver as he leaned across the console and voiced his concern. With the door safely closed and wheels spinning, John stared at Craig, who glared back, devoid of emotion.

Chapter Twenty-Five

'Those Cockneys will think you're a right head case when they get a load of that black eye and those bruises, mate.'

'And if you tell them 'you should see the other bloke' they'll think you won the fight and won't mess with you.'

'The birds down there might take a shine to your shiner you know.'

'If you tell your new mates a local copper did it, they'll probably organise some kind of protest march for you. Bloody students.'

'Tell them there was a fight outside the chippy and all the fish got battered!'

Sully and Andy each chuckled at the other's humorous observations, while John smiled as he drank a sweet cup of tea then winced sharply as the bruise on his face caused momentary discomfort. He felt nauseous as he watched Sully tuck enthusiastically into a fried sausage that oozed fat as he cut it in half and dipped the end purposefully into the yolk of an equally greasy-looking egg. His mouth full, he spoke while he munched down the breakfast he had dubbed 'the last supper' and shifted in his seat. The chair legs squealed on the grimy floor of the café located opposite Birmingham's Digbeth bus station.

'It looks a bit better than it did a couple of days ago, mind you, but not much. At least he didn't kill you.'

Sully swallowed hard, grabbed a piece of buttered toast and stuffed it into his mouth to prevent more misplaced words from exiting. The pressure on the West Midlands Police to solve the mysterious whereabouts of Matt Douglass had increased since the discovery of a stolen car outside the Birmingham City Mission that had been linked to the missing teenager. A library card, the most unlikely of documents imaginable in the name of the subject of their inquiries, had been unearthed, having been wedged inside the glove box of the red Mark II Ford Escort parked beside a long-expired parking meter. The police established that Matt had been driving the stolen car for several months and believed he had chosen to offload the vehicle rather than risk being caught in possession during his visit to London. That theory, coupled with the fact that his suitcase was no longer stored in the boot, as Mrs Douglass had noted, made perfect sense to officers convinced he had travelled south by other means. The Evening Mail reporter who had covered the initial missing person complaint appeared to believe there was mileage in the story and penned a tabloid-style follow up piece that included additional sobbing quotes from the distraught mother. Notepad in hand and pen at the ready, the eager newshound had visited Rosemary Douglass with a photographer in tow to stage an image aimed at amplifying the gravity of the story. In a twist that had terrified Stephen, the reporter knocked on his neighbouring door to request an innocent comment to help determine Matt's character. In a moment of complete shock, Stephen had blurted out that Matt kept himself to himself and the two rarely spoke. Underwhelmed by such bland words, the journalist declined even to jot down the quote in his notebook, let alone use it in his final article. Stephen was spooked and now wanted to close the chapter on Matt Douglass. He hushed his voice and leaned in, resting both elbows on the cheap paper cloth covering the café table.

'Look, we keep saying 'don't talk about it' but we keep fucking talking about it. I know you were just insinuating Sully, but we have to stop. Maybe we got away with murder, maybe this has all blown over and we're all too jumpy, maybe that wanker is out there somewhere wondering who did this to him; I don't know. John's leaving today and you're starting a job next week, so maybe this is some sort of landmark change or something. We'll see less of each other in the pub because we're busy doing other things, so please, let's put a stop to mentioning it. Please!'

The pensive silence between the four friends served as an agreement to observe Stephen's wishes. Two weeks and a handful of hours since they had carried out vicious retribution for the sexual assault on Siobhan Murphy, they agreed they would never speak of those violent moments in the cut through again, or of Matt Douglass.

Andy peered to the side of the table and inspected a pair of large suitcases placed side by side next to John's chair.

'Your whole life in just those two cases? I suppose you can come home and get more things if you need to, but that will get a bit expensive. I've got more than that packed for my trip.'

They could all appreciate why Andy was taking advantage of an offer to spend some time in picturesque Tenby on the idyllic Welsh coast in a caravan his parents owned and had finished renting to tourists for the summer season. His mother was concerned by his seemingly fragile mood of late. Of the four of them, Andy had suffered the most frequent bouts of anxiety in dealing with their secret.

John looked at his watch. Only an hour remained until he left behind his childhood friends, all that was familiar and safe, the city he called home and essentially his youth, for what he anticipated would be a life-changing experience at university in the capital. He knew that Victoria bus station on Buckingham Palace Road was his destination on the National Express bus. Beyond that, other than a tube train trek to digs near the Isle of Dogs, his future remained somewhat blurred.

'Look, lads, I don't want to sound ungrateful, but why don't you lot go home now. We're not going to have any tearful goodbyes as I get on the bus and I can't imagine you standing there waving like you're my mom as the coach drives off. I appreciate the lift Sully, and thanks all of you for coming to see me off, but, well, you know.'

They did know. Sully dug into his wallet and produced a note to add to an assortment of coins from his pocket to cover the cost of the breakfast and placed the total down loudly on the table beside the worn plastic salt and pepper shakers. After all, the price of his sizeable full breakfast dwarfed the cost of the teas consumed by the others. John stood up, followed by Stephen and Andy, creating a chorus of metallic squeals from the dragging chair legs. Sully's embrace engulfed John and following a hearty slap on the back that unintentionally aggravated a bruise from the fight with Craig, he exited, thanking the peroxide-haired server behind the counter for her service to a blank response. Andy had dreaded this moment and was thankful for its spontaneity. He hugged John and having extended an open invitation to the six-berth caravan by the beach at Kiln Park, said his goodbye.

Stephen wasn't going so quietly. He waited for the door to the busy street outside to close behind Sully and Andy. He stared tearfully at John.

'I love you. You know that, right? And I also know you understand what I mean by that.'

John did know. He smiled, the defiant English phrase 'stiff upper lip' immediately springing to mind as his facial muscles twitched and fought to fend off any outward show of emotion.

'It isn't easy being Stephen Taylor you know. Poof, queer, homo, iron, bender; all those words people use. I was watching *Minder* on telly the other night and Terry McCann had to look after a bloke who was gay. Him and Arthur Daley were worried about being alone in the room with him, assuming he'd make his move, corrupt them, turn them into queers. That's how it is, John. People are idiots. I overheard a bloke in the pub the other night talking about the risk of catching AIDS off the toilet seat if there were any poofs working in his office.'

Stephen sniffed loudly as he continued.

'When I told you, or I asked you how long you'd known, you were caught off guard and I know it wasn't the easiest thing in the world to deal with, especially as we were on the back of a bus and going to see The Smiths. The thing is, you just accepted it. You never judged me, or acted differently towards me. I was still your mate, Stephen.

'I don't mind Sully and Andy making their silly references. I know they mean no harm. But they've both had the awkward 'so long as you don't fancy me' chat with me. I mean, can you imagine? Sully! He has enough trouble pulling birds.

'I've been visiting a pub in town, and a couple of nightclubs too. I wish you could have come with me. Maybe next time you're home? There are straight blokes who go there too, but only those who don't have hang-ups or misconceptions. The clientele of The Jester will indeed watch your arse as you walk up the long flight of steps to the exit, but they'll also know you're not interested. Anyway, once you're gone, I plan on spending more nights there than in the Bull with Terry and Arthur. There's nothing for me in the pubs of the suburbs, or midweek football matches at the Moorlands.

'So, like I said, I love you, my friend.'

Before John could respond, as stubborn tears insisted on trailing down both bruised cheeks, Stephen grabbed him by the shoulders and planted a firm kiss full on his lips. The hush that paused the bustle of the busy café and etched shock on the faces of the crusty clientele was broken only when the door to the main street outside flew open and Sully's flustered face appeared.

'Oy! Rock Hudson. Enough with the goodbyes. Let the boy go to London.'

Chapter Twenty-Six

Despite having spent countless solitary nights in soulless accommodation during three decades of business travel since the early nineties, John Garland had never felt so alone.

He surveyed the sterile bathroom of his cramped Premier Inn hotel room that was littered with instructional signs posted on lurid green or purple placards.

Please keep this door closed when in use, as steam from the bathroom can activate our sensitive smoke alarm.

Smoking anywhere in this room will result in a £100 charge.

Our smoke alarms are super sensitive and will go off.

You could re-use your towels if you're staying more than one night.

There was even a caution that hot water might spray from the shower. The jet of water that washed over his naked middle-aged body was indeed hot, but also soothing. John felt the heat intensify on the back of his reddening shoulders before arching his head backwards to soak his hair and then engulf his face, both eyes now shut tight. All John could see was his friend Stephen Taylor, lifeless, perforated by tubes and needles, his final breath working its way tortuously through a fatally broken body.

John routinely applied a trusted mechanism for dealing with such grief. It always worked. He had employed it to desired effect at the funerals of both his parents, first at the bland mandatory church services and later when their ashes were scattered on a hillside overlooking the sleepy seaside town that had been their adopted home for twenty-five years. They had moved there, almost on a whim, less than a year after John had departed for London, lauding the slower pace of life compared with the nation's second city, while making John's visits to see them more picturesque and convenient.

Dad had left them first, the evil of cancer claiming another of its multiplying victims on the tenth anniversary of the terrorist attacks on the twin towers that had shocked the world. Within a week, his heartbroken life partner joined him in a mysterious destination the vicar delivering the eulogy assured all present was a much better place, though John questioned that declaration. Not once, on either occasion, did John waver and allow an emotional memory of either of them to darken his stream of closed consciousness. Not once did he reminisce over a pleasant childhood memory that might spark a stirring of heartache, of Dad proudly selecting John's first cricket bat at Eric Wilmont's sporting goods store, or of Mom smiling as she slipped her son an extra few pence when he was short of the price of a packet of football stickers.

While his sister Jane wailed, supported and comforted by her dutiful husband, and John's wife Ellie sniffled into a dampened tissue, he stared blankly at the church alter, or at the delicately stitched robes of the mournful vicar, or out to sea, devoid of emotion. Bottle it up, stiff upper lip and all that bollocks. It might have been a British stereotype, a failing perhaps, but it worked for him. No tears, no emotion; no regret that they would never speak again, just a stoic stare into the abyss to suppress an underlying pain that he knew would erode with time. Heartless, Ellie called him, and perhaps he was, but he reserved the right to deal with death and the grief it generated in his own detached way.

But not any longer, it seemed.

John's face crumpled and his eyes welled and burst open with a flood of tears as he clasped his hands to the side of his head, defiantly fighting to fend off the overwhelming grief that poured from his soul. John's back slumped against the cold white tile lining the shower cubicle and he slid down slowly, unable to resist the buckle in his knees, barely noticing the pain of the shower gel container scraping his skin as he slumped into a defeated haunch. The hot water rained from above as fluidly as his tears poured free. Shaking and crying uncontrollably, omitting short coughs and sharp sniffs, John succumbed to grief and rocked gently in the lonely corner of the shower.

He could no longer see the old Stephen Taylor he once knew. The catalyst for John's disabling sorrow was the overriding image of his friend lying lifeless in a morbid hospital ward he had visited earlier. There was a person in there, he thought, inside that motionless vessel. There was still a lifetime of love and affection bottled up inside that carcass that could bring smiles and happiness to reams of people who were supposed to be touched by Stephen's personality in the years to come. That warmth would never again enlighten the lives of others; they would be denied. The world would never smile again because of Stephen Taylor. That wasn't fair. It simply wasn't fair.

John banged the side of his fist against the plastic moulded floor of the shower cubicle and let out a deep defeated sigh. He paused, collected his thoughts and banished Stephen's dying image. Resentment now overriding his grief, he pounded his white-knuckled fist again; and again, this time more loudly and with greater frequency, hammering the shower floor angrily as he let out a loud guttural scream. He didn't care if the apologetic hotel staff came calling to either complain or to inquire as to his wellbeing. He pounded once more, and again, shouting out in helpless frustration. They could give every fucking guest a free night's stay due to his inconsiderate actions for all he cared.

John held his head in his hands, closed his eyes and allowed the jet of hot water to cleanse his body of salty tears and emotions. He sat there for probably twenty more minutes, his legs now spread out in front of him, his skin now smarting from an irritating scratch. He cared little for the passage of time as he reconciled that Stephen Taylor would soon be gone from the world, his beautiful spark extinguished forever, long before it was supposed to expire. John grieved, not for his own sorrow, but for Stephen and the fact that he would be denied the days, weeks, months, and years that should have lain ahead. What had Stephen been planning to do this week or next, he wondered? What enjoyable experience, liaison, adventure or emotion was Stephen being denied, now that he was pushing against death's door? It just wasn't fair.

John wrapped a starched while towel around his overheated skin, his fingers pruned in response to the lengthy time spent beneath the jet of water. The shower head dripped intermittently, its faucet returned to the off position. Drying his torso and wincing as he rubbed the towel against the abrasion on his back, John randomly recalled the image of a favourite family pet from his childhood subconscious. One minute his faithful dog had been pulling happily on its lead, tail wagging in cheerful appreciation of a daily walk, the next he had been struck down by illness. Euthanasia soon overwhelmed a once lively puppy as it rested its head one final time to a quiet chorus of grieving goodbyes. Its tail wagged one final farewell. John cursed the memory and slammed shut the door to the bathroom in frustration at a second defeat to sentiment. Again, he cried, defeated. Pulling on the last clean pair of Marks & Spencer boxer shorts he had packed for his visit, he wiped away the latest intrusion of tears and sniffed defiantly, determined to regain his preferred cold-blooded state. He entered the four-digit code that unlocked his smart phone and scrolled through recently dialled contacts to select a number. He had time to wrestle his head and arms into a plain black t-shirt before he spoke.

'Hi, it's me. Do you think you could come here? Now?'

The evident pain and hurt in John's voice negated the need for an explanation. They were both experiencing the same miserable emotion, after all.

'It really would help. And.'

He hesitated for a moment, wiping the end of his nose with the back of his hand while inhaling sharply.

'And I really would like to see you.'

Chapter Twenty-Seven

'Oh, for fuck's sake, doesn't anything work anymore in this place?'

Detective Craig Jones stabbed the return key on his computer keyboard several more deliberate and forceful times with an exasperated middle finger then sat down, defeated by the failure of his printer to accept and produce a simple one-page document.

Silently and somewhat sheepishly, the office cleaner, whose late-night vacuuming had just tested Craig's patience to the limit, unplugged the cord that straggled its way across the room to his overworked Hoover from a nearby wall socket. The instant he inserted the printer lead back into the electrical supply, Craig's machine clicked noisily and whirred out half a dozen quick copies of the desired one-page report. Craig glared at the cleaner predictably before his brief anger morphed into a farcical laugh. He shook his head at the ridiculous conclusion to what had been a frustrating day.

'Time to call it a night, boss? We can make last orders if we leave now.'

Craig chewed the inside of his cheek and surveyed a cluttered desk of papers, documents, dusty old files from the mid-eighties. In his hand, he juggled a rusted metal dog tag hanging from an equally time-eroded chain that had been removed from the skeleton exhumed on Gas Street and tossed it onto the eclectic pile. PC Tim Carrack, more commonly known as Crack by his colleagues at Steelhouse Lane Police Station in Birmingham city centre, stood expectantly beside the desk, hopeful of a pint to close out the long day.

'You're a bad influence Crack, but yeah, fuck it. Let's see if we can't get a couple in. I can't get my head around this. There's something not right here, but I'm buggered if I can figure it out tonight.'

Craig slipped on a distressed brown leather jacket that was draped across the back of his battle-worn office chair and motioned to the cleaner, who was now coiling the vacuum cord as he wheeled the machine towards a small closet in the corner of the room.

'Hey, Gunga Din. Make sure you empty the bin under my desk this time.'

Crack laughed and muttered a racial slur under his breath as the pair exited, turning the lights off as they left to deliberately plunge the office inconveniently into darkness.

'So, boss, what's not making sense? Anything I can try to help with?'

Crack always referred to Craig as 'boss' and he liked that about the young constable. A moniker more familiar than Sir, which was reserved for formally addressing a superior, was commonly employed throughout the ranks. In their working relationship, Crack was an eager and courteous copper, learning the ropes and showing respect to those who had earned it. He reminded Craig of his younger self, still naively blinded by ideals and not yet exposed to the negative realities of combating crime in the city. In his enthusiasm to help, and win personal favour, Crack had volunteered to liaise with officers in the neighbouring town of Solihull who were responsible for investigating the assault on Stephen Taylor, so he could report back all findings to Craig.

As they called the lift to the fourth floor to begin the descent to the lobby and take the short walk to the Jekyll & Hyde Pub, Craig laid out the bare bones of the case of the skeleton found in the basement of the Gas Street offices.

'Ah I don't know Crack. It's probably simple enough, but like I said, something doesn't feel right. That dog tag we found on the remains has the name Matt Douglass stamped on it. It isn't a real military tag, just one of those things that used to be a fashion accessory. Back in 1986, I knew a Matt Douglass and had just started on the force when his disappearance was being investigated. Well, actually, we had a quick sniff around and decided we couldn't find him.'

Crack was intrigued and Craig noted the look of fascination on his expectant face as the PC waved him through the opening lift door and then out into the lobby, trailing him, spellbound by the revelation.

'Okay, there's more to this than just a missing persons case. Douglass was a prick. A real arsehole judging from the brief interactions I had with him back when we were eighteen or nineteen-years-old. He was a bully, a troublemaker, he had some form, and he was tied to an established crime family in the area. He was known to harass girls at the club where he worked as a bouncer and there was a rumour going around that he'd sexually assaulted some bird on the dance floor at a club or somewhere. Not a nice lad by all accounts and to be honest, when he went missing, nobody lifted a finger to find him. His mom kicked up a bit of a fuss, but he'd nicked a car and buggered off to London, so we let it go. Good riddance, as I'm sure you can appreciate.'

Crack was now nodding inquisitively as he held open the door to the pub and once inside, eagerly grabbed two drinks menus that listed an array of draft and bottled beers. Craig pointed to the tap of Purity Mad Goose Pale Warwickshire Ale as he caught the barman's attention, while Crack noted the Sameul Adams American lager he had drunk frequently when visiting America on holiday might have been misspelled on the menu, but was still well worth consuming. He encouraged Craig to continue.

'Anyway, while we might have even hoped he was dead, we never concerned ourselves with whether he was or wasn't. He never came back here, which we were all happy about. I met today with an old colleague who retired a while back and he wasn't too surprised to learn that he might have turned up buried beneath a load of concrete. A classic underworld hit, right? At least back in the day that was how they did things. I was amazed that when they dug up and relocated the Kennedy Memorial from Smallbrook Queensway a few years ago during all the regeneration they didn't find any bodies from the Krays gang that the Fewtrells once ran out of town. We had a book going on that, you know.

'I'm having dental records run. If it is him, there's no sign of a gold tooth, which I remember Douglass having, but then somebody would have probably yanked that out anyway, either as a sick souvenir or to make a few quid from the scrap gold I'd imagine. He never returned from London as far as we know, so it doesn't quite fit like it should. There's just something bugging me. I don't know.

'Anyway, young Crack, cheers to you and your pending rise through the force!'

The pair chinked glasses and drank a significant dose. Craig sat back in his chair beside a table near the entrance, where both rested their pint pots and let out a stressed sigh as he stared at the ceiling. Crack was distracted for a moment by a young woman dressed in a smart and seductive outfit he termed a business power suit, her legs sheer in nylon that peaked his interest. She smiled provocatively as she caught him staring as she clicked past in high heels that guided her to the exit. Crack shook himself back to reality before he urged Craig, now supping his pint contentedly, to divulge more information.

'So, I don't understand what bothers you, boss. If it is this Matt Douglass you knew, which it sounds like it could be, then your theory makes sense and you can put the case to bed. After all, nobody cared much about him in the old days anyway from what you said. Is his mom who reported him missing still alive?'

Craig laughed at the reference to the eighties as being 'old days' when in his mind, they still felt like recent times. Rosies, a nightclub in Solihull, used to hold eighties music nights that Craig frequented when in his late twenties, but these days their hippest retro spotlight shone on the nineties, so perhaps the years of his youth were indeed regarded as ancient history.

'No, his mom died a fair while back, so she's long gone. I doubt there's anyone alive that cares about him to be honest. I remember at the time she was his only close relative in terms of parents or siblings.'

Craig finished the pint that had been on his mind since he had eagerly consumed a similar pair at lunchtime and rose to return to the bar to repeat the round. He waved off the protests of his subordinate, who was eager to dip into his own wallet. Once back in the quiet corner of the pub, he resumed talking after Crack had finished texting on his smart phone.

'I would put this to bed, but something came up today that makes me suspicious. Douglass disappeared the day after The Smiths – please tell me you've heard of them - played a gig at the Odeon in town. They don't have bands there anymore, but it used to be a great place for live music. I saw everyone there. Zeppelin, Queen, Sabbath. Well, never mind.

'So, I sold my ticket to that gig, because I'd split up with the girlfriend I was originally going to go with, and sold it to... can you guess?'

Crack's open jaw and nodding in disbelief confirmed he did.

'Yeah, so I flog this lad my ticket and he's never seen again, which is a little disconcerting. I never told anyone at the time because my colleagues back then didn't seem to care and I was the new lad on the beat. I was there to learn, not to solve the crime for coppers who'd been at it for years. Now, I'd leave it at that and put it down to coincidence, but, like I said, something came up today that has me wondering.'

Crack pulled his chair up, closer to the table, his trainee intrigue and enthusiasm on full display, and started on his second pint.

The young woman sauntered past again, deliberately plotting her course to skirt the edge of their space. She smelled of the cigarette smoked outside during a pause from her evening with friends, who chatted noisily in the opposite corner. Crack failed to notice her pass by as he coaxed more revelations from Craig.

'So, the old case files from the Douglass disappearance in 1986 were pretty bland, but I noticed a statement from a bus driver, Winston Roberts. He thought he'd seen our missing person not far from where Douglass lived the night he disappeared, but that was disregarded at the time. Our bus driver is still living in the same council house as back then, so I went and saw him today and if he's right and he did see Douglass then it was nowhere near where the body was found. Of course, he could have gone missing later, maybe down in London, and then been buried in those offices, which is why I was going to ignore his witness statement as well, but then he mentioned something else. He said he'd seen four lads in the same vicinity at that time, running towards a shortcut through some trees that led from the main Stratford Road to where Matt Douglass lived.

'Now I wouldn't pay that much attention either, but get this. I knew those four lads, if they're who I'm thinking of. One of them was most likely Stephen Taylor, who lived next door to our missing mystery man. You know that name of course.'

The confused look across Crack's face melted into a smile of realisation as he connected the name with the vicious attack on which he was keeping tabs. Craig watched the young PC's eyes open wide as he made the association between the Stratford Road reference and the location of Stephen's near fatal assault from the prior weekend.

'Smart lad! Eerie, isn't it? We've got Matt Douglass, and we've got people I knew who also knew him, all those years ago, all in the same vicinity of the attack that's left Stephen Taylor clinging to dear life. And, purely from my own personal knowledge, I can tell you there was a lot of friction at the time between Douglass and those four, so there was no love lost. He'd been bullying Stephen for yonks, and like I said, he was a nasty bastard. Something has to be missing from our investigation, doesn't it?

'And get this. Those lads I knew all got together in Brum this week, which isn't all that strange since they're here to visit Taylor in hospital. But I'm working the crime scene yesterday, and who do you think shows up on Gas Street, poking around outside, asking questions?'

Crack landed his glass forcefully on the table as he quickly swallowed a mouthful of Sam Adams.

'You're joking! Really? Fucking hell. I can see why you're a bit suspicious, boss. It makes you wonder, doesn't it? So, what next?'

Craig laughed as he downed the dregs of his second beer and stood up, tapping the right-hand pocket of his jacket to confirm the presence of his car keys. He rested his hand above Crack's glass, preventing him from hurriedly downing the remainder of his pint.

'What's next for me, young Crack, is getting my head down for some much needed and, if I might say so, some much deserved kip. For you, however, the night has in store whatever that bird in the corner who can't stop staring over here at you has in mind.'

Craig stood up, winked at Crack and gestured towards his vacated chair, encouraging the young woman to make the first move as he headed for the exit.

Chapter Twenty-Eight

John Garland collapsed onto the first unoccupied seat on the number ninety-two bus half coughing and half chuckling to himself as he caught his breath. He could barely remember the last time he had run to catch a bus. Whenever it was, the fare had certainly not been as extortionate as one pound twenty to travel a distance he might have walked was he not late for planned eight o'clock beers with Mike Sullivan and Andy Morris. In fact, he couldn't remember the last time he had used the form of transport that had been a staple of his youth, relying these days on taxis, the London Underground and occasionally chauffer driven cars to navigate London. He cursed at the discomfort of a cough he noted was caused not by cigarettes, as it would have been during his youth, but by his lack of general fitness and procrastination when it came to spending that promised time in the local gym. John gazed around the lower deck as his breathing steadied, noting the vast improvement in the quality of bus seating. Sharp deep red backs to comfortable seats covered in a blue material flecked with a pink and orange motif bordered almost on luxurious compared with the graffiti-tarnished interior he once knew. John focused briefly on the passenger opposite and nodded as the elderly gentleman tipped his brown trilby hat and smiled, as if politely welcoming him to the National Express West Midlands travel experience.

John stared down at the aisle between them, noting that even the floor of the bus appeared to have been hygienically treated. He was now frowning in confusion, searching his memory banks to identify that familiar face opposite. His mind ran through images of teachers, men that watched Moor Green while leaning on the barrier around the pitch, blokes in pubs, ticket collectors at the train station, bus drivers. Hold on a minute. John looked up and stared back across the aisle, the satisfaction of a recalled identity clear from his expression.

'Blimey! Winston!'

The man rocked back and forth and almost appeared to be bowing such was the exaggerated extent of his nodding. He smiled broadly.

'Yes, Sir, it is indeed!'

The West Indian accent that used to dance around the buses John caught almost daily during the years of his youth rang as broadly as it had back in the seventies and eighties. The hair that used to protrude from beneath that trademark hat had thinned and greyed.

'You know, I'm sorry, I can't recall your name, but I do remember you and your friends, who always caught my bus into town and even before that, I think you used to catch my bus to go to junior school.'

John stretched out a hand and introduced himself with a hearty handshake he never imagined would be delivered so genuinely for an anonymous bus driver whose relevance had slipped from his memory decades ago. Winston encouraged John to sit beside him and requested a brief summary of the years that had passed since times that truly seemed a lifetime removed from the present day. They laughed at how Winston insisted on passengers either finishing or discarding their chips from Jack's before riding on his bus, and the times John and his comrades would stagger through the concertina doors, barely able to alight due to the effects of alcohol.

'I'm sorry to hear about your friend. I was there when he got off the bus and those hooligans chased after him.'

John had been poised to end the jovial conversation as quickly as it had begun since his stop outside the Bull's Head was in sight and he needed to bid farewell and end his short journey. Instead, somewhat taken aback by Winston's revelation, he remained seated.

'What do you mean, Winston? You know who did it? The police are looking for them you know.'

Winston patted John gently on the shoulder, a large hand with long wiry fingers squeezing into a tense muscle in a reassuring gesture.

'It's okay my friend, I've told them everything I know. There were other witnesses too. One lady up on the top deck who had been annoyed by their behaviour on the ride back from town and the bus driver, an Eastern European man who they screamed abuse at before they got off. I thought nothing of it until I read about the attack in the newspaper and then I went to my local police station straight away. I told them it must have been those three boys.'

John was stunned into silence. He knew from his conversation with Craig Jones that he was keeping tabs on inquiries and surely Winston's witness account must have provided significant information. He watched as the Three Horseshoes pub, some two or three stops beyond his intended destination blurred by as the driver increased speed to guarantee making the traffic light at the junction of the Stratford Road and School Road as it turned amber.

186

Winston peered over his shoulder to confirm the location of other passengers before lowering his tone.

'I met with a DI Jones earlier today and I should tell you, he also asked about another case, one that was apparently unsolved from the eighties. It's quite a coincidence I should see you on the bus tonight because I mentioned you, although like I said, I couldn't remember your name.'

John was conscious that he was now staring in utter confusion at Winston, who relayed the tale of how he was helping police with their inquiries. John felt uneasy at the prospect of what he was about to learn regarding unexplained events from 1986. He took a deep breath as he regained his composure and encouraged Winston to explain.

'I went to Solihull police station on Monday and all they asked me about was what I saw late on Friday night. I gave a statement, descriptions as best I could; my eyesight isn't getting any better with age, you know. That's why I stopped driving the buses when I did. Anyway, earlier today, that DI Jones, who I'm sure I remember from around the same time you were catching my bus as a teenager, visited me at home. I'm retired now and I was out cutting the lawn in the back garden when my wife answered the front door.'

John felt the same impatience that had agitated him that fateful night when Stephen Taylor struggled to spew out the details of the sexual assault on Siobhan Murphy and felt his knuckles whiten and his nails dig into his hands. The College Arms passed by as the bus crossed the suburban border from Hall Green into Sparkhill. John listened patiently, struggling to hold his composure.

'He wanted to know about that poor friend of yours but then asked if I remembered him from a night back in 1986. Well, to cut a long story short, I did remember what he asked about. He was asking about some Matt fellow.'

'Douglass,' John chimed in, prompting an acknowledging nod as Winston adjusted his trilby hat.

'Yes, that was the name. At first, I didn't remember the name when the policeman mentioned it, but the description was clear enough. A big bully, who used to cause all kinds of problems on the buses, particularly harassing young girls travelling home alone at night; we all knew him, all us drivers. Never liked him and thought he was trouble.

'The night they said he went missing was my last night that summer before I went on holiday for two weeks. I remember the date

187

of the following day even now because it was the first time I was going back to Jamaica to visit my family and it's my wedding anniversary. It was a very special day for us. August 30, 1986. My wife and I had been saving up for years. I remember it was terribly expensive!

'Anyway, that night, I was working the last bus shift and after a quick game of dominoes at the terminus bus depot, I got a lift home from another driver. It was well after midnight I remember, as my wife was upset I hadn't come straight home. As we drove down the Stratford Road, we saw that Matt, erm, Douglass, right? He was getting out of a car, didn't look too sober and staggered off into those trees near where your friend was found at the weekend. I hope I didn't get you and your friends into any trouble, but I mentioned I vaguely remembered that you might have been on my bus that night. I said I was fairly sure I saw you again, crossing the road, after I saw that other lad get out of the car. In fact, we would have run you over, if we hadn't slowed down. I wouldn't have connected the dates, had it not been for me taking that holiday the next day. And what a wonderful trip that was! Well, anyway, apparently, he was never seen again, that Matt character. DI Jones told me he'd gone off to London looking for work.'

John shook his head, pretending to dismiss the significance of the witness sighting so many years ago and agreed that the line of questioning did appear unusual.

Winston continued: 'It was such a long time ago, I can't imagine how it was tied to the attack on your friend a few days ago, but then what do I know?'

Winston thrust out his hand suddenly as the bus approached a large Victorian building that used to house a lively pub named The Mermaid, which now stood forlornly boarded up and crumbling as it succumbed gloomily to the elements and a tumbling economy.

'Well my friend, I have to jump off here to change for the number thirty-seven bus to go and see a friend. It was nice seeing you again.'

John mustered a hearty smile in reply, shook hands and then waved as Winston stepped down onto the pavement. Then he slumped back into his seat, closed his eyes and attempted to decipher the likely consequences of the unexpected and potentially catastrophic witness that had crawled out of the woodwork. He tapped the right-hand pocket of his jeans where he always kept his mobile phone and cursed its absence, remembering having left it on the bed on his hotel room. He wouldn't be able to text either Sully or Andy to explain his tardiness.

- - - - - - - - - -

'Where the bloody hell have you been? Didn't get lost, did you? We've both been calling and texting you.'

Mike Sullivan's inquiry hovered somewhere between exasperation and mockery as John Garland wandered into the Bull's Head more than an hour later than advertised. John swivelled on his heels and headed to the bar, having first placed a copy of that evening's Birmingham Mail on the tall table beside them, folded deliberately to expose a relatively anonymous page four story. Sully and Andy dug into the text of an article that ran below a headline proclaiming: SKELETON FOUND IN GAS STREET BASEMENT. Andy prodded a finger against the newspaper as John returned.

'This is what we saw Craig investigating yesterday. You're not collecting cuttings about your ex-girlfriend's husband, are you mate?'

John was unwilling to indulge in Andy's banter, no matter how innocent the intent of his comments. The revelation that Winston Roberts had placed the four friends guilty of a vicious murder at a place only they knew was the scene of the crime and had exposed that truth to Craig Jones, of all people, served to strip John of his sense of humour. He glanced around the pub that was as sparsely furnished with clientele as it was on any typical Tuesday night, noting the closest patron was not within earshot.

'I'm late for good reason, which I'll come to in a minute, but it's this story that concerns me.'

Sully interrupted before John could explain, laughing as he spoke.

'I'd be concerned too if that prick Craig Jones was investigating. Have you read the crap he's spouting to those reporters? Comes straight out of a 'don't tell them anything' textbook from what I can see. And as for you being late, my crafty Cockney friend.'

Sully's jovial repartee was halted immediately as he stared disbelievingly at the newspaper and glanced at Andy, noticing a look of concern across his face. John had brought a borrowed pen back from the bar with him and had crudely crossed out the first word of the Mail headline and written a name in its place. The block letters now

189

screamed out '*MATT DOUGLASS* FOUND IN GAS STREET BASEMENT.'

'Fucking hell, John!'

Andy tore the story from the page and screwed up the paper urgently, stuffing the crumpled ball into his pocket. He wiped the stains of newsprint from his hands onto his jeans.

'What does that mean? You said...'

'I said we make no mention of what happened unless things have changed, which they have now. I have something to confess, or to tell you that you need to know.'

Sully and Andy exchanged concerned glances again then returned their collective focus to John. They stood before him, a captive audience spellbound by intrigue but in fear of what they were about to learn. John deliberately lowered his voice.

'Do you remember that bloke Stephen was seeing? The one who died seven or eight years ago? It was to do with complications from AIDS.'

Both remembered, though neither had attended the memorial service for their friend's partner.

'Stephen needed someone to talk to after his friend died. He arranged to meet me in a place just outside London, a pub in Beaconsfield. It was a straight shot up the M40 for me and an easy train ride out of Brum for him. It was the last time I saw Stephen, actually.'

John paused and sighed in regret.

'His boyfriend's name was Paul Booth, if you don't remember. That night of the Smiths gig, he was at Stephen's apparently, waiting for him to get home. Stephen's mom had no idea what was going on and thought he was just a friend who needed a place to stay that weekend. He was a couple of years older than Stephen. They were together until Paul left Brum for a few years to go back to where he was from originally, Bolton or Wigan or somewhere like that. Then he came back and they were on and off for a while. As time went on, they became, I don't know, mutually exclusive I imagine you'd call it.

'Stephen had to get something off his chest after Paul died. He told me that Paul desperately tried to calm him down after what happened that night between the four of us and Matt Douglass in the cut through. When Stephen told him everything that we'd done, Paul convinced him they had to move the body.'

John looked at Sully and Andy to gauge their reaction. He imagined if he had a ping-pong ball, he could toss it at Andy and even a poor aim would find his gaping open mouth. Sully appeared more intrigued than shocked. John continued with his revelation.

'They dragged Matt along the path and across the wasteland to some garages. Do you remember those at the back of his house? Well, then they put Matt in the boot of his own car, took they keys, which were in his pocket, and drove into town. Stephen still had a set of keys to Silver's offices because he hadn't mailed them back in yet. He dumped the body in a hole that was going to be filled later with concrete. I don't know if you remember, but we'd been told a while before to stay out of the basement because there was work going on down there. Then he dumped the car where he knew it would be found since it was nicked anyway. Bloody brilliant if you ask me.'

John glanced at his two friends, eager to solicit a response, the most sobering of which was delivered by Andy, whose suddenly ashen complexion suggested he might collapse unceremoniously to the floor. He gripped the tall table between them for support, while Sully reached out an arm to steady him. Andy's voice was hushed to a barely audible whisper and trembled in unison with his hands.

'So, so we did kill him then. I mean there's, there's no doubt about it?'

John nodded and shrugged, regretfully confirming their guilt, remaining silent to allow Andy to process his emotions.

'It's just that. Well, I suppose I always hoped. You know, never found a body and all that. Fucking hell lads. We really did. Well, I suppose we always knew we did but... Jesus, I need a smoke.'

Sully was shaking his head in disbelief and intervened before Andy had an opportunity to calm his nerves outside, blocking his exit with an outstretched arm.

'No. Not Stephen. You're fucking kidding! He was shit-scared afterwards, probably more than we were.'

John threw his hands up and hunched his shoulders.

'I know mate, I know. But somebody moved the body, didn't they, because all those explanations we came up with were all shit when you think about it. He didn't survive the kicking we gave him, he didn't crawl away and drive off to London, and he didn't decide to never call his mom. This makes perfect sense and I wouldn't have expected it of Stephen either, but that's what he told me happened. Why would he confess to this, especially at a time when he's just lost

191

his long-time boyfriend? He just had to get it off his chest and so he told me. He swore me to secrecy and until now I've honoured that. I'm sorry I didn't say anything to you earlier this week, but I didn't think I needed to. Andy, I'm sorry this is how you have to find out. Sorry that you have to find out at all.'

The trio stood in silence that lasted until Andy intervened.

'You know, I've laid in bed, unable to sleep, countless nights over the years and there's one thing that's always bugged me, something that didn't add up. It fits perfectly with this explanation. Do you remember, Stephen told us he couldn't use the back-bedroom window of his house to look down on the cut through and see if there was any movement, or to see if Matt made it back to his house next door?'

John and Sully racked their brains, eventually recalling Stephen's explanation from the first night the four petrified friends had reconvened in the bar at Moor Green Football Club. He had told them that because his mother slept in the back bedroom at number five Stonor Croft, he had been unable to investigate from a prime vantage point.

'Well that's crap,' exclaimed Andy. 'If you remember, when we were hiding from Craig and the other copper after we hung the mannequin a few weeks before that, we were in that back bedroom. It was the spare room and his mom's room was in the front. He must have been lying. He definitely would have had a clear view of the cut through and the garages at the back of his house. So maybe him and his friend Paul did go out there and move the body.'

John and Sully nodded in agreement before Sully slowly and deliberately analysed the theories. He waited until a passing former workmate sharing polite pleasantries had moved on to battle the fruit machine that jangled away in the corner. There was an opportunistic tone to his words.

'Now, I don't mean to sound heartless boys, but what I see here, is we have is one dead accomplice and another who...'

Sully paused in a moment of sadness for his mortally wounded friend, unable to find words to describe the anticipated fate of Stephen Taylor. He drummed his fingertips on the table and waited a moment before continuing, his voice noticeably tempered by sorrow.

'Anyway, it's fair to assume neither of them, Stephen or Paul, can be prosecuted or even questioned. Again, this is far too, I don't know, calculated or cold, but we're in the clear basically. If these remains are indeed identified as Matt wanker Douglass – and let's not forget what he did to deserve that kicking – then we can come clean and tell Craig the copper the truth and divert any suspicion away from us.'

Andy's previously pessimistic demeanour shifted dramatically. He had been sipping on his pint continuously during Sully's reasoning and was now resting his glass thoughtfully on his bottom lip. He landed the pint pot confidently on the round wooden high top table.

'Fucking hell, lads, yes! We should just tell Craig. Tell him we know the body is Matt Douglass and how we know. We'll tell him that Stephen and Paul were responsible for everything. He'll end his investigation. This whole thing that has been hanging over our heads almost our entire bloody lives just goes away!'

Sully held up his remaining beer in a celebratory toast and chinked glasses with Andy's offering, but stopped short when a more cautious John failed to reciprocate. There was apparent dissention in the victorious ranks.

'No, it isn't that simple. We have to let Craig's investigation run its course and then if or when we need to, we can tell him about Stephen. He might never figure out how the body got there and it could just remain a mystery. Right now, that knowledge is our best bargaining chip.'

Andy was unrepentant.

'I'm sorry, but I'm telling Craig! You bastards have called the shots all my life and now I'm taking control. I'll get the next round of beers in as well, since I haven't paid for one since we all met up. My mom and dad gave me a few quid when I told them I was going to the pub again tonight.'

Andy cringed almost immediately at the ridiculousness of the source of a grown man's additional funds. Sully smirked, as did John, neither meaning to belittle their friend, but struggling to suppress the humour of an adult attempting to command his friends while spending mommy and daddy's pension at the pub. Andy continued to speak, this time a little sheepishly.

'What did you mean by bargaining chip?'

John adopted a look of seriousness.

'If things were as simple as we've just discussed then I'd agree with you, Andy, and we could tell Craig. But things aren't that simple. Do either of you remember Winston?'

Sully stopped short of suggesting the wartime prime minister might be implicated. Andy pondered and inquired.

'Wasn't that the name of the old bus driver on the ninety-two?'

John proceeded to relay the tale of how he came to ride all the way into Birmingham city centre on the bus after his alarming chat with Winston, vacate the lower deck briefly and then board the same bus back to the suburbs again, much to the bemusement of the returning driver. The journey excused his lateness and explained the reasoning for not confessing all to Detective Inspector Craig Jones.

'If we go running to him now, it's obvious we're trying to get ahead of the game and ward off any likelihood of guilt. Worst of all, Winston's account puts four of us, not just Stephen and Paul, at the scene. And we were there yesterday, checking out where the body was buried and that must look as suspicious as fuck.

'He'll think he's got us bang to rights if he puts all these pieces together. Then he'll separate us and interview us independently and someone will slip up. We need to all tell the same story, but not until we absolutely have to, and then we'll be in the clear. There's just a couple of variations we have to make.'

Sully and Andy readily agreed as John explained.

'First of all, when or if we do tell Craig, we have to say that all three of us met Stephen at the pub where I met him, okay? I'll have to work out the exact date. It was The Swan in Beaconsfield, which is easy to remember. Look it up online to see some photos. It's an old fifteenth century place. Let's say we all sat outside in the beer garden. I drove and you both did too. Stephen made his own way there by train. Don't get inventive and claim you picked him up from the station or anything silly like that. Just basic details. The rest can be a bit of a blur because of the circumstances, and say you had something simple to eat, like fish n chips or shepherd's pie, or the lasagne. No regaling the fine beers they served or the wonderful menu, just a simple pint and meal.'

The alibi seemed simple enough to construct. Andy remembered the time he frantically memorised almost every listing in the Radio Times for August 29 and 30 of 1986 and then remained awake for the next two days, unable to sleep, convinced he would soon be shackled in chains.

'Secondly, and I don't like doing this, we definitely have to pin the murder on Stephen as well. Moving the body is the lesser crime. We can't tell Craig that four of us kicked the shit out of Matt

194

Douglass, but that Stephen and Paul Booth are guilty for dragging away the corpse. We need to tell him we all hung around the bus stop having a few cans after the gig, which, he'll figure is why Winston saw us. We were walking home when Stephen ducked into the woods, as he always used to, to get home, cursing about Matt and how he'd bullied him. He was bullshitting as far as we were concerned about how he was going to kill him one day, but then with the benefit of Dutch courage, must have been true to his word and given him a kicking, maybe with the help of Paul Booth. You don't even have to remember his name really.'

The contemplation of John's apparently fool-proof plan was broken as bells sounding and lights flashing celebrated the emptying of the pub fruit machine as the jackpot was breached for the first time in many a week. Coins pumped out like rapid machine gun fire and a supportive cheer went up from the few drinkers that remained at the bar, more in hope of a free pint bought by a perhaps generous lucky winner than in genuine rejoicing. The fortunate gambler scooped up his winnings and exchanged handfuls of coins for a wad of crisp notes, a pint and a whisky chaser that was only soberly toasted by the disappointed barflies.

The scheming trio polished off their drinks and agreed to retire for a relatively early night. The following day they were already committed to meet Craig and Siobhan for lunch in Solihull; an awkward liaison initiated by the wife of the investigating officer and the returning former boyfriend from London. Surely since all were now mature adults having carved out lives and families of their own in the many years that had passed since their formative teenage years, they could behave civilly in public around the table of a popular pasta franchise restaurant.

The three friends stood outside the Bull's Head in a sparse car park and reviewed the story that solidified their alibi one more time. John underlined the power of the ace in their pocket.

'Remember, we can't mention this to Craig yet, especially not at lunch tomorrow in front of Siobhan. We should see what he has to say and then get together afterwards to devise a plan. I think we're in the clear boys.'

Sully and Andy nodded as they processed the logic. Kicking his heels in the dirt, John broke their concentration.

'I really don't feel like going straight back to that bloody hotel and sitting there unable to sleep. I'll walk down your way first if you like lads, then wander back from there. I haven't walked these streets in a long time.'

Andy was quick to usher John away in the opposite direction.

'Oh, no you don't, mate. I know what you usually get at the end of walking someone home from the Bull's Head and I'm not into that kind of thing and I don't think Sully is either. Be off with you and I'll see you at lunchtime.'

All three laughed loudly and went their separate ways.

John looked back over his shoulder, relieved to see Andy walking confidently down the Stratford Road away from him as he chatted away with Sully. His friend was the weakest link whom he feared might break under pressure if their alibis were ever put to the test under questioning and the threat of prosecution. Andy turned and seeing John staring, blew a kiss, grabbed his crotch and spun away, laughing.

'He'll be just fine,' John tried to reassure himself under his breath.

Chapter Twenty-Nine

Siobhan Jones rarely offered more than a polite hum or affirmative nod in response to her husband Craig bemoaning his day's work for the West Midlands Police. The pair conversing around teatime was a rare enough occasion itself and Siobhan cared little for the rundown on the latest serious crimes to befall the region. She peered inquisitively over Craig's shoulder as he sprinkled a tenderised steak with a concoction of spices. She declined to offer advice, protesting that she had no cause for criticism and was merely curious. Not since her teenage years had she eaten a dead carcass, remaining true to the *Meat Is Murder* ethics of The Smiths, whose influential album of the same name now seemed further in the past than she cared to admit. Neither had she been prepared to grill, cook nor barbeque such an offending item, even for her husband, children or dinner guests, much to Craig's frustration. More than occasionally, he was press-ganged into serving as a reluctant cook in the kitchen as a result. Siobhan was removing the cork in a fragrant bottle of Rioja when Craig's monotone summary of the day's events gripped her attention.

'What? Who did you say? A dead body?'

Craig turned from his peppered-steak and smiled as he reached for a knife to continue butchering the raw flesh.

'And I thought you weren't listening! I said the skeleton we found in Gas Street looks like it's Matt Douglass. You remember, that head-case who lived next door to Stephen Taylor and used to be a bouncer at some dodgy clubs in town.

'There's something odd about the whole case, but I've had dental records checked and sure enough, it's him all right. I've got his teeth and a dog tag that was still around his neck.'

Siobhan stood frozen to the spot in the kitchen. Gripping the wine bottle tightly with one hand, she stared at the pool of red wine that was pouring like blood across the countertop, overflowing from her spilled wine glass. Her eyes welled with tears and her breathing intensified.

'Fucking hell, love, what a mess. Are you going to clean it up, or what?'

Siobhan snapped out of her momentary trance, careful to avoid facing Craig as she fumbled for a roll of paper towels from a cupboard, concerned he would investigate the petrified look of fear on her face as she fought back tears. She mopped up the wine sporadically, eventually stuffing the sodden towels into the plastic drawstring bag of an overflowing pedal bin, which she hurriedly removed and took outside to the dustbin. Once on the pathway between the house and garage, Siobhan crouched down, convinced she was about to vomit. She fought the gag reflex and managed to compose her emotions and her bodily functions as she stood up straight and took a deep breath. Then suddenly, a sick grinning golden-toothed image of Matt Douglass that had been suppressed for decades flashed before her and she retched violently, regurgitating her earlier glass of wine and a barely digested red pepper and onion quiche unceremoniously against the wood-panelled garden fence.

'Bloody hell, Siobhan, are you ok? I didn't think my steak would have that effect on you.'

Craig had been concerned by his wife's sudden exit and having followed her outside, now rubbed his palm gently and genuinely up and down the middle of Siobhan's back in an all too rare show of tenderness. Their relationship had been devoid of even a hint of such affection for far too long.

'I'm fine, really. I think it was what I ate earlier. You don't have to worry, but thanks. Could you get me a glass of water?'

Craig hustled inside, dutifully ran the cold tap and once Siobhan returned to the kitchen, handed his wife the tall glass. A few moments later, he continued with his work story, apparently oblivious to the squeamish nature of his next revelation.

'If you look in tonight's Mail there's a story in there about finding the bones, though we hadn't confirmed it was Matt Douglass when I spoke to the reporter. The really odd thing about the skeleton, and we haven't told anyone this, especially the media, is that the middle finger on his right hand had been hacked off, maybe post-mortem, maybe before, and there's no sign of that finger bone at all.'

Siobhan slammed the empty glass down with urgency, rushed to the sink and again vomited uncontrollably; coating a colander full of green beans that Craig had strained and left there moments earlier.

Chapter Thirty

The mushroom and risotto fried balls came served in a quaint stainless steel mini fryer basket with a rocket salad on a wooden board. Siobhan Jones admired the thoughtful presentation of the appetiser she had selected from the Bella Italy menu as she poked one of the spherical delights with a fork and blew lightly to cool it before enjoying a subtle taste. Her morning activity had caused her to work up an appetite she needed to satisfy at least temporarily before the arrival of her lunchtime guests. She was almost half an hour early for a rendezvous she now regretted organising between her husband Craig and their three friends of yesteryear Mike Sullivan, Andy Morris and John Garland. Bringing the group together around the table again for the first time since 1986 had seemed a natural element of their collective grieving for a comatose Stephen Taylor, but now Siobhan sat hoping one or all might construct a convenient excuse for cancelling.

As Siobhan adjusted her knee length skirt, she again convinced herself that Craig would not notice that the black tights she now wore were a completely different colour from the skin tone nylons she had left the house wearing earlier that day. He might have been an inquisitive policeman with a natural nose for solving crimes and collecting incriminating detail, but rarely was he so observant when it came to his wife. Those original tan tights had been discarded in the bin of a nearby hotel room, torn beyond being presentable enough to wear during a fervent exchange with her lover in a moment of uncontrolled passion. At the Boots store in Solihull's Touchwood shopping centre, she had hurriedly purchased a pair of the same brand as a replacement. Only when she came to slip them on in the public toilets before arriving at Bella Italy did she realise her glaring colour error. She smiled mischievously as she tasted the last of the fried balls, recalling her illicit morning liaison that had been as spontaneous as it was delightful.

Siobhan's lustful recollection was broken as a smiling waitress eagerly removed the empty plate and mini-fryer basket from the table and presented a bill for the appetizer, which Siobhan paid for immediately with two crisp five pound notes, waving away the potential return of any change. She contemplated scrolling through meaningless social media updates on her phone to pass the time, but instead observed a grey-haired couple she estimated were in their late fifties as they entered the restaurant. He wore an awkward multi-coloured sweater and she a dress that clung to her a little too tightly for such a relaxed lunch setting and a woman of her vintage. Siobhan loved people watching. Neither wore a wedding ring, so she imagined each was either divorced or widowed and from their cautious demeanour, perhaps they were in the early stages of a relationship. She wondered if they had met on an Internet dating site or via the more traditional route of a pub, or an introduction through mutual friends. Had she bought the gaudy sweater as a gift for him, or was it his attempt at creating a look less dour than his nondescript grey corduroy trousers? Had she agonized over the appropriateness of her fitted dress, or had she brazenly sought to peak his interest? Siobhan sighed as she wondered if she would ever be that woman, single again later in life, her long and uninspired relationship with Craig finally at and end. She watched the couple intently and candidly as they ordered from the menu.

Speak of the devil and beside him the equally roguish figure of John Garland. Their movements awkward and self-conscious, the pair manoeuvred between the maroon and blue painted tables of Bella Italy, disturbing the occasional diner in the process, heading in her direction. Both fumbled awkwardly over which chair to select, Craig eventually positioning himself beside his wife, while John sat across from the unhappy couple. Siobhan took a perverse pleasure in listening to how Craig and John had inadvertently arrived at the shopping centre entrance at the same time. She imagined their uncomfortable attempt at making small talk during the walk to the restaurant, both no doubt relieved to have finally arrived. Yet now here the three of them were, faced with an uneasy first meeting together since that night at Peacocks long ago in 1986 when Siobhan and John had set the wheels in motion to begin their whirlwind romance and end Siobhan's destiny with Craig, at least temporarily.

'Well this is bloody awkward, isn't it?'

Sully could always be relied up on to break an uncomfortable silence and on this occasion, he brought welcome comic relief to the situation. He and Andy had been trailing John and Craig through the mall, arriving only a moment later. Sully slapped John on the back and caused the metal legs on a chair to screech against the floor as he sat down authoritatively and ushered everyone into a more acceptable seating arrangement.

'Well at least nobody needs an introduction. I'm bloody starving and I know this place does a decent salmon dish, though they're a bit pretentious and it's down on the menu as 'salmone' for some reason. There's a couple of good ciders too if everyone wants a change from lager, which I know I do.'

- - - - - - - - - -

Siobhan's attention had wandered from the general conversation over lunch and she was watching two women who looked no older than their late teens, one constantly wrestling her son of about two-years-old, who was intent on removing himself from a high chair. Having lost her patience, the young mother instructed the waitress to remove the boy's macaroni and cheese since he had done little more than poke at it with his fingers and the child was now crying and reaching in the direction of the departing server. An older woman at an adjoining table, who Siobhan noticed spoke in a light Brummie accent that she tried desperately to conceal, shot a judging stare at the young mother, tutting and shaking her head at the behaviour of the boy. He was soon lifted up and strapped into a pushchair, which seemed to improve his mood. Siobhan smiled at the youngster, who held up a stuffed Elmo character from Sesame Street in reply. Siobhan smiled at the mother too, but all she could muster was an exasperated response. Siobhan wondered if she regretted having a child at such a young age. She wore skin-tight black leggings that once upon a time might have been worn as an attractive fashion item, but now served a means of pure convenience during a daily struggle to successfully play the role demanded of motherhood. Her long dark hair was most likely pulled back tightly and wrapped in a bun for the same reason. Siobhan conceded that she too was trapped, albeit in a different version of bondage. She glanced forlornly at Craig, whom she realised appeared to be speaking to her.

'Are you with us, love? Honestly, you never seem to listen to a word these days. I was just telling this lot about the break in the case for Stephen's attackers.'

Siobhan scowled, annoyed by the patronising nature of Craig's comment.

'One of my PCs has been talking to the lads at the Solihull nick and they've arrested a lad this morning, a right nasty piece of work with plenty of previous. He hasn't admitted anything, but they know it's him because a couple of strong witnesses came forward. There's two others involved and we'll get them as well, once the first lad breaks. Bloody kids they are, only teenagers.

'Look I know it's no consolation, what with Stephen being as bad as he is, but it looks like we're going to get the bastards.'

Maybe Craig wasn't so bad after all, thought John. The assault was beyond his jurisdiction, yet he was actively pursuing the case. He and Stephen had briefly been friends outside the tight-knit group before John, Sully and Andy were introduced, but once Stephen's sexuality had been disclosed, Craig had kept his distance. Perhaps Craig was acting just to appease Siobhan, but even if that was his motivation, John had no complaint. They all thanked Craig for his attentiveness and casually discussed the crime and its likely outcome. John considered pressing Craig for details on one of the witnesses he knew to be Winston Roberts, but given the fact he had also provided information on the events of 1986, thought better of lighting that touch paper. He glanced quickly and often at Siobhan, who either seemed to be ignoring or not noticing the attention he paid her.

The reunited group swapped embellished tales of their fallen friend as they ate, evoking an eclectic range of emotions, as memories of his colourful life became harshly contrasted by the bitter image each recalled of Stephen lying close to death in a sterile hospital ward.

Then Craig changed the subject.

'What do you lot remember about Matt Douglass?'

The collective silence served to fuel Craig's suspicions that the disappearance of Hall Green's bullying bouncer might in some way be linked to the three friends who now sat before him. Unwittingly, his wife had delivered the trio for an impromptu interrogation, regardless of the relaxed public setting. John appeared thoughtful, Sully concerned and Andy tried to conceal a near-terrified demeanour. Siobhan was thankfully confident that the mention of her assailant's name would not cause her to throw up her salmone, which as Sully had observed, came slightly burned on the skin side, which detracted from the light taste of a nice salad of beans greens, olives, tomatoes and cucumbers. She accidentally knocked an unused spoon from the table and the noise as the cutlery clattered on the wooden floor created a welcome break from the awkward silence.

'What do you mean? He was an arsehole, as I'm sure you remember.'

John's reply prompted agreement from around the table and led Craig to divulge more information, though he remained suspicious of the initial reaction to his question.

'Those remains I told you we'd found on Gas Street, when I saw you the other day. It turns out to be Matt Douglass.'

Craig paused, again hoping the three friends might incriminate themselves, but this revelation proved too dramatic and provoked an almost instant response. Had he divulged such critical information so brazenly during the interview of a suspect down at the station, his colleagues would have voiced their dismay at his poor technique.

Neither Sully nor Andy possessed the confidence to confront Craig head on, so John quickly recognised it would be down to him to lead the conversation.

'You're shitting me! I heard he'd gone off to London and just never returned. That's what people said at the time if I remember rightly. Dead! Blimey. I can't say I'm very upset considering what a prick he was, but, well, you don't wish that on anyone, do you?'

The waitress returned with the bill, which Craig and Sully both reached for and they argued as to why each should pay the entire cost as a treat for the others. The distraction allowed John to look at Siobhan to gauge her reaction. She was staring at the floor and her concerned eyes met John's only briefly before she returned her gaze to the couple in their fifties she had observed while alone earlier. They had split the cost of their meal and he was now helping her up from the table with an affectionately outstretched hand and they linked arms as they left the restaurant. Siobhan hoped they planned to work off their lunch calories in a romantic fashion.

John supposed Siobhan must have confided in Craig at some point during their marriage, recounting that night she was assaulted by Matt Douglass. Perhaps she had, but then again, perhaps not. After all, why would Craig be so callous as to even utter his name before a group of people with his wife present? Siobhan appeared uncomfortable, but not distressed.

'Craig, you were saying?'

Craig and Sully's credit cards now sat amicably side by side awaiting an equal portion of the cost of the meal. The police detective continued, prompted by John's apparent interest.

'Well, there's some information that wasn't in the Mail last night if you saw that story, which is that apart from identifying the skeletal remains as Matt Douglass, we've found that one of his fingers

203

appears to have been torn off, amputated if you like. It's a mystery why that was done, but it's a pretty gruesome thought. The lads at the station have come up with all kinds of theories, like…'

'Okay Craig, there's no need. I think we get the picture.'

Andy's interruption was as welcome as it was unexpected from the most nervous of the three friends concealing vital information.

'That's a rather unusual way to dispose of a body, burying him in a basement, beneath a load of concrete. What are you thinking? He was knocking around with some undesirable types back then, so I suppose it could have been any one of Birmingham's criminal lowlife.'

Craig nodded affirmatively, slightly disappointed that his line of questioning had failed to unearth a more intriguing response. He thought to himself that perhaps the consideration his one-time associates might be complicit in the death of Matt Douglass was nothing more than a far-fetched theory. His logic was fuelled by a nagging suspicion caused by the witness Winston Roberts placing them at the last-known sighting of the deceased and by their unexpected appearance on Gas Street earlier that week. Perhaps those sightings were simply coincidences and the criminal underworld was indeed guilty of the murder and crude burial. Craig resolved to set his suspicions aside, but remained equally prepared to revisit them if necessary. He laughed to himself as he sized up Andy and tried to imagine Nervous Nellie in the act of killing and then burying and desecrating a dead body, hacking the finger off a corpse to save as a sick souvenir.

'I mean it does look like some of those unsavoury characters back in the eighties might have done this. It's their style. To be honest, and this is strictly between us, my bosses just want confirmation that it's him, which I can give them now, so we can close the case. We're not going to go running around after some of those old villains hoping for a conviction.'

Craig leaned in to the table and glanced cautiously over both shoulders.

'There's always been rumours at the nick about the influence those old gangster-types had within the force, whether it was a beat copper they'd bought off, or one of the governors upstairs. I had offers to keep things quiet when I was first out on the streets, but I wasn't interested. You either swing one-way or the other.

'So, if there's nobody out there who honestly cares about what happened to Matt Douglass and there's still the odd, excuse the pun, skeleton in a someone's closet, this will be put to bed quickly. The truly nasty pieces of work from back then are either inside, or retired on their ill-gotten gains, or were bumped off by rival gangs at some point. Nobody wants to dredge up the past.'

Craig was about to conclude when he checked his lean back into his chair and rested his elbows on the table, talking again in a hushed tone.

'Your old gaffer Tony Silver will probably have to answer a few questions down in his bath chair on the coast, since the skeleton turned up in his old pad. Did you see him on the news? Quite honestly though, so many people had access to that place over the years, plus the workmen who poured the concrete in the foundations who will never be traced; he's not going to get more than a quick visit from the local force.'

Craig pondered for a moment as he made the intriguing connection between his observation underlining the ease of access to Silver's and the fact the three characters sat beside him had all been furnished with keys at the time of the Douglass disappearance. The correlation was not lost on John, Sully and Andy either.

Craig clasped his hands together forcibly enough to startle the waitress as she cleared the last of the group's plates from the table and Siobhan reached out instinctively to prevent the crockery from falling to a likely demise.

'Anyway lads, that's about it from my end. I'm pulling a late shift at the station, so the sooner I get over there the sooner I'm done. Skeletons from the eighties create a lot of paperwork and are more trouble that you'd believe.'

The grasp of Craig's departing handshake felt warmer and more heartfelt than either Sully or Andy had anticipated. Since Siobhan had turned her back, distracted again by the small child and Elmo, Craig raised both fists in front of John and ducked his head sharply from side to side, mimicking a boxer. He leaned forward to inspect the left eye he had bruised on their last meeting decades earlier and smiled as he held out his hand.

'Looks like no permanent damage then. No hard feelings either, I hope?'

John laughed and shook his head.

'Nah, no worries. It was a long time ago, a very long time ago in fact.'

The old adversaries shook hands, but maintained eye contact that betrayed a lingering element of mistrust. They were hardly going to hug and become best friends, after all.

Chapter Thirty-One

'No, it was definitely 1981 when it only cost two pence. I remember because Stephen had that Rasta Blasta, you remember? He played his tape of that bloody Soft Cell single, over and over and he pissed off all the other passengers. By the time we got around the full circuit of the number eleven bus route, I knew every word to that fucking song.'

Mike Sullivan assumed an overly camp pose and in as close a falsetto voice as his croaking vocal chords would allow, mimicked a chorus of *Tainted Love*, the best-known song by the eighties synth-pop duo.

Andy Morris conceded that Sully was right. It had indeed been longer than either had first thought since Birmingham's bus company had bizarrely empowered the city's population of under-sixteen-year-olds, and those who could pass themselves off as such minors, to travel as far as they desired on any of their double-decker vehicles within the West Midlands for the token fare of only two pence. The generous gesture unintentionally proved the catalyst for a wave of school truancies since a day spent riding the top deck for a bargain price far outweighed the alternative of sitting in a stuffy classroom. The number eleven, known as the Outer Circle since its 27-mile route followed what had once been greater Birmingham's suburban borders, proved the most popular bus for those skiving off school. Tracing the entire route that weaved around the postcodes could last more than three hours and navigating the full circuit ensured the passenger was returned to the original point of embarkation.

Now Sully and Andy found themselves back on the top deck of the number eleven bus, bound nervously for a hospital pilgrimage to see Stephen Taylor that neither was prepared to admit would likely be their final farewell. Andy had decided his visit earlier that week had been too brief and traumatic and that he owed his old friend a more fitting goodbye.

They gazed beyond historic Sarehole Mill to a patch of grass where they once spent countless Saturday mornings kicking around a football while arguing over disputed goals, or trying to hit a cricket ball beyond the farthest fielder and into the River Cole during summer months. Andy banged his head gently against the window as they passed Swanshurst Park and he recalled the bittersweet memory of a fruitless fishing trip with a defiant Stephen, who was adamant that the park's murky pond could provide an appetizing evening meal if they allowed patience to prevail. He closed his eyes, overcome by sadness. Predictably, Sully jolted Andy from his thoughts.

'Two pence! Bloody hell! For what we've paid to catch this bus today, we could have taken a taxi back then and still had change left over for a bag of chips. Daylight robbery it is.'

Andy shrugged. His reminiscing had taken on a more sombre mood.

'I wish we could go back. Not that far to when we were only thirteen, but to that summer before we all went our separate ways. You know, before…'

Andy's voice trailed off. He felt the soothing palm of his friend ease the tension between his shoulder blades and a comforting voice now whispering rather than belting out in its usual intrusive tone.

'I know mate. I've often thought about that. I'd go to Woolies to buy that Smiths single so that maybe John never goes gaga over Siobhan, or I'd tell Stephen not to buy extra tickets to see The Smiths, knowing that Craig is going to give one to Siobhan. Maybe I'd spend all my time convincing John to go to university up here rather than down in London. You can drive yourself crazy thinking about all the different scenarios, mate.'

Sully paused and stared out the window himself as the Swanshurst Pub and an all-girls school of the same name blurred past. He remembered playing matchmaker between Stephen and one of the school's students whom he assured his friend was 'a sure thing' and then being perplexed when the promise of passion failed to materialise. He recalled too how a stag party in the upstairs room of the pub livened by a racist and homophobic opening act comedian and a pair of ropey strippers had failed to titillate Stephen, who on that occasion drank himself into a near-comatose state before the night was done.

'There's a lot I'd tell Stephen too. I used to think it was funny to yell 'backs to the wall' when he came into the pub, or make jokes about queers. Attitudes weren't like they are now, were they? No tolerance, no acceptance, just nastiness. I had a hard time accepting that the kid I'd showered with after football matches for years and after P.E at school, and crashed in the same bed with occasionally after a pissed-up night out was gay. I just thought about how that made me look and what people might think about me, having a friend who was, you know, like that. I suppose we were young and didn't know any better, but I'm ashamed of how I felt, even if I tried to just make jokes about it at the time. I should have told him since then, especially because my attitude really did change, but I never did. I really regret that.'

Sully slumped back in his seat and tried to avoid making eye contact with Andy, who had rarely experienced such a heartfelt pouring of emotion from his friend. Andy stared, solemnly. The second time, Sully caught Andy's gaze, the acceptance that he was journeying to see Stephen for the final time shattered his previously stoic façade. Sully closed his eyes, covered his face with both hands and fought back tears caused by the loss of his friend.

'Hey, hey, it's okay. You can tell him how you feel today at the hospital. He might be sleeping, but he'll hear what you need to tell him.'

- - - - - - - - - -

Craig Jones pushed back slowly from the large whiteboard that dominated the wall beside his desk. Thoughts rotated in his mind at the same slow and deliberate pace as the casters on his chair turned before he came to a gradual halt a distance from where he could still read every word and study every photograph on the board before him. His hands were clasped together symmetrically; his fingers straight and aligned, his thumbs resting below his chin, while the tips of his index fingers hovered below his nostrils and seemed to be unintentionally stroking his moustache. Glancing up from his nearby desk, PC Tim Carrack considered at first glance that the atheist detective inspector might be seeking divine intervention, his hands posed as a child first learns to pray. The young policemen thought better of making a wisecrack, instead reclining to observe his mentor at work.

Craig's face was the epitome of concentration. He frowned, scowled and opened his eyes wide then returned their sharp gaze to a narrow focus. He shook his head, nodded and blew intermittent sharp bursts of breath and long sighs through his now drumming fingers.

Before him, a marker pen summary of the mysterious case of Matt Douglass lurched down from the wall. Names, dates, people, places, eye-witnesses, theories, friends, family and accomplices were all afforded a strategic position within the puzzle. At the top, centred but stuck to the board carelessly at an awkward angle was a menacing

209

archive mug shot of the recently discovered deceased. Taken following an alleged assault charge that was dismissed before the appointed court date, the photo depicted a then 17-year-old Matt Douglass, smirking as if already confident that the renowned crime family for which he had been working at the time would ensure the filed charges were dropped. His hair bleached almost white stood in short spikes and his trademark sleeveless t-shirt hung from his toned shoulders.

Craig Jones broke his concentration and turned squarely to face PC Carrack.

'Nasty piece of work he was, Crack. Bad news, bad person and there were a lot of relieved people when he disappeared. He was small time of course, but with the potential to become a real problem. He had the backing of the Rourke family, so he would have been untouchable for quite some time. Then he vanished, which is one of the things still eating away at me.'

Craig resumed his praying pose and scanned the board again for what felt like the thousandth time since dental records had confirmed the skeletal remains unearthed on Gas Street were indeed those of Matt Douglass.

John Garland's name and photograph sourced from the Driver and Vehicle Licensing Agency database hung there too, underlined in red during a moment of angry recollection rather than to differentiate him from Stephen Taylor, Mike Sullivan and Andy Morris, who also took their place among the rogue's gallery. Each had been identified as being present at the last known sighting of the deceased by witness Winston Roberts, who was documented off to the far left of the board, listed among the incidentals of the case.

A timeline began on Friday, August 29 the night The Smiths had thrilled a raucous audience at the Birmingham Odeon when the subject was known to have been among the attendees. It progressed slowly to a confirmed Douglass presence at the Garryowen after-hours pub and then to the Stratford Road beside the cut through to Stonor Croft where Winston Roberts had seen him exiting an unidentified car. Garland, Taylor, Sullivan and Morris had been placed there too. The timeline stalled in the early hours of the following morning. The trail went cold for a period before a distraught Rosemary Douglass insisted to sceptical police officers that her darling son was missing. Then, other than a library ticket connection made between an abandoned stolen car and the deceased, the subject had faded conveniently from memory until his unexpected resurfacing from a concrete tomb.

'Ok Crack, hear me out on this one. Something about those four reprobates I used to know is really bugging me, but I can't connect them to a suspicion of murder or disposing of a body or any involvement in this, no matter how hard I try. They might well be involved, but I have a theory that fits without them, and the chief wants this wrapped up. I can give him that, so, here's what I think.'

Craig took one final fleeting look at the collage of conspiracies before swivelling his chair to again face the young PC, who was eager to discover the likely conclusion.

'Pissed up Matt Douglass, who was seen staggering out of a car not far from his home by a witness who is as reliable as he can be all these years later, sleeps off a bout of drinking in the back of his car. Actually, a car he stole several weeks previously. Maybe he doesn't want to disturb his poor old mom, or can't be arsed to let himself in and clamber up the stairs to bed. His suitcase for the trip to London is in his car already, so he can stretch and wake up and head off to London nice and early the next morning. Being pissed up, he forgot a package in his bedroom that he was supposed to deliver to someone in London. We never did retrieve that package from his old mom back in eighty-six. I remember nobody considered that necessary.'

Crack nodded affirmatively, following every step outlined by his detective inspector.

'Garland, Sullivan and company just happen to be getting off the bus when our witness sees them. After all, that isn't so far-fetched considering they'd been to the same Smiths gig and they all live in the vicinity. What *is* far-fetched is the theory that those four tossers, even together, could take down that big bastard. Is this making sense?'

PC Carrack nodded again in confirmation.

Craig rose slowly from his seat, leaning one hand against his desk for stability as he stretched out a back that ached from being cramped for a prolonged period, while reviewing the theory before him. He stepped forward and prodded the second stage of the timeline with an authoritative middle finger.

'This is when I think he was killed. These two weeks when his mother believed him to be in The Smoke. Maybe he was down there and strayed onto the turf of some of the capital's undesirables. After all, there was a bitter battle going on between the Rourkes and some Cockney mobs back then.

'Suppose he was done over in London and dumped on the Rourkes' doorstep to send a message. It wouldn't have been the first

211

time. Those animals traded foot soldiers a few times like that. I could buy that and I'm sure our gaffers would too.'

Craig reached both hands over his own shoulders, which he massaged firmly while grimacing as he looked again at the board. His pause allowed PC Carrack to contribute to the theory.

'So, boss, then the Rourkes take the body and bury it in the foundations of a listed building that they quite rightly think will never be disturbed. One of their blokes runs his business out of those offices, so nobody ever knows. You didn't mention the finger that was cut off, but surely that just adds to the mob connection; a gruesome message sent from the Cockneys to the boys in Brum.'

'Exactly! I thought that same thing about old Tony Silver, who owned the Gas Street offices at the time. He was known to be connected to the Rourke mob, or at least had dealings with their nightclubs. I spoke to him on the phone and he says the concreting of the basement happened sometime in the mid-eighties. He used a local Irish firm to do the work, cash in hand and all that. It was probably some of the Rourke contractors, so we'll get nowhere pursuing that line. There's no paperwork to record when the concrete was freshly poured, or who did it. But again, I'll bet it was around that time Douglass was likely done over in London.'

'And nobody ever cares anyway, except for Mrs D, who pops her clogs a few years later.'

Craig searched for the reference to Rosemary Douglass, buried among the scrawl of different coloured marker pens.

'Here. In nineteen-eighty-nine she wanders through the pearly gates and the days of anyone being concerned about what happened to Matt Douglass are over.'

Craig took a step back from the tangled mess of information, names and photographs and folded his arms across his chest, twisting his wrist slightly as he peered down at the hands of a stylish antique-style watch that had somehow ticked beyond the hour of ten o'clock.

'I think we've cracked it, Crack. You and me should celebrate with a decent ale or two. I hope that late night menu is still available at the boozer.'

Craig patted his back pocket to confirm the presence of his wallet, but swivelled on his heels as the pair was poised to exit. He reached to the top of the whiteboard and grabbed at the photo of Matt Douglass, screwing it into a tight ball that was then tossed into a nearby wastebasket.

'There. That filth is where he deserves to be. I mentioned the rumour about him assaulting some bird at a rock concert, or a nightclub, didn't I?'

PC Carrack nodded inquisitively as he held the office door open for the detective inspector, recalling the reference but not the details from an earlier conversation, intrigued to learn more about the undesirable character.

'Well, I remember a few weeks after his old lady had made probably the third or fourth complaint that we weren't looking hard enough for her beloved, we pulled in a bouncer from one of the Rourke clubs on an assault charge; another one that didn't stick if I remember rightly. Anyway, as a matter of routine really, we pressed him about missing Matt and he remembered boozing in some pub or other with him, most likely the Garryowen. It was all very bland until he told us how Douglass was bragging about how he'd got himself crushed up against some tart in a short skirt on a packed dance floor, or at a gig or something like that and he'd fingered her. Right there in public, with her unable to put up a fight. Then he slipped off into the crowd and carried on enjoying himself. Fucking disgraceful.'

PC Carrack cringed and shook his head in mutual disgust, staring ominously at the middle finger he had used to press the button that called the lift to the fourth floor. He wondered if that revelation might be linked to the missing middle finger of the discovered skeleton, but just as his mentor had done back in the eighties, thought better of solving a mystery on behalf of his more experienced superior.

- - - - - - - - - -

'Are you two lovebirds interested in taking part in the pub quiz, or are you going to get a room?'

John Garland excused himself from the passionate embrace he thought was secluded from the other patrons of the Saracen's Head Pub and grinned mischievously at the smirking quizmaster who stood before him holding out a sheet of paper and an assortment of pens. Coming up for air they used to call in their teenage years.

'No mate, we're fine thanks. The lady and I are finishing our drinks and we already have a room, which we'll be retiring to shortly.'

The paper and pens were offered once more in a hopeful gesture, but were again rebuked.

John laughed and straightened his slightly crumpled shirt, peering around the edge of the alcove that hosted the illicit rendezvous and shifted deeper into the corner to hide from view. Another passionate kiss proved too tempting to resist.

A few minutes later, a booming voice announcing the humorous names of several teams poised to answer an eclectic series of general knowledge questions interrupted the romantic liaison. John resisted the next demand for his lips.

'You know, while it would be very erotic to see how far we can continue this here, in public, I do have a room upstairs. It would be just like old times, together again in Birmingham like when we were younger. I bought a few bottles of wine from Sainsbury's when I got here and there's a couple left. If you don't mind drinking from plastic cups, we can enjoy a much more intimate time upstairs.'

The invitation accepted by the subtlest pouting of her lips, John eagerly rose from the alcove, modestly covering his pronounced arousal with her handbag, causing her to laugh provocatively. She willingly took his hand that led her across the pub in the direction of the back stairs that in turn led to the Premier Inn hotel rooms.

Chapter Thirty-Two

John Garland was laughing so hard he was in tears. A hand clamped across his mouth failed to mute the hysterics as he coughed uncontrollably, gasping for air, while shaking his head in disbelief. For a moment, he sat upright and regained his composure, but then quickly doubled over again, urging Mike Sullivan to restrain from adding further illustration to the hilarious anecdote that had triggered the fits of laughter. Andy Morris approached from the car park of the Three Horseshoes, debating which of Sully's notoriously endless catalogue of yarns had proved the catalyst for such merriment. He also wondered why his two friends were sat outside the pub on a patio overlooking the main Stratford Road without a lunchtime pint beside them.

'Sorry mate, we don't open for another ten minutes.'

Andy had his explanation from the young man dressed in an anonymous starched white shirt and equally bland black suit trousers, who stopped him at the foot of a short flight of steps that led to the patio. Andy motioned his intention to wait outside, along with his two friends.

'Alright, Andy. Have you heard this one? Sully's going to kill me one day with his bloody stories. I thought I was going to die laughing just then.'

John inhaled and exhaled loudly as he was finally able to glance at the mischievous grin stretched across Sully's face and shoot back only a laugh and a smile, compared with the gut-wrenching reaction that had caused his belly to ache. He checked the time on his cell phone, impatiently cursing the minutes that remained before opening hours commenced. They had not anticipated a change in lunchtime venues translating to having to wait for a beer.

'You have to tell him that Sully, if you haven't already.'

Andy sat beside them on a wooden picnic-style bench, straddling the weatherworn seat and looked inquiringly at Sully, who appeared deep in thought.

'You know, I don't think I've told Andy that one. It only happened recently and I don't think you've been back from Wales since.'

Sully barely needed a second prompt to again recall a visit he had made to an early summer barbeque hosted by Craig and Siobhan

Jones a few months earlier. Holding court to tell one of his many and often-embellished tales was his favourite pastime, be it at parties, in the pub, or often in the company of his children, usually much to the dismay of his embarrassed wife.

'So, a while back, sometime in May, just after the FA Cup Final it was, I bump into Craig and Siobhan in Waitrose. They're squabbling away in the cereal aisle, arguing over Shreddies or Frosties, or something like that. Anyway, I haven't seen them for yonks, so I stop and say hello, which is a bit awkward really. I mean, Siobhan on her own is fine, but Craig, well, I feel like I can do without ever bumping into him to be honest.

'So, we give it all the old polite chat and I'm just about on my way when Siobhan goes and invites me and the missus to some garden party they're having the next weekend, since the weather forecast is good. You know, a chance to enjoy the fine weather in case the summer is short and all that. Of course, she's only being polite and I can see from Craig's face that he's annoyed that she's asked me. For that reason alone, I decide to definitely go along.

'It turns out to be an okay afternoon. Plenty of burgers and hot dogs and all that on the grill and some fantastic hummus a woman who works with Siobhan had made. Never thought I'd be a fan, but I was, scooping up loads of the stuff with some Doritos.'

True to form, Sully's yarn had spun long enough that the trio were ushered by the blandly dressed barman into the pub, its doors now propped open to welcome all-comers. Three poured pints and a distribution of menus later, the friends relaxed around a large table in a corner as Sully resumed, much to Andy's intrigue.

'So, anyway, Siobhan has her cousin visiting from Ireland and he's doing all the cooking, wearing a chef's apron and everything. Being the perfect hostess, Siobhan's opening beers and pouring wine and juggling that with greeting everyone who comes along. There's probably about thirty of us, just chatting away in their garden. Now Craig is visibly pissed off that he's surplus to requirements and not tossing the burgers or whatever. You know what a prat he could be. He hasn't changed. He can't just relax and have a few cans and let the party take care of itself. He has to try and do something to make some sort of meaningful contribution.'

Sully shifted in his seat, shaking his head in anticipation of the punch line, while Andy smiled expectantly, glancing at John, who had again covered his face with both hands as he chuckled to himself.

'So, off Craig disappears and a few minutes later, returns with a plate of Ritz crackers and a big serving of pâté that he's cut up into slices. So, all the food is on a big table near the grill and everyone's casually helping themselves, but Craig has to walk around with this plate he's carrying and offer everyone some of the pâté. Never been a fan myself, so I decline, but plenty of the other guests tuck in.

'I notice pretty soon that there's a few twisted-looking faces and a few people secretly spitting the stuff out into napkins, but everyone seems too polite to say anything. Good old Craig is delighted with himself. He doesn't notice and he walks around the garden convincing just about everyone to have a taste.

'It's about now that I see the Jones family dog, a little yappy thing that had just been wandering around getting fuss from people, is trailing Craig everywhere. He's pawing at Craig's leg, begging for some of the pâté, yet up to this point he hasn't bothered anyone else for a bit of their burgers or anything.

'Craig gets to Siobhan last and there's not much pâté left, but there's enough for her to take a piece and a cracker. Craig has this pathetic satisfied look of having proved his worth to the afternoon and smugly walks off to get a beer from the kitchen. He's almost there when Siobhan shouts and stops him in his tracks. Now, I'm stood about half way between the two of them, so she walks towards him and he walks back and when they meet, I can hear what they're saying.

'She asks: 'who bought the pâté with them, Craig?' She's not eaten any of the piece on her plate and has a disgusted look on her face. Craig looks a little bemused and shakes his head, saying 'well, you'd left it in the fridge, so I thought somebody had better serve it.'

John could contain himself no longer and again with tears in his eyes, excused himself from the table, his laughing audible until the door of the gentleman's toilets swung closed behind him. Sully tapped his wrist with two fingers, assuring the overeager barman that they would place their food order in a matter of minutes, before continuing with his tale.

'That's when Siobhan drops her plate, the pâté, burger and all the trimmings falling onto the grass, and the dog leaps in and scoffs the pâté like it's the greatest food ever invented.

'Turns out that twat Craig had only gone and sliced up one of those big sausages of soft dog food that was in the fridge for their mutt and served it to everyone at the party! Fucking hilarious it was. What an idiot! No wonder people didn't like it, but plenty of them had politely eaten it.'

Andy sat back in his seat, chuckling in disbelief, his reaction more contained than the hysterics that had overcome John, his mood tempered by the previous day's sombre visit to see Stephen Taylor still lying comatose in an anonymous hospital bed. Andy leaned forward and prodded a finger at the appetizers section of the menu.

'I guess we won't be ordering this for a starter then.'

Sully spied the list of offerings inquisitively.

'Pâté! Bloody hell, no. Not for me, thanks. Maybe I'll take some home in a doggy bag!'

- - - - - - - - - -

Craig Jones had seriousness written all over his face as he entered the Three Horseshoes, his attention caught by the three people who had asked him to meet them for lunch as they laughed raucously in a far corner. He paused at the bar to order a pint of Guinness and although he stood with his back to the trio, their quietened demeanour assured him they had observed his arrival. Craig had been wondering all morning why Sully had texted him just after nine o'clock, asking if he would meet them for lunch. After all, they had sat around the table at Bella Italy only two days earlier after an absence of some thirty years and not once had there been a hint of enthusiasm for a repeat reunion. Craig watched his pint settle before casually wandering over to join John, Sully and Andy, who had uncharacteristically just rejected the barman's offer of a second round of drinks.

'So, what are we now then chaps, best buddies?'

Craig's mood was in stark contrast to his relatively jovial farewell from Bella Italy. He had fought with Siobhan numerous times during the short period since that lunch meeting. First, after leaving the restaurant, he had called her mobile as soon as he had cleared the car park beneath Touchwood and accessed a clear phone signal. He accused her of flirting with her former lover John, of laughing at Craig's expense during a period of the conversation she couldn't recall, and blamed her for unnecessarily gathering the group of them around the table in the first place. He viewed John Garland now with disdain, wondering if he and his wife had resumed an affair he believed had ended decades earlier. If they had, Craig resolved coldly to destroy them both. Their fight resumed late that night, once Craig returned home from work, lubricated by a couple of pints and whisky chasers sunk at the pub. The next was tempered by a foul mood exaggerated by an ache in Craig's neck caused by sleeping on the living room sofa after Siobhan had locked him out of the bedroom. A bolt across the door had originally been employed to prevent their daughter from accidentally ambling in at an inopportune moment when she was a child, but now served a less pleasurable purpose. He had made a mental note to pry it loose with a screwdriver the following weekend.

Craig was in no mood to be pissed about by three people whom his instinct told him knew something about his active case that they were failing to divulge, or in particular by one he feared was again screwing his wife. Craig might have convinced himself and PC Carrack that the Silver Skeleton mystery had been solved, but the request for a second lunch date with Craig was cause for suspicion.

John broke the silence with a completely unexpected revelation.

'We know who killed Matt Douglass.'

Craig wiped the foam from the head of his Guinness that had clung to his moustache in dramatic slow motion with the back of his hand. He slowly licked one remaining drop with his tongue that snaked out of his mouth and back in again like a lizard tasting the atmosphere. His eyes bored into John as he rested his pint purposefully on the table and smacked his lips together at the bitter taste. He sat down slowly and deliberately.

'What? What did you say?'

John glanced at Sully and Andy before offering an explanation the trio had rehearsed tirelessly throughout Thursday afternoon in Sully's living room. The Saracen's Head Premier Inn hotel bathroom mirror had also been subjected to an increasingly confident patter on numerous occasions. If there was any trepidation in John's mind, it did not filter out through his voice.

'We know, Craig. We know. That's why we asked you to meet us here. We wanted to say something on Wednesday, but for some reason, with Siobhan there, it just didn't feel right. You told us your crime family theory and, well it just didn't feel like the right time or place to contradict that.'

Craig's heart was racing. He had been unable to banish the witness report supplied by Winston Roberts of their presence near the last-known sighting of Matt Douglass and their sudden appearance on

Gas Street as coincidences. He could call for back up and arrest all three of them and conduct questioning at Steelhouse Lane Police Station in an intimidating environment. Yet why, he wondered, after their previous conversation had ended with Craig admitting that this case would likely be tied to a tit-for-tat war between rival Birmingham and London gangs, would they inject themselves into the inquiry? John provided a revelation that almost knocked Craig off his chair.

'It was Stephen. Stephen Taylor. He killed Matt Douglass.'

Craig stared, open mouthed at John, frowning as he reviewed the affirmative expressions on the faces of Sully and Andy. He paused, took a sip of his Guinness and then a substantial gulp. Rarely did Craig find himself lost for words and he masked his dumbfounded reaction with a series of sips of the smooth velvety liquid.

Sensing a caustic mood at the table, the barman, who had seen his customers stack the lunchtime menus on an adjoining table, nervously approached to take their order, hovering close by.

'Three Ploughman's please mate,' said John sharply.

'Make it four,' added Craig, who was agitated by the interruption, without looking up from the table. 'And four more pints in a while too.'

Craig was unaware that John, Sully and Andy had each abstained from consuming more than their initial drink, for fear of clouding their rehearsed explanation and their judgement.

The prolonged silence, while briefly broken, was unnerving Andy, who felt as though he might crumble at any moment. Craig's pondering was anything but a tactic to lure one of the three friends into incriminating themselves, but it almost served to that effect.

Craig resumed the praying pose he had held for several minutes when reviewing the timeline of Matt's disappearance back at the station. This time his deliberation was more pronounced, his long fingers reaching up to his frowning forehead. As he stared one by one at John, Sully and Andy, he closed his eyes and shook his head. He was certain he was missing something and that one if not all were guilty of wrongdoing, but the urge to close this sorry chapter seemed to be overriding a personal vendetta against the three, and specifically against John Garland. Craig was gripped by an undertone of regret as he finally spoke.

'Strange as it sounds, that makes sense. I wouldn't have thought he had it in him, but I can appreciate the motive.'

Any mild panicking subsided, yet nobody dared contribute to Craig's surprising opinion for fear of altering his logic and volunteering information that might contradict his theory.

'Hated queers didn't he, Matt Douglass? Really hated them. He always had it in for Stephen. I used to see that, even during the brief time I was around you lot. I rode a bus back from town once, in uniform, because there'd been all kinds of hassle on the late-night buses and our chief wanted us to be more prominent in the community. I think everyone except me was pissed up on the top deck and I remember Matt giving Stephen tons of abuse. He was a nasty bastard. It didn't matter that I was there in uniform. He wasn't intimidated.

'Getting back to the point though, how did Stephen do it? He wasn't exactly Bruce Lee.'

The scraping of Craig's chair against the tired wooden floor caused the other three to jump nervously. The pondering policeman moved aside to allow the barman to deliver the second round of drinks, then gestured his index finger in a clockwise motion, encouraging John to continue to enlighten him.

It was the ambiguity of the components of the case that had forced the trio's hand when they might have gambled on Craig settling for blaming an organised crime vendetta; the fact they had been placed near the cut through on such a pivotal date, the lack of conviction they sensed in Craig's theory, the suspicion that he still harboured a grudge against John, and the unfortunate timing of their innocent appearance on Broad Street at the point when the skeleton was discovered. They were aware that Craig knew they had been in the vicinity of Matt Douglass that fateful night, placed there by a bus driver returning home from work, but Craig had no knowledge of Winston Roberts sharing that revelation with John. As the permutations swirled around his head one more time, John decided to gamble and use that element to their advantage to tie up all the potentially incriminating loose ends. In a moment of improvisation, he decided to stray from his well-rehearsed script.

'Well, I think we might have been there just before Stephen killed him.'

Sully and Andy retained their composure, their exterior totally calm but for the tell-tale flushing of cheeks as John deviated from the agreed plan. Sully wanted to kick him beneath the table.

'It was the night of the Smiths gig. We'd caught the bus home with Stephen and he was terribly upset about Matt. He'd been at the gig, he verbally abused him; said some of the usual bollocks about him being gay. You know. Like you said, you'd witnessed it too. Matt had bullied and tortured him for years, since they were little kids. Stephen used to talk about wanting to climb through his bedroom window at night, since he lived next door, and stab him to death. Stephen had a great big antique sword on the wall of his bedroom and I used to worry he'd grab it one day and go hunting for Matt. We all thought he was just saying it out of anger, but perhaps he was honestly considering doing that.

'Anyway, that night, we got off the bus near the cut through to Stonor Croft. You remember? It was where some jokers murdered a mannequin and you were the investigating officer.'

John was gambling, hoping Craig's mood might have mellowed during the course of three decades, but he just stared back at him, unimpressed.

'I'm sorry John, but let's not forget what we're talking about here. It's not the place where you tossers hung a dummy and had a lot of laughs at other people's expense and spent fun times as kids any more. It's the place where your friend was beaten unconscious. There's been a rape, maybe two, maybe more that haven't been reported, some cases of indecent exposure and who knows what else happen on that path. They should flatten it and build houses on there because it's a fucking miserable place these days.'

John's shoulders slumped as he now starkly visualised Stephen, assaulted in that spot, his eyes closed for what would likely be the last time. He realised there was nothing remotely humorous about the place where his friend had fallen.

'I'm sorry, lads. Really, I'm sorry. I didn't mean…'

Four Ploughman's lunches arrived at the table. As the barman passed out four sets of cutlery he had been wrapping in single-ply napkins to constructively pass a quiet lunchtime shift, the table remained silent. Each plate was crammed with a large chunk of cheese, a warm bread roll, pickled onions, slices of raw onion, two ripe tomatoes and half an apple and in a separate ramekin dish came a side of Branston Pickle. The lunch looked far more appetizing than the prospect of food had when first ordered under such gut-wrenching circumstances.

'Some English mustard too, please mate.'

Craig didn't break eye contact with John as he spoke to the server. He beckoned him to continue.

'I was going to mention that Sully and Andy went to see Stephen in hospital again yesterday. He's lying in the same position he was when we visited him on Monday. The doctors are just monitoring him, listening to the beeps, making notes on charts and pumping him full of fluids and painkillers, but that's about all. They haven't given us any indication that his condition will improve. We just have to hope. We just have to wait and hope.'

Nobody spoke, observing a contemplative silence. John made the most of the pause to compose himself before returning to his explanation.

'Right, so we left Stephen by that cut through and went home, assuming he'd wait for Matt to clear the path before using it himself, after all, he was usually shit-scared of him. But it turned out he went along and found him having a piss against a tree, with his back to the path. In a sudden moment of rage, he cracked him over the back of the head with an old metal chair he found lying there. The blow stunned him, maybe knocked him unconscious. Stephen was so furious that years of pent up rage came out and he gave Matt a right kicking. He kicked him full in the face while he was trying to get to his feet, and his head snapped back and broke his neck. That's what he told us.'

Craig now wore a poker face, eager not to play his hand as brazenly as he had done at Bella Italy.

'What about Siobhan? She went to the Smiths gig with you lot, didn't she? Was she there, just before this happened?'

This was a line of inquiry the foursome had failed to consider, despite its glaring relevance, but Sully barely skipped a beat as he trotted out a convincing explanation.

'Taxi. She took a taxi home from town. She was off to Ireland early the next morning, so said she couldn't hang around with us. We were going to doss about after the gig, which we did, after we got off the bus. She went home instead.'

Craig's manner surprised John, Sully and Andy. He seemed almost as relieved as they were to be closing this chapter, but in truth, he knew only a fraction of their culpable secret that continued to eat away at each of the three friends. Craig gave the thumbs up to the barman in approval of the arrival of mustard and the spread before them. All Craig required now was an explanation and a series of pieces that fitted snugly into the jigsaw. Growing in confidence, the conspiring three friends carved out more intricate lies as Craig posed questions to tie up loose ends.

'How do you know all this anyway? Have you known about this for all these years?'

The phantom visit to a pleasant pub in the London commuter belt was flawlessly recalled without over complication and the revelation of Stephen's now deceased lover and accomplice in moving the body was dovetailed in to the anecdote. They explained how Stephen and Paul Booth chose to move and bury the body rather than risk being linked to its discovery, while Craig conveniently connected Stephen's possession of keys to Silver's offices where he once worked and the skeletal remains had recently been unearthed. Craig mulled over the convenient explanation.

'Why the finger? And what happened to it?'

Blank expressions. Nobody had an answer to that conundrum and the trio had previously agreed while creating their conspiracy that tying up every loose end would appear suspicious. Craig was content to gloss over the mutilation.

'Who knows? To be honest lads, I have bigger fish to fry. That sounds blasé, but there's a lot of shit going on in Brum right now that I need to devote my time to. Believe it or not, an old skeleton from the eighties ain't a priority if it's considered related to a bunch of old criminals who aren't around anymore, which could still be the report I submit. It sounds like this crime rests with Stephen and I'm sorry to have to say this, but you know where I'm going with it, if I say he might not wake up from his coma. Sorry for putting it so blankly, but this secret could die with him. In that case, nobody's going to prosecute a couple of dead blokes.'

Despite being reassured by what he was hearing from Craig, Andy felt compelled to pose questions of his own. There remained concerns from his perspective as well, which he felt would surely be addressed soon enough if the detective probed further.

'Craig, are we in any trouble? I mean we concealed this for a number of years after Stephen told us. I suppose we've been harbouring a murderer and the knowledge of a murder we didn't report, though we could just have written it off as a drunken story.'

Craig shifted in his chair and nodded as he sliced into his large wedge of cheese and garnished it with a generous addition of Branston Pickle.

'Yeah, you're all guilty and I should run you in right now really. I mean, you said it, Andy. Harbouring a criminal, suppressing knowledge of a murder. I suppose though, you could deny all

224

knowledge of any of these conversations, there's no real evidence, just circumstantial and all that. There's honestly a lot more substance to the other theory.'

Craig contemplated further as he sipped at his Guinness.

'I could do one of two things. I could follow the tack that's already being discussed back at the station, that this is related to old organised crime activity, or I could provide a fresh theory. I could go down the path suggesting that Stephen and this other bloke, Paul Booth you said, are responsible. A resolution is all anyone really wants.'

Craig rocked back on his chair as he pondered a potential outcome.

'I'll be honest; I don't want to cloud the waters where the prosecution of Stephen's assailants is concerned. A good defence lawyer would paint a pretty unfavourable picture of Stephen with this knowledge and gain some sympathy for those three tossers who attacked him. This doesn't go beyond this table, okay? I can pretend I know nothing about Stephen being involved and can push the rival crime family theory and the Rourke connection through as being gospel.'

Three assuring heads nodded, confirming their compliance, while each contained an overwhelming burst of relief at Craig's proposal.

'The coincidences are staggering, though, aren't they? Stephen Taylor assaulted in the same place where you say he killed Matt Douglass and that chair you mentioned. The Solihull officers found an old rusty chair at their crime scene. I don't know. It's all very bizarre.'

Craig shrugged as he buttered his large roll and stuffed it greedily into his mouth. Using his hand to shield the others from having to watch him chew, Craig announced in muffled tones that he had a confession of his own to reveal.

'I sold my Smiths ticket to Matt Douglass you know.'

They didn't know. Sharp glances were exchanged around the table, each pair of eyes keen not to betray an admission of concern and the gradual realisation that Craig had inadvertently been the catalyst for that tumultuous night's events back in 1986. Craig was too busy munching to notice anyway. He bit into a pickled onion, blinking his eyes rapidly at its tartness.

'I originally wanted more than face value for the ticket because they were so hard to come by, but I was pissed off with you John, which I'm sure you can understand since you'd stolen Siobhan from me. So, I told Matt he could have the ticket for whatever it was, a fiver, on the condition that he gave you a smack or two to make up the difference.'

Surprised by the revelation, John put down the slice of apple he was poised to bite into. He was about to declare that Matt Douglass had never so much as given him a slight slap and had passed up the perfect opportunity to carry out that order before and after the Smiths gig when Craig divulged further details.

'I had second thoughts after that PC I was working with at the time told me I'd regret being into a character like Matt Douglass for a potential favour somewhere down the line. He was right, so I told Matt to back off and not bother you. I remember I spoke to him on the phone just before he went off to the Smiths gig.'

John nodded and ate the apple as he talked with his mouth half full.

'Well he must have understood because he never bothered me, he just continued to harass poor old Stephen.'

Craig seemed unconvinced. He commented on the unexpected but pleasant sharpness of the Ploughman's cheese before returning to the topic of Matt Douglass.

'I've been thinking about that summer and I remembered he said something odd on the phone. He said he'd leave you alone, but he'd thought of something he'd enjoy doing that would be far worse and traumatising for you than attacking you physically. He said he'd get you another way. The bloke was a lunatic. I never really understood what he was on about.'

- - - - - - - - - -

As some men are in the compulsive habit of doing, Craig checked the zip fly on his trousers once more as he exited the toilets, knowing very well he had sufficiently adjusted his clothing before returning to the bar. John had settled a lunch bill everyone lauded as being great value for money considering the generous size of the portions, but he boiled with rage inside at Craig's revelation about Matt Douglass. Craig had caused Matt to be at the Smiths gig. Craig had put the idea of hurting John, whether physically or emotionally, in Matt's head and that alone, as far as John was concerned, meant Craig was guilty of triggering this entire miserable episode. Craig was the reason Siobhan was sexually abused and Craig was the reason Siobhan had failed to return from Ireland, ending her relationship with John. The responsibility for the appalling assault on Siobhan, Craig's future wife, lay firmly at her husband's feet.

Sully cursed the fruit machine that had just swallowed the last of his pound coins without reward. He slung his jacket over one shoulder as he followed Craig, who held open the pub door for both he and John. They found Andy outside, leaning casually against a wall in the car park watching his addictive cigarette smoke glide off into the sky as if he was without a care in the world.

As the group was poised to say their goodbyes, Craig glanced at the smart phone he had told his constable he would not be checking until after lunch, no matter how often it buzzed silently in his pocket, which was had been more frequently than he had expected. As he scrolled quickly through the messages, scanning the list for priorities, one stood out from the clutter of correspondence.

'Oh, fucking hell, no.'

Three inquiring faces gazed in his direction, their intrigue quickly replaced by a heart-breaking realisation before Craig even spoke.

'It's Stephen. I'm sorry, lads. He's gone.'

Chapter Thirty-Three

'Thank you, Dad! Thank you! Thank you! This is fantastic!'

John Garland smiled contentedly as his daughter spun around excitedly in the kitchen, its dizzy background blurring on the screen of his smart phone.

'This gig has been sold out for months! How did you get tickets?'

John was disappointed by his enforced absence from Vicky's eighteenth birthday party, but the convenience and capabilities of FaceTime provided a consolatory opportunity to still interact with his daughter via their devices. Her excitement and laughter was infectious as it surged through the screen and caused John to smile more broadly than he had done since learning of the death of Stephen Taylor earlier that day. He had planned to explain why his visit to the Midlands would be further extended, since he had agreed to pitch in with tidying up the personal affairs of his friend, but decided against tempering his daughter's happiness.

'Well, you've met my business partner Dom. He knows a few people and they know people, so I was able to get a couple of tickets. The Arctic Monkeys aren't quite The Smiths in my book, but I thought you'd like the tickets. So, Happy Birthday, love. Who are you taking to the gig with you?'

Vicky's phone tilted to one side and smiling predictably at the camera was Vicky's best friend, Sophia.

'Hi Mr Garland! Oh, my god, those tickets are incredible. Seats right near the front too! Thank you! Thank you!'

Vicky joined her pal and the pair proceeded to dance together around the kitchen in another spinning celebration selfie.

'Hey, Dad, that's the doorbell. Hold on and let me talk to you in a minute, okay?'

Vicky hurriedly discarded her phone on the kitchen counter and dashed towards the front door, Sophia in tow, hoping some of the several boys they had met during occasional visits to the local pub had accepted their party invitation. As she sped past the living room, Vicky saw her mother out the corner of her eye and slid to a brief halt on the polished wood floor.

'Oh, Mom, I've got Dad on FaceTime in the kitchen if you want to talk to him. He just called me from his hotel to wish me happy birthday.'

Ellie Garland had received the sad news of her husband's friend Stephen Taylor, whom she had never met, via a text from John earlier that day. Frustrated as she was at being left alone by John to chaperone a house full of teenage drinkers likely to party long into the night and stressed by the anticipated worry of damages and breakages, she felt an obligation to offer her condolences in person. She set her wine glass on a decorative coaster atop an antique wooden side table and rose from her comfortable armchair, reaching for the remote control to switch off a television show she had been only half-watching. She and John might have been suffering a tumultuous marriage for longer than either was prepared to admit, but she still cared for him and knew that beneath a stoic exterior, his heart would be aching. She made her way dutifully to the kitchen.

Throughout the past week, Ellie had followed the breaking news in the Stephen Taylor case through multiple visits to the online portal of the Birmingham Mail. She had also assumed a vague interest in the eerie mystery of the Silver Skeleton, once John explained that he had known the deceased as a teenager and frequented the office where the remains were found, and also had a prior connection with the investigating officer, who was now married to the former Siobhan Murphy.

As she entered the kitchen, Ellie tried to recall the last time she and John had communicated via any medium other than texts and emails during one of his many trips that took him away from home on an almost weekly basis. No such occasion came to mind. When John first used to travel, back in the distant past of a happy marriage, he and Ellie would talk daily, irrespective of the cost of a transatlantic phone call or the logistical challenges of making contact from Asia, America or Australia. The calls were often playful, rich with colourful descriptions of faraway lands and on occasion erotic, temporarily filling the void in intimacy caused by the physical distance between them. The rapid advances in technology initially enhanced those interactions, but gradually, as their relationship waned, relatively impersonal emails and texts became commonplace and in time, the expectation. Then, despite the advent of Skype and FaceTime, contact slowed to a bare minimum. These days, Ellie was more surprised than expectant when it came to receiving travel updates from her husband. Their paltry communication mirrored their threadbare sex life.

The sporadic texts Ellie had received during John's enforced return to Birmingham included some intriguing inside information regarding the Douglass and Taylor cases. She had cringed at the confidential revelation of the unpublicised missing middle finger from the excavated bones and also knew that a suspect was helping police with their inquiries regarding the assault on poor Stephen. John never once called with updates, preferring to text during convenient moments of downtime. She might have been his wife, but Ellie had been relegated to the same category as business contacts John would only correspond with while in line waiting to order a coffee, or while held up at a red traffic light with a void of thirty seconds or so to fill. So rare in fact had their personal interaction become that Ellie now seized on the opportunity to chat with her husband face to face, encouraged as much by the novelty of the occasion as any genuine affection.

Ellie picked up her daughter's phone, confused for a moment that all she could distinguish from the screen was what appeared to be a ceiling, presumably of John's hotel room. There was no movement, but she could definitely hear voices, more than one in fact. One was clearly a woman's voice.

- - - - - - - - - -

Before John could speak, Vicky was gone. He called after her, wanting to again wish her a happy birthday, but she was already rushing along the hallway to discover the identity of the first arrival for her party. John wished he could have been there to celebrate with her. He placed his phone on the polished surface of his hotel room desk and laughed at his daughter's frivolity.

John reached across to switch off a black oscillating fan the hotel front desk staff had kindly delivered earlier that day to help combat the summer heat. As he stretched and yawned, its whirring blades gradually fluttered to a halt, the room by now cooled to a more comfortable temperature. He also turned off a muted television that was wedged within an open-plan wardrobe that furnished his economically designed room with shelves to accommodate clothes, a spacious rack for hanging his shirts, convenient tea-making facilities, and a hairdryer mounted beside a half-length mirror. John rose from

231

the chair and stood by the edge of the bed. He gave his appearance an approving glance in the mirror.

'It's okay, you can come out now.'

The bathroom door opened and an attractive brunette in her forties glided seductively into the bedroom. She wore a loose-fitting black silk robe, which was short enough to reveal the lace tops of her black nylon stockings as she walked, treading cautiously in impractically high-heeled shoes. John clearly displayed his appreciation and enthusiasm.

'My god, you look incredible. Last night was fantastic, but something tells me tonight is going to be, well, I don't think I can find the right words.'

An authoritative finger, its long nail manicured a deep red rested over John's lips.

'Last night was just an appetizer. Tonight, we're going to enjoy the main course. But first, pour me a glass of wine. You know, I'm feeling quite sentimental, being here together. Perhaps we should do some of the things we used to do when we were teenagers.'

John laughed and his imagination shifted into overdrive. He grabbed two small plastic cups and retrieved a bottle of Marques de Riscal Rioja Reserva 2008 that he and his lover had opened the previous night. They had failed to drink its entire contents due to the passion that had consumed their evening. John began to pour as he recalled some erotic moments from their past.

'Do you remember that time you phoned and convinced me to come round rather than go to the pub because your parents had gone out? You tied me to their bed. That's something we could recreate if you're feeling a little bit kinky. Or I could tie you up this time.'

His lover smiled and ran her finger seductively over his as she accepted the plastic cup of wine. She perched provocatively on the edge of the bed, crossed her legs and ran her free hand suggestively from her knee down to the strap of her high heels that wrapped around her ankle and back up her nylons again, never breaking eye-contact with John.

'But I don't want to leave scratch marks all over you again, not now that you're married. I was thinking more of a certain position that you thought wasn't possible until we tried it, and perhaps something we used to do together in the shower.'

John beamed an expectant smile, the couple's lustful memories provoking a feast of possibilities for the evening ahead. Then

232

suddenly, as John began to fill the second cup full of wine, the jovial face of his daughter Vicky appeared unexpectedly on the screen of his phone, causing John to jolt his hand in a panic and send intrusive red liquid spilling across the desk.

'Bloody hell! Vicky!'

Alarmed, John grabbed his phone, pulling its camera's focus close to his face, while urgently ushering his equally startled companion back into the bathroom with his unseen hand, her awkward heels impeding her flustered progress. Panicked, he tried to compose himself as red wine dripped intermittently onto his socks from the desk.

'Sorry love, you made me jump. I thought we'd ended the call.'

'No, silly; you'll never figure out technology, will you? I just put the phone down and left the call open while I answered the door. You left your phone on too. I've got to go because people have started coming to the party. I just wanted to say thank you again. Thanks so much for the tickets. I love you Dad. Bye!'

'Vicky! Hold on! Hold on!'

The screen on the phone went blank to confirm Vicky's departure. John sat on the bed in concerned silence for a moment. Had Vicky overheard the conversation between her father and his lover? John played the events of the past few minutes through in his mind. No, he thought. Definitely not. Vicky would never have chatted so cheerfully had she just caught her father red-handed, talking so explicitly. Much to his relief, he determined that both phones must have remained connected, but conveniently untouched by either party.

A slightly less seductive figure emerged cautiously from the bathroom, now in stocking feet and carrying her challenging shoes, opening the door fully only once John waved the offending phone aloft to confirm its now benign status.

'Did your daughter see or hear us?'

She perched on the edge of the bed beside John, seeking reassurance, her exterior broadcasting irresistibility, but her emotions in turmoil, suddenly detached from the planned passion for which she was dressed.

'No. Well, I didn't get to ask her as she had to go, but she wouldn't have acted as nonchalantly if... No, everything's fine.'

They both laughed in relief.

'Kind of killed the moment though, hasn't it?'

233

John took her hand, carefully examining the red nail polish that was one of many accessories that had so aroused his senses only a few minutes earlier. One finger at a time, he traced the contours of her hand, sighing regretfully as he mulled over how their relationship might have played out had they both made different choices over the years. He stared at her, searching for the perfect words to convey his feelings. John was poised to speak when a finger again rested across his lips.

'I know. You don't have to say anything. I know.'

She retrieved the two plastic cups, handing one to John and after a silent toast, they both sipped the smooth velvety liquid. They sat for a several minutes, contemplating the remainder of the evening, sensing the onset of a mild buzz as the wine gradually diminished and the alcohol took effect. After a while, she slipped her feet back into the eye-catching pair of high heels, stood up and walked the short distance to the door, which she opened, surprising John.

'What are you doing? Where are you going?'

Undeterred, she stepped outside to the corridor and beckoned John provocatively with a teasing index finger and a mischievous smile as the hotel room door closed between them. John grabbed a white plastic swipe card room key that had been spared a wine covering on the desk and hurriedly followed.

The second-floor landing appeared empty until John swung around to his right. There she stood, outside the door to the fire escape exit, further down the corridor, illuminated by fluorescent ceiling lighting, radiating the erotic beauty that had captivated John earlier when she first emerged from the bathroom. John walked towards her, as aroused as he was apprehensive. Two arms draped around his neck as she kissed him and whispered seductively in his ear, her warm breath a forgotten sensation from a time that seemed a world away sending a sharp tingle down his spine.

'I don't know about you, but the thrill of perhaps getting caught is really having an effect on me.'

Before John could respond, she knelt before him.

- - - - - - - - - -

234

'Mom, where are you going?'

'Out! Out, for the night, Vicky. Just try not to wreck the place while I'm gone.'

Vicky Garland was as shocked as she was delighted by her mother's unexpected and unexplained exit as the front door to their home slammed shut. She had begged her parents to approve a house party without adult supervision since the wish to host friends in celebration of her eighteenth birthday had first been voiced. Now, here she was, alone with Sophia and two of the desired male guests invited from the local pub, with the assurance of many more revellers and perhaps some unpredictable gate-crashers to come. It now promised to be a spectacular night.

Ellie Garland cursed the unresponsiveness of her remote car key fob, its battery long overdue for replacement, as she thumbed the button several agitated times before the indicator lights flashed and a gentle click signalled that the doors of her BMW 5-Series had opened. She slumped into the driver's seat as she tossed her mobile phone and handbag onto the empty seat beside her. She placed the key fob in a storage slot beside the gear lever and pressed the button that started and gently revved the two-litre turbocharged four-cylinder engine. Ellie sat back, rested her head against the cream-coloured leather sports seat and closed her eyes, searching for a moment of tranquillity. She sat there for perhaps five minutes, remaining as calm as the fury raging inside her would allow.

Her concentration was broken only when three inappropriately dressed teenage girls wandered up the driveway giggling, not noticing the plain middle-aged woman sat within the purring sleek vehicle, their excitement at arriving at the neighbourhood's fashionable Friday night house party blinding their vision to all around them. Ellie heard the chinking of an assortment of bottles of alcohol transported to the doorway in supermarket carrier bags with stretching handles. She opened her eyes to focus on the bargain bottle of Sainsbury's red wine she grasped with both hands. Unscrewing the top, she took as large a swig as she could stomach before coughing at the effects of the acidity. She pulled the lid off an empty travel mug sat in the centre console cup holder and roughly wiped the remaining few drops of the morning's coffee from inside with a paper napkin before emptying the contents of the wine bottle into the mug. Once the electric window had lowered on the driver's side, she hurled the empty bottle out onto her front lawn.

Ellie gripped the steering wheel angrily with both hands then without a destination in mind, engaged the gear lever and slowly drove away down the driveway, muttering under her breath.

'You know what Vicky? Do what the fuck you like to the house. Your father has wrecked the home, so it really doesn't matter anymore, does it?'

Chapter Thirty-Four

'You have to press the send button, boss.'

PC Tim Carrack was trying to be as helpful as he was sarcastic. If Detective Inspector Craig Jones would simply email his final report on the now apparently solved case of the mystery skeleton unearthed on Gas Street, the pair would be finished for the week and the younger policeman could rush off to meet the woman he had recently started dating. He was already half an hour late, but took solace in the fact she was content drinking in a pub nearby with friends to whom he would be introduced for the first time, if he ever managed to vacate Steelhouse Lane police station. He turned away in dismay as Craig instead saved the email in his drafts folder.

'Maybe I should hold onto this until Monday morning Crack, just to be sure. I want to sleep on it. Sure, it does the trick and solves the case, but it can wait until Monday. In fact, until Tuesday, since I'm taking the day off on Monday.'

PC Carrack shrugged. He hoped Craig had failed to notice him glance beyond his shoulder to spy the clock on the far wall, its hands ticking further past the meeting time he had arranged with his romantic liaison.

'Don't worry I won't keep you much longer. It's that bird from the pub the other night, isn't it? A bit of alright, she was.'

Tim rubbed both eyes with the base of his palms, expelling a wide-mouthed yawn as he wondered how long or short a time he was still expected to commit to the end of a long and exhausting week. They had solved the unearthed skeleton case, or so he thought. Their colleagues in Solihull had identified and arrested three youths who would now face far more serious charges than either of those apprehended had anticipated since Stephen Taylor had died, the hospital tubes and machines that had been keeping him alive now redundant. Tim was ready for the weekend to begin.

'Promise me one thing though Crack. Don't go marrying her. It's not worth the aggro; believe me. I thought my missus was the be-all and end-all when I was your age, younger even, but that's all youthful bollocks. When it comes down to it, you're much better off just looking after number one. None of that till death do us part shit.'

Tim reached optimistically for the jacket draped across the back of a nearby chair, but rested his elbows back on his desk as Craig picked up a cloth and began wiping clean the whiteboard detailing the timeline of missing Matt Douglass. He continued to talk as he slowly created a blank canvas.

'My wife's having an affair you know. I'm sure of it. She thinks I don't notice things, but I do. I'm a fucking detective, aren't I? Just the other day, she was wearing different coloured tights from the ones she'd worn when leaving home only a few hours earlier. She must think I'm a fucking idiot.'

Craig paused, hanging his head, his back to Tim as he faced the now vacant board mounted on the wall. Saying those words out loud, airing his frustrations for the first time to another soul, caused his previously infuriated grievance to become tinged with sadness. He sighed, defeated at the reality of his lost marriage. After staring at the floor for a short while, Craig turned slowly and smiled at his young constable.

'You're a good lad Crack. I don't mean to unload this on you and you shouldn't be missing your Friday night of fun because of me. It's just that, I got a text from a bloke I know today, owes me a favour or two. I think you know the sort. He's not a friend, more of an acquaintance, you might say. I had him sit in that pub in Shirley, the Saracen's Head, where one of our possible suspects John Garland is staying while he's up here from London. I paid for the bloke's beer for a couple of nights, so it was a top job as far as he was concerned. Anyway, earlier today he texted me a few times and descriptions from things he'd seen at the boozer. Last night he observed a woman fitting the description of my wife: slim, forties, brunette, 'killer dressed' he said. Getting it on with some bloke who fits the description of John Garland she was. Then they went off to the hotel at the back. Same woman, same bloke and similar deal tonight; they're there right now. And I'm sitting here working, like a cunt.'

Craig's relatively calm reaction to such an earth-shattering realisation surprised and in a sense, unnerved Tim. He would have expected the detective, whose moods and mannerisms he had come to know and predict, to rage and curse and storm into an uncontrolled frenzy. Instead, Craig appeared relaxed and contemplative.

'So, if my wife has rekindled the feelings she had for a former flame, just five minutes after he's showed his face after being gone for god knows how long, then that doesn't say much about my marriage, does it? There's been plenty of other opportunities for them this week as well, and I've had my suspicions. That's why I put that grass in the pub. So, if I think of something before Tuesday to tie John Garland to the skeleton crime scene, perhaps I'll have a reason to completely change that report before I email it to the top brass.'

Craig dug both hands into his suit trouser pockets and stood staring at Tim, who sat in silence, staring at the blank whiteboard, uncertain of how best to respond to his detective's discovery and apparent plans to prioritise personal retribution over what he had communicated was a genuinely solved case. Sensing his mood of conflict, Craig grabbed Tim's jacket from the back of the chair and handed it to the young constable.

'Anyway, young Crack, you be off. I just have a few more notes to scribble down here and then I'm done for the night too. Text me if there's any talent in the boozer hankering for a middle-aged miserable copper who is most likely going to get hammered drunk tonight. Oh, and thanks for listening.'

The door to the office closed. The eager Tim, grateful to be heading for the exit, sent an apologetic text to his waiting date as he hurried down the stairwell that would carry him out to the street quicker than if he waited for the slow-moving lift.

Alone in the office, Craig picked up a black washable marker pen and began composing an alternative theory to the one detailed in his pending report, the official line concluding that Matt Douglass had been disposed of and buried as a result of an organised crime dispute. Murdered in London, shipped back to Birmingham sans middle finger, which could possibly have been posted home earlier to deliver a warning, and his body concealed by a local criminal element not versed in engaging the assistance of the authorities in seeking to resolve such matters. He would be dismissed as a foot soldier casualty in a turf war of yesteryear. That was a plausible conclusion, one that would wash with those eager to put the case to bed. The local media hacks, titillated more by the headline-grabbing discovery than they were eager to solve the mystery, might press initially for resources to be poured into bringing the killer to justice. The police would shrug their shoulders and admit they had drawn a blank. The Silver Skeleton would soon fade from the headlines and besides, Craig and his colleagues had cemented firm enough relationships within the hierarchy of the journalistic fraternity to sufficiently influence the level of eagerness reporters might show in a crime of dwindling merit.

The Silver Skeleton unearthed on Gas Street would become a legend, perhaps even a myth over time.

Then there were the once influential crime families, whose power had diminished with the advent of city centre regeneration and the influx of overseas capital and franchise hotels, bars and restaurants replacing their mini empires. Their comfortable lives of retirement out beyond the suburbs were rarely probed or troubled these days, other than when documented by the occasional throwback magazine article, or revisionist book glorifying and exaggerating the crimes of decades gone by. It was like Ronnie Biggs meeting Jack Slipper again. Time to bury the hatchet and agree to call it a draw.

By emailing his report, Craig would choose not to lay the blame at the door of Stephen Taylor and his lover Paul Booth. Plausible though he considered the theory that the pair had murdered and buried Matt Douglass, he had no wish to expose that speculation beyond the confines of his office and a handful of suspected accomplices.

Yet there he stood, black marker in hand before a blank white board, mulling over new information that had come to light to cast doubt on the explanation provided by John Garland in the Three Horseshoes pub earlier that day. John claimed that he, Mike Sullivan and Andy Morris had listened to an improbable confession to the murder and removal and burial of the body of Matt Douglass professed by the now equally deceased Stephen Taylor. While the Taylor theory tied all the pieces together conveniently, it also cleared the remaining trio of any major wrongdoing. Craig had dug a little deeper, his inquisitive nature never satisfied, and he had unearthed some problematic inconsistencies that gnawed at a suspicion of conspiracy. On his computer, he pulled up three recently retrieved archived driving license records from the DVLA in Swansea and transferred the information the white board, circling it in red marker pen.

Neither Stephen Taylor nor his supposed accomplice, the equally conveniently dead Paul Booth, possessed driving licenses at the time of the alleged murder, August 29, 1986. Paul passed his test some three years later and records indicated that Stephen had never so much as applied for a provisional license and was known to be a regular bus and train traveller. Mike Sullivan, on the other hand, held a license and John Garland had failed his first test only weeks earlier, meaning either could have driven the body to its Gas Street resting place, but not Taylor or Booth. Sully even owned a car, one in which Craig had himself once been a passenger that fateful night at Peacocks.

Craig scrawled additional information that potentially incriminated the trio, opening each line with a tidy bullet-point, focusing primarily on John and Sully.

- *Placed at possible crime scene by witness Winston Roberts.*
- *Attended Smiths gig along with Matt Douglass on night of disappearance.*
- *Held keys to office building where skeletal remains were discovered.*
- *Ability to drive and access to a car.*
- *Motive... bullied.*
- *Known associates of Matt Douglass.*
- *Who has the finger and why?*
- *Fucking my wife?*

Craig stopped and wiped away the final point before snapping a photo of the list with his smart phone. Then he cleaned the board completely, pouring a splash of a strong-smelling liquid chemical onto the cloth to ensure all traces of the notes that contradicted the report he was delaying submitting were eliminated from even the faintest view.

He eased his jacket over two aching shoulders, popped a sharp mint into his mouth to counter the taste of stale coffee and loosened the large-knotted tie he still loathed wearing, even after such a long period of time on the job. As Craig slipped his phone into the inside pocket of his crumpled jacket and caught the armpit aroma of a long shift, his mobile buzzed. Reluctantly, he retrieved the device, cursing himself for being too conscientious at the end of a tiring day. Craig was pleasantly surprised to see a text message not related to work, but from PC Tim Carrack. He was even more delighted by its content.

Boss. She has a friend who ain't too choosy! At O'Neill's til about 11.

- - - - - - - - - -

'You can't beat a nice cup of tea, can you, mate?'

Andy had to agree. The smooth taste of PG Tips, not sugared like Sully's brew that had barely dissolved three heaped spoons full, served as a soothing means to end an arduous day. He had been relieved when Sully filled up and plugged in a Kenmore electric kettle when they arrived home, not because he could not stomach any more of the bland American bottled beer that remained in the fridge, but because his alcoholic intake of the past few days had been more than double the total he might normally consume in a full month. The entire reunion of old friends seemed to have taken place in local pubs. Both sipped their warm comfort drink in appreciative silence, each still digesting the stark reality that one of their best friends, Stephen Taylor, had taken his final breath through a hospital life-support machine tube earlier that day.

They had spent the afternoon with John and Siobhan, alternating between grieving and debating how best to clear up Stephen's personal affairs, from informing colleagues and acquaintances of his demise, to the question over what would become of the now vacant property he owned. In the absence of any next of kin, Siobhan had discovered she was the executor of his will and had arranged for its reading the following week. John, Sully and Andy had broken the harrowing news of Stephen's death to Siobhan in person, relieving her husband Craig of the duty he routinely dreaded as he returned to the office to work a long shift. The carefully chosen words Sully had prepared proved unnecessary. Just the sight of the solemn trio, arriving unexpectedly at her front door on a Friday afternoon, delivered the message she had anticipated, given Stephen's critical condition, but dreaded nonetheless.

Andy blew gently on the surface of his tea, cooling the recently boiled brew.

'Do you think Siobhan and John have, you know?'

Sully smiled in response and shook his head.

'Nah, mate, I think John would if he got the chance, in fact I know he would, but Siobhan moved on, a long time ago.'

Sully placed a spoon on the glass-topped coffee table between them, creating a small puddle of tea before slurping a cautious amount of the swirling brew as it slightly burnt his lips.

'I shouldn't tell you this, so this is in confidence, okay?'

Andy placed his mug on the same low table that divided Sully's living room and shifted on the settee, perching on the edge in anticipation of his friend's pending revelation.

'So, I saw Siobhan out in town a few weeks ago. Occasionally I meet with clients of mine for a drink, to go over their financials in a more casual setting. So, we're in some boozer in town, like I said, and Siobhan is in there with a handful of work colleagues and they look like they've had quite a few. It turns out they've been in there since knocking off work early to make the most of happy hour. It wasn't long after the pâté incident at their barbeque, so since she's in such a lubricated mood, when we get chatting after my client leaves, I mention Craig's unfortunate appetiser. Well, to cut a long story short, that opens the floodgates and she can't stop moaning about her bloody useless husband. A few drinks later, by which time she's had way too many, her friends ask me if I'll make sure she gets home in a taxi since I live not far from her. So, sure, I agree to help out and no sooner are we in the cab than she starts sobbing about Craig and how she's been seeing some bloke she used to work with and I'm suddenly the proverbial shoulder to cry on. I'm there soaking up enough confessions to embarrass a priest and the cabbie is enjoying a right earful too. But get this; she's been seeing this bloke for almost three years. Three years! She's all concerned that Craig is going to find out, then starts laughing hysterically that she's married to a detective who can't see what's going on right under his nose. It was an eye-opener; I'll tell you that much.'

Andy shook his head at the lurid disclosure. As he sipped on his cooling tea, he wondered why so many married couples he knew self-inflicted torture in this manner. He much preferred his simple single existence in the relatively remote calm of the Welsh seaside. Siobhan and Craig appeared to be at each other's throats and the relationship between John and his wife Ellie was apparently irrevocably strained. Only Sully and his better half seemed content, although their existence ran along parallel lines, crossing only it seemed, from what Andy observed, for mealtimes, parenting duties and when tucked up in the matrimonial bed. Each indulged in different interests, divided household chores and moved in separate social circles. Perhaps that was their secret to marital bliss, but a sad solution if true. Andy's deliberation was broken by Sully shuffling back to the kitchen, peering into an almost empty mug on the way and returning with a warm teapot insulated by a knitted cosy in the blue and white colours of Birmingham City. Andy breathed in the refreshing aroma of the richly steeped brew as Sully poured and mixed in a carefully measured compliment of milk from a small chilled cardboard carton, clammy to the touch having been left beside the fridge on the kitchen counter.

'I owe you an apology mate.'

Sully's words bemused and intrigued his friend. He pointed in the direction of the small tin canister that sat atop the wooden mantelpiece and sat back, stirring a generously heaped teaspoon of sugar into his own second helping of tea. Andy purposefully dunked a custard crème and caught a few falling crumbs with a cupped hand as he bit into the biscuit.

'You mean the tin?'

'Yeah, mate. The other day, I didn't mean to snap, but after we'd just been to see Stephen and all that, well, I just wasn't in a good mood. So, I'm sorry. Go take a butcher's, if you like. Oh, but try not to drop the lid this time. Those rusty hinges have been dodgy for quite a while, so you have to be careful with it.'

Andy rose gingerly from the settee, shooting an inquisitive glace at Sully, who ushered him on with a wave of the back of his hand. Andy lifted the canister cautiously and prized open the detachable lid, setting it down on the mantel. Inside, just as there had been a few days earlier, were an assortment of five and ten pound notes and a scattering of pound coins. It was again the cigar-shaped item, wrapped in tissue paper that intrigued him. Just as Andy reached inside to remove the cylindrical object, Sully spoke.

'That's Matt Douglass's finger.'

Andy reeled back instantly in shock, dropping the tin, which clattered loudly as it bounced and came to rest on the concrete hearth, spilling notes and coins that rolled in random directions across the polished wooden floor of the Sullivan living room. Andy stood rigid in the pose of an animal frozen the glare of car headlights, staring at the floor and the horrific finger-shaped item that came to rest beside his feet. Sully sat back clapping and laughing raucously, his tea slopping from the sides of his filled mug as he kicked the legs of the table in front of him.

'Bloody hell, Andy! I'm just messing about, mate. Your face! You should see yourself. That's not a finger; it's dope you dope. Drugs, you know, marijuana.'

Andy bent down cautiously, retrieved the object and sniffed it tentatively, its distinctive aroma confirming Sully's revelation. He tossed the small package into Sully's lap and returned to the settee, perplexed as he took a reassuring sip of tea.

'Jesus Sully, you almost gave me a fucking heart attack!'

Andy listened to a jovial Sully's explanation that his son smoked the weed for medicinal purposes to help combat a recently diagnosed panic disorder, the symptoms of which had apparently dogged him since his junior school years. The nervousness had contributed to him twice failing his driving test. Sully and his wife would occasionally slip spare change and the odd note into the canister to fund the practice, which was frowned upon by most and remained illegal. The remedy had proven effective, so was endorsed enthusiastically by Sully, who had sourced a regular supplier of the soft drug, which he had quickly discovered was readily available in most local pubs on most evenings.

Still agitated by Sully's prank, Andy ignored him and grabbed the television remote control and flicked through channels until he came across an old Clint Eastwood movie from the seventies airing on a retro movies channel. Both watched as an out of control relic of latter day policing relentlessly pursued his criminal prey. Only when the adverts interrupted their viewing did Andy speak.

'Dirty Harry, remember?'

Sully did indeed remember. The 1971 classic had provided each with an alibi when it was broadcast on terrestrial television in the early hours of the morning of Saturday, August the 30th 1986. At a push, Andy could still recall the full listing of programmes from the Radio Times from that weekend, having imprinted the shows on his memory to serve as his indelible alibi.

Now he wanted to grieve again, not only for Stephen Taylor, but also for Matt Douglass and for their carefree teenage years that ended that fateful night. Andy might have escaped the prison sentence the four assailants who committed a frenzied murder all those years ago rightfully deserved, but he felt he had lived a life confined to terror, constantly in fear that the felony of his past would be unearthed and incarcerate the twilight chapter of his existence. Andy closed his eyes and expelled a relieved sigh, appreciating that the discovery of the skeleton of the victim and a lie apparently believed by the investigating officer appeared to have at last granted him parole from his life of trepidation. He sipped more tea before looking inquiringly at Sully.

'Do you believe John?'

Sully shrugged, nonplussed, before Andy elaborated.

'It's just that, if I'm honest, I've realised John is a pretty accomplished liar. It's been great seeing him after all these years, don't get me wrong, but there's something about him I just don't trust. He was always a bit of a scoundrel, but he's also really dishonest from what I've learned this week.'

Sully motioned for Andy to mute Dirty Harry's gunfire that intruded from the television. His mood was now more thoughtful as he encouraged Andy to continue.

'If you go back to that summer with Siobhan, he was also still seeing Rachel whenever he got the chance. Now he's cheating on his wife with Rachel and it isn't just a casual affair, but a full-scale operation that includes friends lying for him, football matches he pretends to watch and even a flat he owns in London. He's convinced Craig that we didn't kill Matt Douglass, which I'm grateful for, don't get me wrong, but I almost believe that lie about Stephen and Paul Booth myself, the way he tells it, and I was there kicking the shit out of Matt along with everyone else. What if the other part of the explanation is a lie as well? What if John moved the body? What if he never actually met Stephen in a pub near London? What if John has the missing finger?'

Sully sat back, caressing the warm mug in both hands, resting his feet on the edge of the coffee table, as he pondered. He sipped and swallowed, blew across the surface of the hot tea and took another thoughtful sip.

'I dunno, mate. He has no reason to lie, does he? I mean.'

Andy cut Sully off, having debated John's explanation at length since it had come to light.

'Of course he does! If the skeleton remains hidden then he has no reason to worry, but since its discovery, if he's the guilty one and if he does have the finger, which by now of course will have decomposed down to the bone, he's in the shit.

'What if Craig had investigated the discovery further and started to suspect John who had a key to Silver's and who could drive, even though he hadn't passed his test at that time? Then all this would have come down on John. You and me had solid alibis. John even told us he didn't go straight home. What if he went to move the body and cut off the finger?'

Sully was nodding in agreement.

'You're right, I remember now he said he went to try and see Siobhan. Bloody hell Andy, you've got a good memory. I'd forgotten that. Either way, though, if Craig has accepted what John told him earlier, we're in the clear, you and me at least. We don't have to worry. If John did go down for this, for all his faults and lies, he wouldn't take us down with him. I'm sure of that.'

Andy rose and began to pick up the scattering of coins and the fallen notes, stuffing them back into the tin box, which Sully topped off with the rolled marijuana. Andy laughed as he replaced the lid, clicking it shut tight before returning the container to its rightful place on the mantel.

'Finger in the box. Jesus, Sully, you gave me a right scare. Anyway, if John is lying, you have to give him credit. Neither of the two he's accusing can contradict his story from the grave, can they? I'd love to know the truth about the missing finger, but to be honest, I'm happy to let that little mystery remain unsolved.'

- - - - - - - - - -

Rachel Turner sat upright in bed with a white duvet pulled up to her neck to conceal her nudity. She smiled slyly as she followed John Garland's awkward manoeuvre around the compact hotel room, watching him almost trip over her high heels and numerous items of discarded lingerie.

'I think some of the other guests might be calling reception to request a free night's stay, you know. I think we were probably a little loud just then.'

John smirked as he returned from the bathroom. He joined Rachel beneath the bed covers and probed at the pillow that had felt too spongy to guarantee a sound sleep during the previous five nights. Rachel slid down the bed and snuggled her lover, resting her head on his shoulder as she traced meaningless shapes on his chest with her finger.

'So, was that the truth, what you said you told Sully and Andy about Stephen moving the body? You never told me that before. It doesn't seem like something Stephen would do.'

John peered down and caught Rachel's eye as she looked up inquiringly, soliciting a response.

'Yeah, of course it was the truth.'

John paused, combing his fingers gently through Rachel's soft brown hair.

'Why would I lie? Besides, Craig believes it, so this whole sorry mess is over now. He knows one thing, will tell his superiors another, which is what they want to hear and that's the end of it.'

Rachel rested her head, again contemplating the explanation her lover had given her after she had travelled up from London to comfort him, as he had requested over the phone in a despairing moment of sorrow. Rarely had she returned to Birmingham since moving away in the late eighties. She had visited the hospital to say a tearful farewell to Stephen earlier that day and before she had even finished exploring the much-altered landscape of the city she once called home, received a text from John with the heart-breaking news that their old friend had died.

'I don't know, it just doesn't fit Stephen, that's all. The finger, especially, doesn't seem like something he'd do. Can you imagine? Hacking a finger off a dead body and then keeping it? Ugh!'

Rachel shuddered as she contemplated the act of desecration. She wondered how the butcher who sliced it free might store a dead finger, its rancid flesh rotting slowly down to the bone. Or perhaps the perpetrator mutilated Matt Douglass purely as an act of aggression or revenge rather than to claim a perverse trophy and disposed of the digit to distance him from any incriminating evidence. She eased herself slowly away from John and reached for one of the plastic wine cups sat on a small shelf beside the compact double bed that now held fresh tap water. She sipped slowly as John stirred slightly, his drifting into a long overdue deep sleep interrupted only briefly as he rolled onto his side and faced away from her.

Rachel stared at her lover uneasily, concerned at the vulnerability of his explanations and the bullish, almost arrogant manner in which he had delivered them. She knew John well enough to detect his devious streak, which had become his second nature, in order to successfully conceal their ongoing affair. A carefully crafted measure of deceit now seemed to have been liberally applied to fashion the explanation of how Matt Douglass came to rest in the basement of a city centre office building. Rachel rocked the switch on the small light that illuminated her side of the bed. As she plunged the room into darkness, she slipped down slowly beneath the duvet, careful not to disturb John, who was now snoring lightly. She wondered what had truly transpired that fateful night at the tail end of August 1986.

Chapter Thirty-Five

Early hours of Saturday, August 30, 1986

Gas Street, Birmingham

Stephen Taylor trembled as he pulled smoke nervously through the filter of his fourth and final Players No. 6 cigarette from an emptied packet he had discarded through the open window of the passenger's seat of a red Mark II Ford Escort. The crumpled box laid beside three chain-smoked nubs, littering a Gas Street pavement among a scattering of similarly discarded chip papers, newspapers, broken bottles and crushed beer cans. He could afford to leave nothing, not even a butt end, in the stolen vehicle. Stephen jumped as an anonymous sound in the distance jabbed at the frayed nerves that were causing him to tremble. Holding the cigarette delicately between his lips, he folded his arms and frantically rubbed both biceps, wishing his hands would generate a semblance of warmth to offset the damp chill of a sodden shirt that had been soaked by a torrential downpour less than an hour ago. He craned his neck out of the window desperately hoping to see the front door of Silver's office block open soon and a figure emerge. He had been inside there himself, ten minutes or so earlier, spooked by an unexpected last breath that had released itself from the crumpled corpse of Matt Douglass.

The movement of a car traversing Broad Street caused Stephen to jerk his head anxiously up to glance in the rear-view mirror and then over his shoulder to confirm that a potentially inquisitive passer-by was not driving along the darkened side road in his direction. The combination of a parked car with its engine running and a feint glow rising from the basement window of Silver's would surely intrigue anyone who might stumble upon the dubious scene. Stephen tried to reassure himself that apart from the occasional remote flicker of car headlights, Birmingham city centre was soundly asleep at a little after three-thirty in the morning. The fear of being discovered and the reason for his suspicious loitering sure to be exposed agitated his already troubled disposition.

'Come on, for crying out loud. What's taking so long?'

Two gloved hands rummaged impatiently through a cutlery draw. The kitchen inside Silver's office block seemed to house every known utensil other than the desired steak knife. There was an eclectic assortment of spoons, forks and knives of varying sizes, but nothing sharp enough to slice open human flesh, let alone mutilate a body. Leathered fingers frantically probed the various sections of a wooden divider, but failed to unearth a suitably jagged implement.

'Nutcrackers! I guess they'll have to do. Maybe that and an ordinary knife.'

The kitchen drawer was closed carefully, deliberately, leaving no hint of a covert middle of the night visitor. The faintest of footprints were wiped clean by a white sleeveless t-shirt that had been removed hurriedly from an old brown suitcase found inside the Ford Escort. No visible traces remained of the brief intrusion, transferred instead to the now grimy garment.

The discarded body of Matt Douglass lay crudely at the foot of a set of creaking stairs that were sparsely covered by ancient musty-smelling threadbare carpet treads. The occasional step had absorbed the blow of the lifeless falling body as it careered down the stairs. The final leg of an unceremonious journey to its ultimate resting place had seen Matt's twisted corpse shoved callously down to the basement of Silver's where he landed with a crack as some bone or other broke on impact. He came to rest just feet away from a hole in the ground that was to be filled with a sloppy mass of freshly poured concrete the next morning. From his mouth, a golden crowned tooth had been jarred loose and spilled out onto the floor. The glistening fang was pocketed as a souvenir.

The owner of the office, Tony Silver, had bemoaned the sheer volume of a cavernous hole, almost four feet deep and twice as far across and wide that needed to be filled and the concrete set before he could put down carpet and install several rows of metal shelving to serve as valuable storage space. Rubble and debris gathered from all corners of the basement and from the rear of the building that occasionally spilled on to the Gas Street canal towpath had been dumped into the cavity, filling perhaps half the chasm. Cracked and splintered wooden pallets sat atop the crude filler, awaiting the incoming concrete. The finished surface would be smoothed to perfection, and a month or so later, once completely set, the entire floor would be painted an anonymous grey to match the room's equally uninspiring walls.

Rigor mortis had stiffened the right arm of Matt Douglass, which was now pinned to the ground by a buckled leather boot, which stamped on his wrist to steady the limb. The jagged metal teeth of the borrowed nutcrackers were gripped around the base of the chubby middle finger on Matt's right hand. With each handle squeezed tightly together, a slow pull on the seized finger created a brittle cracking sound. The bone was eased crudely from the socket of the knuckle. Carefully applied force, in sharp contrast to the urge to viciously tear the finger from his hand, and a waggling of the nutcracker popped the bone loose to the sound of more splintering. Still pinning the arm to the cold stone floor and pulling the finger taut, the simple dinner knife, despite its bluntness, was effective enough to puncture the stretched skin and flesh surrounding the knuckle. After a few stabs, the full finger broke loose, causing its butcher to stagger backwards unsteadily, stopping just short of teetering into the ominous looming hole in the floor. Held aloft, illuminated by a dull single bare light bulb, the amputated digit made for a gruesome prize.

'There! No more fishy fingers for you, you bastard.'

- - - - - - - - - -

Stephen Taylor breathed a palpable sigh of relief as the front door to Silver's offices opened and closed as quickly as it did quietly. He hurriedly wound up the passenger side window and leaped out to the pavement, his foot crushing the blue and white striped cigarette packet he had discarded earlier. He fumbled the car keys nervously, almost frantically, as he unlocked the boot, two rusty hinges disturbing an eerie silence on Gas Street as they creaked loudly. Stephen was clearly agitated and annoyed with John Garland.

'What the hell took you so long? You said you'd be quick, but I was out here for ages like a sitting duck. If the police had come by, we'd have been.'

Stephen's voice trailed off as he tugged at the edges of a dog-eared material that lined boot of the improvised Ford Escort hearse that had transported Matt Douglass to his final resting place. They planned to ditch the lining, along with any other items that tied the car to the deceased, in the canal that ran parallel to Gas Street, just the other side of an imposing stone wall. John had used all the threadbare blankets liberated from Stephen's father's disused garden shed to camouflage the body within the hole in the office. Stephen watched as John appeared to unwrap a small object from a soiled white t-shirt and stuff it hurriedly into his jeans pocket before opening the car's curb-side rear door and return the article of clothing to the brown suitcase as he hauled it from the back seat. Before Stephen could challenge John regarding the identity of the mystery item, a car turned off Broad Street and made its way gradually in their direction, two slightly offset yellowish headlights leaping from dipped to main beam, illuminating and incriminating the two dazed figures.

From the open boot, John grabbed a long black-painted metal bar that formed part of the car jack and gripped it menacingly in his right hand, holding it concealed from view by his side as the vehicle approached.

'No John! What are you going to do, kill someone else?'

John shot Stephen a disbelieving glance as the car came to a halt.

'Need a hand, lads? Everything ok?'

The driver was a middle-aged man, who smiled from inside a smart Jaguar as he offered some assistance. A gust of alcohol-fuelled breath wafted over the concerned pair.

'No, there's no problem mate, just fixed a flat tyre. We're okay, thanks.'

John raised the metal bar as he spoke, to illustrate the invented inconvenience. Looking dishevelled and exasperated, each covered in dirt and blood that had dried to the extent that the dim streetlights disguised its appearance as that of more grime, they both appeared convincing. Stephen had nudged the out of place suitcase with his foot to beneath the Escort where it was hidden from view. The Good Samaritan had little reason to question their explanation.

'Oh, hard luck lads. That's no fun on a miserable night like tonight.'

John agreed and threw the bar into the boot where it landed with a frustrated clang.

'I know. Luckily, I think we're done, just before the heavens look like they're about to open again.'

The man waved farewell and beeped his horn twice as he drove away, instigating a brief moment of panic. Once his car had faded from view, John and Stephen urgently retrieved the suitcase and tore free the boot liner. They hurried along the towpath to sink the final pieces of evidence in Gas Street Basin. With the putrid waters of the Worcester and Birmingham Canal, they washed away the betraying marks of murder that stained their skin. They would drown all assorted items that linked them with Matt Douglass, which for good measure included the jack and accompanying iron bar.

Chapter Thirty-Six

Ellie Garland sat calmly, axe in hand. She stared solemnly, not focusing on the souvenirs and artefacts that were the travelogue of her husband John's numerous overseas business ventures of the past three decades, but staring blankly through them. There was a boomerang, a wooden Tanzanian drum with a taut goatskin head, porcelain from China, silk from the Jim Thompson House in Bangkok, an Irish Hurley and even a piece of the Berlin Wall, its authenticity debatable. The confines of his home office were crammed with photographs, memories, maps, posters, and antique paintings, all of them apparently more important in John's eyes than the one thing Ellie considered of more worth; their marriage. Even their daughter Vicky had shown more respect for her father's office than the remainder of the family home, its door securely closed and its contents immune to the carefree damage that had been inflicted upon several rooms during Vicky's raucous eighteenth birthday party the previous night. Ellie no longer cared. She had chosen to vacate the premises before the frivolities kicked into high gear and had now returned to a scene apparently abandoned by Vicky, her partner in crime Sophia and any other revellers who might have been guilty of such carefree partying. They were nowhere to be found, but Ellie had other things on her mind.

In one quick and decisive motion, she swung the axe, which John used to occasionally chop logs to fuel the open fire in their mock Tudor living room, in an arc above her and brought the steel head crashing down, driving it angrily into the target of her frustration. The axe tore through the tortoise-shaped Kerala wooden box that sat in the middle of John's large mahogany office desk. The teak antique, edged in brass decoration, which John had nurtured carefully home from a visit to India years before, splintered into countless pieces that shattered across the room. The carefully crafted artefact, previously securely locked by a brass key that was always closely guarded upon John's person, was opened unceremoniously.

Ellie wasn't finished. She gripped the axe with both hands and with a force that almost threw her off balance, hurled the weapon in the direction of the wall at the opposite end of the office. It came to rest with perfect if unintended precision, embedded in John's forehead having shattered the glass protecting a prized photograph of him shaking hands with the famous manager of some or other football team that John's company had sponsored more out of fandom than business acumen.

Ellie surveyed the deep gash that the axe had torn through John's pristine desk and the remains of the Kerala box, which had been destroyed almost beyond recognition. Previously, she had avoided the reality that every dark facet of his clandestine life she suspected lived within that box. Now those hidden secrets were exposed to the outside world and, more importantly, awaited her prying eyes.

Ellie had already convinced herself that John indulged in occasional liaisons with Siobhan Jones, the woman she would mockingly paint as his first and only true love to sometimes spike their frequent arguments. She had no proof of course, but a work colleague had conveniently sat in close enough earshot of John and an attractive brunette with a mild Brummie accent at a Café Nero in Mayfair several months earlier to report back her concerns to Ellie. She had tolerated the affair and considered her own occasional infidelity a suitable form of revenge in response to John's continued indiscretion. Fuck John, thought Ellie. If he could have his little tart on the side, then so could she. Her flings were meaningless and proved to be unfulfilling, but they fit the bill perfectly where the purpose of vengeance was concerned.

And now, before her, there she was. Siobhan Jones, or Murphy, or whatever the fuck she was called. Ellie had never so much as laid eyes on a photograph of her before. She was the slut that was sleeping with her husband. There were photos of her in a cosy flat in London, its location betrayed by the quintessential view that only one of the many picturesque squares that were dotted around the more salubrious edges of the capital offered. The initials R.T. were scrawled on the back of the first of several photos of an erotic tone that Ellie viewed and then tossed aside. She was disgusted at her husband's betrayal that seemed to have run a longer course than even she had suspected, based on the changing fashions and haircuts of the cheating couple in the series of risqué photographs. Clearly John and his lover had indulged in secret liaisons for the past few years, if not longer. She had always wondered and worried what Siobhan looked like. She spat on one photo of the attractive brunette, slimmer and taller than she, wearing provocative lingerie that had no doubt served to indulge her husband in a night of illicit lustful romance.

Beside the photos, she spied a necklace looped through an expensive looking heart-shaped piece of silver jewellery. She pulled it closer with disdain so that she could decipher the initials *JG & SM* that were etched into the trinket.

Ellie fought back bitter tears, wounded by the betrayal of the man who had willingly signed the standard registry office contract betrothing his undivided loyalty to his new wife and soon to be born child back in the nineties with a delighted lying smile on his face. She tore the photos of John and his lover in two and then in two again and again until she could obliterate them no more. Her instinct was to destroy every one of them, consigning the indelible memories to a shredded grave, but Ellie controlled her rage. She put four or five aside. She thought she might have plans for them.

Ellie retrieved what appeared to be a handful of meaningless items that had spilled from the box. There was a worn old key ring depicting a cartoon rooster and tasteless wording that read 'Bionic Cock' around the edges of the fob. There were three keys attached, of no apparent relevance, though one of them appeared to be a car's ignition key. Ellie put them aside, along with the handful of surviving photos of her husband and his lover. A faded old ticket stub from a concert at the Birmingham Odeon to see John's favourite band The Smiths was added to the pile, along with another anonymous key, this one loose and unbeknown to Ellie, still able to open the ageing front door to the former Silver's offices on Gas Street.

Then Ellie probed a dog-eared envelope that had fallen from the damaged desk to the office floor, coming to rest at the foot of a bookshelf that housed volumes of catalogues relevant to John's business. She peered curiously inside as she bent to retrieve it, brushing off dust that had built up on the wooden floor. The thin adhesive on the envelope, which appeared never to have been licked, had eroded with time and was likely as old as the browned newspaper clippings it held. Ellie recognised the name in the headlines. The stories told of a missing teenager, Matt Douglass, and his anxious mother, frustrated that the authorities were ignoring her pleas to search for her son. Ellie wondered why John would have saved and concealed these clippings from his youth, along with the other random items. Were they all linked somehow, all parts of a mysterious puzzle? Two pages from an old issue of the Radio Times were folded neatly beside the newspaper cuttings. Ellie noted the date of the television listing matched the date of the Smiths gig: August 29, 1986. These surely must be the pieces of a puzzle, perhaps ones that would prove incriminating if in the wrong hands.

Intrigued, Ellie delved further into the remnants of the shattered Kerala box and discovered an envelope she had missed, not as old as the one she had found previously, taped to what used to be the bottom of the wooden container. She peeled it free and noted it was oddly labelled *The Love Nest*. The startling content, which Ellie recognised as a property deed, leapt from the pages as she read. She scanned the information quicker than was possible to fully digest the unbelievable revelation that her husband apparently secretly and deviously owned a second property in London. She sat back in John's imposing leather office chair, stunned by the disclosure of a legal document that now trembled in her hand. She slammed the paperwork on the table, shaking her head in disbelief as she retreated from the desk, her feet pedalling the castors backwards until she came to an abrupt halt against the wall of the office. She wept, almost silently, uncontrollably.

Ellie might have sat there for fifteen minutes, perhaps longer, coming to terms with the evidence before her. She cautiously picked up the deed again and deliberately this time, explored the information.

Ellie was numb. Did her husband have the tart from the photographs she again viewed with disdain holed up in a swanky London flat? The deed was dated from a summer when John had cancelled the Garland family's planned annual holiday to the Greek islands, citing unexpected financial difficulties blighting his previously profitable business. Ellie recalled she had been shocked by John's apparently plummeting revenues that year, but accepted his explanation and sensible fiscal decision to instead enjoy a long weekend break with their daughter on the Isle of Wight. Clearly his funding for the now revealed love nest had been sourced at the expense of his family's pleasure.

When on earth did he find time to lead such a double life between raising his own family and the pressures of work and long hours at the office, wondered Ellie? She laughed, mocking herself as much as acknowledging the absurdity of the realisation that John had probably rarely stayed late at the office. Of course, his overtime hours were spent in the clutches of his lover, and most likely, so were many of the Saturday afternoons when he purported to be following the weekly fortunes of Fulham Football Club. Ellie tossed the property deed onto the pile of papers unearthed from the wooden box in disgust.

She felt defeated. She cast her mind back to a Saturday afternoon the winter before last when she saw on television that a match John was attending had been abandoned at half time due to the sudden failure of the ground's floodlights. That evening, John had sauntered in through the front door of their family home, bemoaning the lack of quality on show, much to her confusion. Ellie had assumed that her husband and his fellow season ticket holder friend Dom must have ventured elsewhere in London to get their football fix and that the alternative match had proven disappointing. Now she suspected she knew better.

Ellie shifted uneasily in her seat as she tried to decipher the magnitude of the discoveries as they related to her marriage, which as far as she was concerned, had now dissolved beyond saving. As she stared at the floor, contemplating the fate of the pile of potentially incriminating evidence she had amassed, her eye caught sight of an item beneath the desk she realised must have been ejected from the Kerala box as it was burst open. She retrieved it gradually with her foot, bent down and inspected the small light tan coloured bag, which measured only a few inches in size. She sat it cautiously upon the damaged desk. Ellie laughed at the jovial moustachioed cartoon character depicted on the miniature sack, which provided a briefly pleasant recollection from her childhood that was in stark contrast to the bitterly dark mood that engulfed her. She had completely forgotten about Gold Nuggets, a yellow-coloured bubble gum that was sold as pretend small pieces of the sifted precious metal in scaled down versions of the sacks prospectors used to gather their spoils during the American Gold Rush. Like most kids of her age, many years previously she had saved the small sacks once the sugary candy had been chewed and discarded and used them to store trinkets and cheap plastic jewellery. Measuring only a few inches high and wide, they had also been ideal for concealing private and secret artefacts.

Ellie anxiously eased apart the yellow drawstrings that were pulled tight and hesitated as she began to turn the sack upside down to spill the contents onto John's desk. She was confident she would strike neither stale golden flakes of bubble gum, nor shiny carats of any worth. Yet gold did come tumbling out. Ellie cringed at the grisly sight of a tarnished tooth, capped in gold. Why on earth would John have kept and concealed such a hideous item?

Then she shook the small sack, completely emptying its remaining contents.

For a moment, Ellie was intrigued by what appeared to be three small bone fragments, but then her discovery caused her to reel back from the desk in shock and disgust. She stared in disbelief at what was indeed a grotesque collection of human bones. In biological terms, which she could still remember from her years at university, they were the distal, middle and proximal phalanges. Instinctively, and more significantly, based on the information John had shared in his texts and emails, and what she had read on the Birmingham Mail website, Ellie knew they were the three joints that formed the missing amputated middle finger of Matt Douglass.

Chapter Thirty-Seven

Ellie Garland was expressionless as she gazed at the polite but slightly agitated FedEx representative. He was almost thirty minutes overdue for his lunch break, and behind the indecisive woman holding an overnight delivery package stood a line of three customers he would be expected to serve before he could tuck into the cheese and pickle sandwiches he had prepared at home earlier that morning. Ellie clutched the package hesitantly.

'If you'd like to consider a cheaper option, it could arrive later next week, rather than on Monday.'

Ellie bit her bottom lip, staring the young man between the eyes, still uncertain and still protecting the purple, orange and white box, which she held tightly to her chest, both forearms crossed and holding it firmly in place.

'Perhaps you'd like to wait over to the side for a minute while you decide and let me serve these other people?'

Ellie snapped out of the trance and spun around suddenly, apologising profusely to the man behind her, who had been watching the hands of a gaudy oversized metallic wristwatch tick by in frustration. A middle-aged woman behind him was clearly exasperated, while a man at the rear of the queue, dressed in a sharp blue suit, sighed in defeat as he glanced again at the screen of a smart phone and chose to vacate the line that had not shortened since his arrival.

'Oh, yes, I'm sorry, so sorry. You go ahead, all of you, both of you. I'll wait. Wait over here.'

Ellie all but jumped to one side, smiling and nodding again, apologetically, to only minor acknowledgement. A heavy frown returned as she reviewed the box she clutched in both hands. The label was addressed to *Detective Inspector Craig Jones, Steelhouse Lane Police Station, Birmingham, B4 6NW*. Inside were photographs, newspaper clippings, a concert ticket, a tasteless key ring and assorted keys. Most incriminatingly of all, packed cautiously within protective bubble wrap, were a gold tooth and the three bone fragments of a middle finger, its skin and flesh long since decomposed. Ellie had chosen not to include a cover letter, believing the contents would speak for themselves when examined by curious law enforcement, though she had included a letterhead from her husband John's company, its logo and business address embossed on high-quality paper stock. When the FedEx clerk had insisted that the package must include the sender's particulars, Ellie had fabricated both the name and the address, which she listed as the clandestine flat her husband owned on Tavistock Square.

Ellie stared forlornly at the package. Her concentration was broken by the voice of the young man behind the counter, who had served the two waiting customers. His patience had thinned considerably.

'Hello? Hello? I don't mean to be rude, but are you going to send that or not? I'm sorry, but I'm starving and I'm ready to go on my lunch break.'

Ellie looked at him blankly and then returned her gaze to the box that she gripped tentatively in both hands. She bit her bottom lip and shrugged uncertain as to whether or not she should mail the incriminating package.

The End.

Lightning Source UK Ltd.
Milton Keynes UK
UKOW04f1639121017
310883UK00001B/70/P